Introduction to Game Programming:
Using C# and Unity 3D

Introduction to Game Programming:
Using C# and Unity 3D

Vahé Karamian

Noorcon Inc.
2016

First Printing: 2016

Paperback Edition:
ISBN-10: 0-9971484-0-3
ISBN-13: 978-0-9971484-0-4

eBook Edition:
ISBN-10: 0-9971484-2-X
ISBN-13: 978-0-9971484-2-8

Noorcon Inc.
Los Angeles, CA
www.noorcon.com

Dedication

To my lovely wife Armineh and
my children Maximilian and Makayla.

Without your love
this book would not exist.

Contents

Acknowledgements.. ix

About the Author xi

Preface.. xiii

Introduction 1

Chapter 1 – Programming Concepts 3
    What Is a Programs?.. 3
    Fundamentals of Programming.. 3
    Object-Oriented Programming Concepts............................16
    Classes and Objects...17
    Encapsulation 20
    Message Passing...22
    Abstraction 22
    Composition 23
    Inheritance..24
    Polymorphism 25
    Modularity...25
    Generics 26
    Interfaces..28
    Delegates 29
    Events 30

Chapter 2 – Brief Introduction to Unity IDE 35
    Interface Overview...35
    Scene View 36
    Game View..36
    The Inspector...36
    Hierarchy Window 37
    Project Window..37
    Creating Our First Game Object..38
    Enter C# Programming and Unity 3D 46
    Publishing Build and Player Settings 49

Chapter 3 – Game Objects and Components........................51
    What Is a GameObject? 51
    Adding and Editing Components..52

Scripts as Components..53
Static GameObjets 54
Prefabs – Concepts and Usage..59
Parent-Child Relationship..60

Chapter 4 – Game Rules and Mechanics 61
Basics of Game Mechanics 61
Simple Examples of the Mechanics......................................66
Physics for Games..71
Enter the Collider Component 72
Collider Interactions 73
Rigidbody 74
Joints 74
Character Mechanics..78

Chapter 5 – Creating the User Interface 131
The Basics of User Interface Design in Unity 5 132
Creating Our First User Interface 141
Enhancing the User Interface 175

Chapter 6 – Creating Battleship..185
Historical Background..185
Game Play..186
Game Plan for Implementation 187
Putting Everything Together - Game Objects 196
Game Flow + Logic...199
Game User Interface 203

Chapter 7 – Delving Into the Code 207
Script – BoardUIVer1.cs 207
Script – BoardVer1.cs...212
Functions Defined in BoardVer1 Class 216
Game User Interface 248

Appendix 1 – Table of Figures..255
Table of Figures...255

Appendix 2 – Code Block Table 257
Code Block Table 257

Acknowledgements

I want to take the opportunity and acknowledge and thank my parents foremost. I am humbled and thankful for the great deeds they have performed towards me. They have endured much for their children and have given up much for the sake of their children. I hope that one day I can repay for their efforts, and be able to be a good parent to my own children.

Secondly I would like to acknowledge every individual that has entered and influenced me throughout my life. These are the mentors from my childhood, followed by my professors at the university and everyone else in between. The good, the bad, and the ugly, have truly shaped and formed my character, personality and wisdom. May the journey continue forevermore!

Lastly, I would like to acknowledge my wife for patiently reading the draft of the book and giving her feedback over the course of the development. The book is nowhere close to a work of art, and for sure it is no romantic novel. On the contrary it is very dry and technical, so thank you for your patience and feedback while managing the household and taking care of the kids, who at the time of this writing are of 2 ½ years and 4 month of age.

About the Author

As a child I was always curious about how things work and what the driving force behind them was. This curiosity eventually directed me into the study of Computer Science. One of the only fields with unlimited potential for creating everything that you can ever possibly conceive of.

In reality, the ability to create your own world and be able to command and control the virtual and the physical environment is what I wanted to do. How to build and control robots, how to make computers think, how to create a simulation and so forth. Long story short, that's how my journey began.

Vahé Karamian holds a master's degree in computer science, his interest include how to enhance Virtual Learning through Virtual Worlds and 3D Environments. He has developed and taught computer science courses since 2011. Topics include Introduction to Computer Science, Java, C#, Python, Data Structures and Algorithms, Operating Systems and Game Design and Programming.

Preface

The book came to be based on several factors. First and foremost, the main objective of this book is to provide a starting point in the field of computer science, and specifically game programming. Second, it is intended as a way to raise the interest in individuals in the field of computer science.

The book is intended for specific audience. It is assumed that the reader has a passion for the study of computer science, and that they have a passion in game design and development. It is also assumed that the reader is proactive and that they would have the ability to engage on a deeper level on their own.

The book is intended mostly for the programmer rather than the artist. There are plenty of books out there specifically targeting the artistic part of game development. This book is written for those who want to give life to those beautiful artistic parts! It is for the magical part of the whole process. It is for the code warrior.

Since the topics discussed in the book are extremely large in breadth and depth, it is impossible to cover every single aspect in one book. Keeping in mind that this is intended as an introductory book for the subject, the content discussed in the first few chapters are generic to the field of computer science, the rest of the book concentrates on game mechanics and how to write computer games.

What other topic would have such an attraction compared to game design and development? The future of Human Computer Interaction is going to be through Virtual Reality and Augmented Reality in the coming years. This books will give you the building blocks for the pathway to the future.

Introduction

This book is written with two objective in mind, first, to introduce the reader to the concepts of programming using C#, second, to put into practice the concepts in a fun and entertaining way by developing computer games and game design concepts.

Even though this is an introductory book, I assume that the reader would have some familiarity with computer programming and object-oriented programming with the C# language. It is also assumed that the reader knows the basics of the Unity 3D environment.

In *Chapter 1*, the reader is given a brief overview on the concepts of programming and object-oriented design terminology. The chapter is intended as a quick reference. For those readers who are already familiar with the basics, it will be a nice quick review. For those readers who are just starting out, it will give a good footing and hopefully make the topics more accessible as you grow in the field.

Chapter 2, is an introduction to the Unity 3D IDE environment. The basic sections of the IDE are explained. The user is shown how to navigate within the IDE and create GameObjects. How to use the transform tools to translate, scale and rotate a GameObject. The Inspector Window is discussed where all of the GameObject components and properties can be modified through the designer and many other useful tips and tricks.

Chapter 3, digs deeper into the concept of GameObjects. How to create them, how to add components, existing or custom. Scripts are discussed and shown how they can be attached to GameObjects and act as components. The concept of a Prefab is introduced and the parent-child relationship within a GameObject is also introduced and discussed.

Chapter 4, the reader is introduced to Game Rules and Mechanics. This is the chapter that sets the foundation and rules for game design and development. It discusses the basics of game mechanics that are used in all games to an extent. Then several examples are built from scratch to illustrate the concepts. Physics, colliders and Rigidbody are also discussed.

Chapter 5, the reader is introduced to User Interface design, and the new built-in architecture for UI design in Unity 5. An overview of the UI architecture is given in the chapter and the examples build in Chapter 4 are used to introduce UI concepts and demonstrate how to build interesting UIs for your game.

Chapter 6, discusses a classic game called Battleship. A brief historical background is given and the game rules and play are discussed. Then the reader is walked through the steps for designing and implementing the game. Game objects, game flow, game logic and the user interface are discussed.

Chapter 7, delves into the C# code that has been discussed and generated throughout Chapter 6 and enhanced in Chapter 7. The primary scripts are dissected, functions are defined and explained and the User Interface for the game finalized.

Chapter 1 – Programming Concepts

What Is a Programs?

A program is a step-by-step instruction that has been designed to solve a given problem. Here is another definition:

"An organized list of instructions that, when executed, causes the computer to behave in a predetermined manner. Without programs, computers are useless."

But the best definition I was given was by my Professor Dr. Lee in the data structure class at Cal Poly:

Program = Data + Algorithm

A program is like a recipe. It contains a list of variables that represent the data to be processed, and a list of directions, the algorithm(s) that perform special operations on the data.

Fundamentals of Programming

Every program needs to store data. In order to store data in a computer, we use what are called *variables*. A variable needs to know what kind of data it is storing, hence a variable needs to have a Data Type.

Data Types

Today's programming languages and frameworks provide several basic data types that can be used to store and retrieve information on the computer. These data types are in general:

1. Numeric
2. Alpha-Numeric
3. Boolean
4. Complex

The numeric data types are represented by byte, short, int, long, float, and double. Alpha-Numeric data types are char and strings. Then you have your Boolean data type, that take either a true of a false value, and finally complex data types that are user defined. Complex or user defined data types are the classes that will be discussed later.

There are 15 different built-in data types in the C# language. The following table will list them out for you and also provide you with the range possible by each type.

Short Name	.NET Class	Type	Width	Range (bits)
byte	Byte	Unsigned integer	8	0 to 255
sbyte	SByte	Signed integer	8	-128 to 127
int	Int32	Signed integer	32	-2,147,483,648 to 2,147,483,647
uint	UInt32	Unsigned integer	32	0 to 4294967295
short	Int16	Signed integer	16	-32,768 to 32,767
ushort	UInt16	Unsigned integer	16	0 to 65535
long	Int64	Signed integer	64	-9223372036854775808 to 9223372036854775807
ulong	UInt64	Unsigned integer	64	0 to 18446744073709551615
float	Single	Single-precision floating point type	32	-3.402823e38 to 3.402823e38
double	Double	Double-precision floating point type	64	-1.79769313486232e308 to 1.79769313486232e308
char	Char	A single Unicode character	16	Unicode symbols used in text
bool	Boolean	Logical Boolean type	8	True or false
object	Object	Base type of all other types		
string	String	A sequence of characters		
decimal	Decimal	Precise fractional or integral type that can represent decimal numbers with 29 significant digits	128	$\pm 1.0 \times 10e{-}28$ to $\pm 7.9 \times 10e28$

The following code block illustrates how to use some of the more common data types:

```
// true or false - one bit
bool   b = true;
```

```
// 0 ... 255
byte    B = 9;

// -32,768 .. 32,767
short   s = 25;

// -2,147,483,648 ... 2,147,483, 647
int     i = 10;

// -3.402823e38 ... 3.402823e38
float   f = 10.0f;

// -9,223,372,036,854,775,808 .. 9,223,372,036,854,775,807
long    l = 34;

// -1.79769313486232e308 ... 1.79769313486232e308
double  z = 13.33;
```

Code Block 1-variables assignment and data types

It is important to understand data types. Each variable you define in your program has to be of some data type. It is important to be able to assign them properly, be able to update and or modify them, and at times, you will want to convert from one data type to another.

Conditional and Decision Making Structures

Then we need some way to make decision inside our program based on some conditions. These are done by the *if..else* statement and switch statement. We can have multiple *if..else* statements. We can also combine *if..else* conditional statements with the switch statement and vise-versa.

```
int x = 4;
if (x > 2)
{
    System.Console.WriteLine("X is > 2");
    if(x<5)
    {
        System.Console.WriteLine("X is < 5 but > 2");
    }
}
else
{
    System.Console.WriteLine("X is <= 2");
}
```

Code Block 2-if ... else structure example

The computer has to execute each if statement it encounters.

The else portion of the *if..else* is optional, and will only execute first if it is defined, and second if the if condition is false. The *if..else* statement can also be nested. This allows the programmer to check for many different conditions. An example would be:

```
if(x>100)
{
    // do something;
}
else if(x>=25 && x<=50)
{
    // do something else
}
else if(x>=10 && x<25)
{
    // do something else
}
else
{
    // do something else
}
```

Code Block 3 - Nested if..else statement

In a nested *if..else* statement, each if condition will be executed in the order they are listed. Once one of the if conditions meets the criteria, its body will be executed, and the rest of the conditions will be ignored.

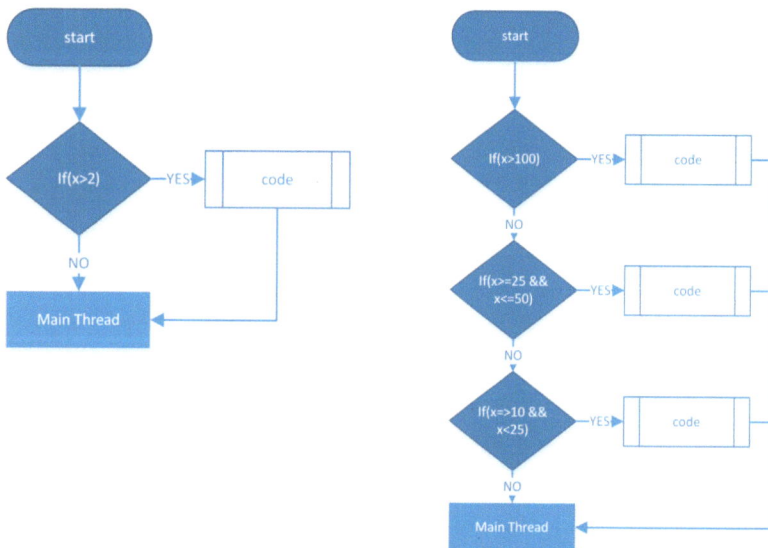

The two diagrams above illustrate the *if..else* condition graphically.

The *Switch* statement is another way to provide decision making inside your programs. It takes in a variable as a parameter, and it defines *special cases*. If the parameter meets the *case*, then the body of the case will be executed. The *default* case is optional just like the else statement in the *if..else* decision structure. If the *default* case is defined, and none of the primary cases are matched, then it will be executed.

```
// x get's assigned a value before this step
switch(x)
{
    case 1:
    {
        // code here to handle case when x = 1
        break;
    }
    case 2:
    {
        // code here to handle case when x = 2
        break;
    }
    case 3:
    {
        // code here to handle case when x = 3
        break;
    }
    default:
    {
        // code here to handle logic when x
        // does not match any of the defined cases
        break;
    }
}
```

Code Block 4-switch statement structure example

One *BIG* difference you will notice between the *if..else* and the *Switch* structures, is the ability to execute multiple code blocks in a switch statement. Notice that each *case* is terminated by a *break* command. The *break* command is optional. If it is present, after the execution of the *case* block, the *switch* structure will terminate. If it is not present, the logic will flow into the next *case* block.

To understand it consider the following: assume the value for the variable *x* is set to *1*. Also assume, that the *break* statement is not defined in the *case* block. When the *switch* statement is evaluated, it will execute *case 1*. Since there is no *break* command present, it will execute the next case block, which happens to be *case 2*. This will continue until a *break* statement is identified.

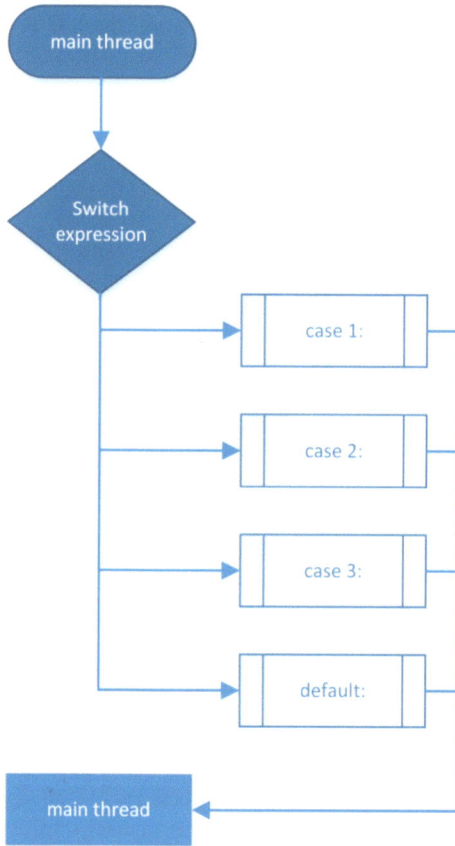

Code Block 2 and Code Block 4 provide a simple example of how to use the decision making statements in the C# language. Keep in mind that the listing display the basic structure, you can extend them to meet complex scenarios.

Loop Structures

Sometimes we also need to be able to loop the same block of code a number of times. This is achieved in a loop structure. There are several loop structures in the C# language:

for loop

By using a *for* loop, you can run a statement or a block of statement repeatedly until a specified expression evaluates to false. This kind of loop is useful for iterating over arrays and for other applications in which you know in advance how many times you want the loop to iterate. The structure of a *for* loop:

```
for (initializer; condition; iterator)
{
    // body of the loop
}
```

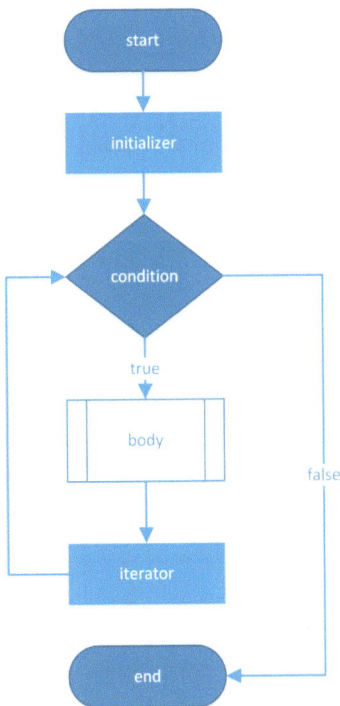

The *initializer* section sets the initial condition. The statements in this section run only once, before you enter the loop.

The *condition* section contains a Boolean expression that's evaluated to determine whether the loop should exit or continue to run.

The *iterator* section defines what happens after each iteration of the body of the loop.

The *body* of the loop consists of a statement, an empty statement, or a block of statements which you create by enclosing zero or more statement in braces.

Figure 1 - for loop diagram

foreach loop

The *foreach* statement repeats a group of embedded statements for each element in an array or an object collection that implements the *IEnumerable* or *IEnumerable<T>* interface. The *foreach* statement is used to iterate through a collection to get the information you need, but it cannot be used to add or remove items from the source collection. This is to avoid unpredictable side effects.

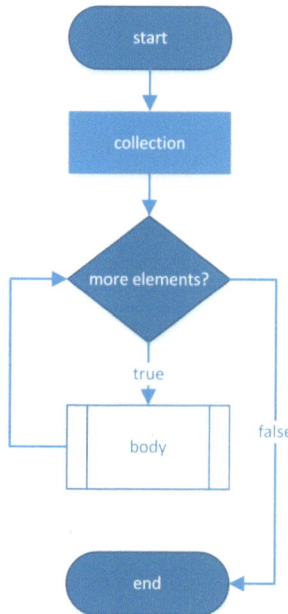

Figure 2 - foreach loop diagram

The embedded statements continue to execute for each element in the array or collection. After the iteration has been completed for all the elements in the collection, control is transferred to the next statement following the *foreach* block.

```
int[] fibarray = new int[] { 0, 1, 1, 2, 3, 5, 8, 13 };
foreach (int element in fibarray)
{
    System.Console.WriteLine(element);
}
```

while loop

The *while* statement executes a statement or a block of statements until a specified expression evaluates to false. Because the test of the *while* expression takes place before each execution of the loop, a *while* loop executes zero or more times.

do-while loop

The *do-while* statement executes a statement or a block of statements repeatedly until a specified expression evaluates to false. Unlike the *while* loop, a *do-while* loop is executed one time before the conditional expression is evaluated.

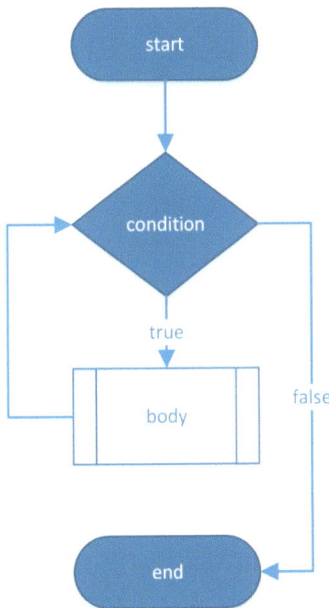

Figure 3 - while loop diagram

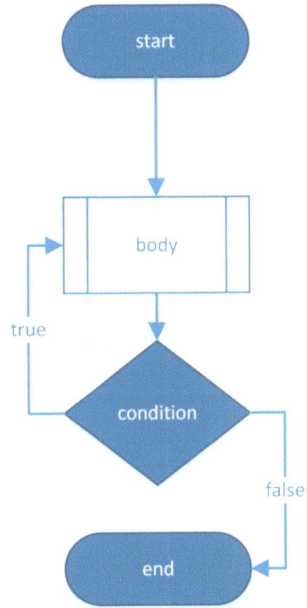

Figure 4 - do-while loop diagram

Every programming language and environment will provide some kind of a looping mechanism. In C# we have four types which have been discussed above. Each loop structure is used for specific purpose as described. The most commonly used loops are the *for* loop, the *foreach* loop and the *while* loop structure. The *do-while* loop is used on special occasions, where you would like to execute the body of the loop at least once before you check for the condition to determine if you want to continue to iterate or move on with the main branch of code.

For instance, the *for loop* structure should be used when you know the size of the elements or the number of times you would want to execute the code block within the body of the loop. The *foreach loop* structure should be used when you want to iterate over a collection set.

The *while* and the *do..while* loop structures are usually used when we don't know how many times we need to execute the body structure of the loop, but, we know the condition for which to exit out of the loop.

```
for (int loopCount = 0; loopCount < 10; loopCount++)
{
    // do something here ...
}

while(x<10)
{
    // do something here ...
    x++;
}

do
{
    // do something here ...
    x++;
} while (x < 10);
```

Code Block 5-loop structure samples

Methods

A *method* in object-oriented programming is a procedure associated with an object class. An object is made up of behavior and data. Data is represented as properties of the object and behaviors as methods. Methods are also the interface an object presents to the outside world. Methods also provide the interface that other classes use to access and modify the data properties of an object. This is known as encapsulation.

A method is a code block that contains a series of statements. A program causes the statements to be executed by calling the method and specifying any required method arguments. In C#, every executed instruction is performed in the context of a method.

Methods are declared in a *class* or *struct* by specifying the access level such as *public* or *private*, optional modifiers such as *abstract* or *sealed*, the *return* value, the *name* of the method, and any method *parameters*. All these parts together are the signature of the method. Method parameters are enclosed in parentheses and are separated by commas, empty parentheses indicate that the method requires no parameters. The following is an example of a method's signature:

```
[access modifier] return-type method-name([parameter-type parameter-name[]])
{ /* method-body */ }
```

The syntax elements are as follows:

- *access-modifier*: determines the degree to which your method is accessible by other classes.
- *return-type*: the type of variable returned by the method (a method can also return an object of a specified class). Your method must return a value using the return keyword, and it must return a value that matches the return-type.
- *method-name*: the name you assign to your method.
- *parameter-type*: the type of parameter passed to your method (a method can also accept objects of a specified class).
- *parameter-name*: the name of the parameter passed to your method.
- *method-body*: the statement that perform your method's task.

```
// The following function takes two floating point data
// parameters, and returns the sum of the two variables
// as another float data type
private float Add(float x, float y)
{
    return x + y;
}
```

Code Block 6-example of a method

By default, when a value type is passed to a method, a copy is passed instead of the object itself. Therefore, changes to the argument have no effect on the original copy in the calling method. You can pass a value-type by reference by using the *ref* keyword.

When passing values by *reference*, the method receives not the object itself, but an argument that indicates the location of the object in memory. If you change a member of the object by using this reference, the change is reflected in the argument in the calling method, even if you pass the object by value.

Here is an example demonstrating parameter passing by reference:

```csharp
// The parameter x is passed by reference.
// Changes to x will affect the original value of x.
static void SquareIt(ref int x)
{
    x *= x;
    System.Console.WriteLine("The value inside the method: {0}", x);
}
static void Main(string[] args)
{
    int n = 5;
    System.Console.WriteLine("The value before calling the method: {0}", n);

    SquareIt(ref n);  // Passing the variable by reference.
    System.Console.WriteLine("The value after calling the method: {0}", n);

    System.Console.WriteLine("Press any key to exit.");
    System.Console.ReadKey();
}
```

Code Block 7 - Method parameter pass by reference

Methods can *return* a value to the caller. If the return type is not *void*, the method can return the value by using the *return* keyword. A statement with the return keyword followed by a value that matches the *return type* will return that value to the method caller. The *return* keyword also stops the execution of the method. Without the *return* keyword, the method will stop executing when it reaches the end of the code block.

To write a program, we use these simple principals and combine them for solving complex problems. Now of course there is more to it than meets the eye, but the basics are the same. There are a lot of other concepts and technical information that has not been presented in this section. This is because, the author expects the reader to be familiar with the basics of programming and that he or she has taken programming courses and is now ready to apply those skills to game programming.

Let's take a look at a simple example that will demonstrate some of the concepts we just discussed. The following program is a simple calculator that will be used to perform some basic operations such as addition, subtraction, multiplication, and division:

```csharp
private static float Add(float x, float y)
{
    return x + y;
}

private static float Subtract(float x, float y)
{
    return x - y;
}

private static float Multiply(float x, float y)
{
    return x * y;
}

private static float? Divide(float x, float y)
{
    if (y > 0.0f)
        return x / y;
    else
        return null;
}

static void Main(string[] args)
{
    float r1 = Add(2.0f, 2.0f);
    float r2 = Subtract(r1, 2.0f);
    float r3 = Multiply(r2, r1);
    float? r4 = Divide(8.0f, 0.0f);

    if(r4==null)
    {
        r4 = Divide(8.0f, 2.0f);
    }
```

```
    string r = string.Format("r1={0}; r2={1}; r3={2}; r4={3}", r1, r2, r3,
r4);

    System.Console.WriteLine(r);
}
```

Code Block 8-simple calculator program demo

At this point you should have a good grasp of the basics. There is a lot of content here if you have not done any programming before. For those who have had exposure to some programming, this was intended as a quick recollection as well as providing a more condensed version of the concepts.

Now that we have a preliminary overview of the basics, we can start discussing modern programming concepts using Object-Oriented Programming.

Object-Oriented Programming Concepts

Games without programming will not be very fun! Programming is what brings everything to life in a game, therefore it is very important to learn and understand the concepts of programming and how to apply them to the games that you intend to design and develop.

Object-Oriented Programming (OOP) is, a design philosophy, a programming model where programs are organized around objects and data, rather than action and logic, everything in OOP is grouped as self-sustainable. Object-Oriented Programming allows decomposition of a problem into a number of entities called objects and then builds data and methods around these objects.

The concept of software objects arose out of the need to model real-world objects in computer simulations. An object can be considered as a representation of a physical item or of an idea that can perform a set of related activities. The set of activities that the object performs defines the object's behavior.

For example, in your game you will have several objects that make up your game. For instance, consider how you might represent a tank

16

in your game. The tank, which is a sort of a vehicle, can exhibit a variety of behaviors, such as moving from point A to point B, loading and un-loading shells, tracking a target, and shooting at the target. It must also maintain information about its characteristics (health, fuel, speed, maximum speed, shell capacity, and etc…) not to mention its current state (location, orientation velocity, inventory, and etc…).

To represent the tank as an object, you would program its behaviors as methods and declare variables to contain information about its characteristics and states. During the game play, the object will carry out its various methods, changing its variables as needed to reflect the effect of its actions. The concept of an object is simple yet powerful. Objects make ideal software modules because they can de defined and maintained independently of one another, with each object forming a neat, self-contained universe. Everything an object knows is captured in its variables, and everything it can do is expressed in its methods.

Classes and Objects

The basic building blocks of object-oriented programming are the class and the object. A class is the blueprint of an object. An object is an instance of the class definition. This will be much clearer as we discuss it and put it into practice throughout the book.

Our world is filled with objects. My car is an object, my bike is an object, my house is an object and my airplane is an object. In fact, any tangible item is an object. Similarly, objects may be grouped together into a class. My car can be grouped into a generic class of cars, all of which have similar characteristics and behaviors. An object can also represent more abstract things – such as geometric shapes, and or transactions.

The easiest way to demonstrate this concept is with a simple example. Let's consider that we would like to model a car. In order for us to achieve this, we would create a class called Car. Our Car class will need to store some information regarding the car object and some methods to represent the behavior of the car object. The following is a visual representation of our car model:

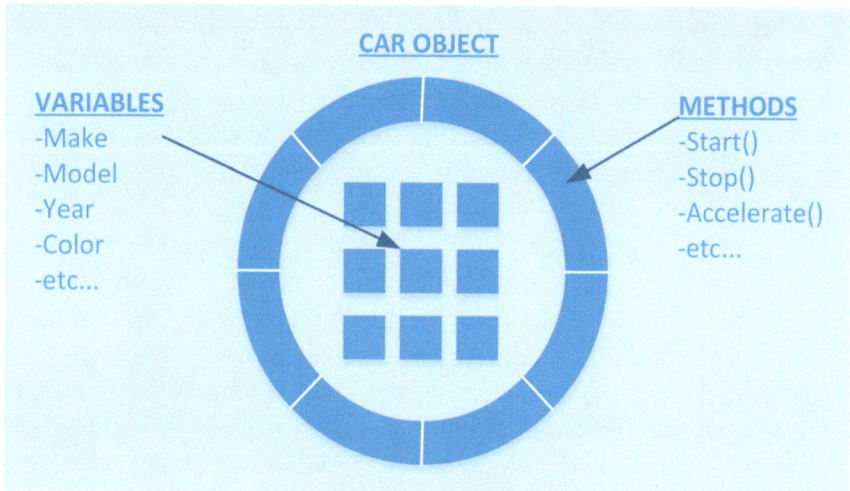

Figure 5-Car Object

Now, in reality, the properties and functions of a modern car are far more complex. But for the sake of the demonstration I have kept things simple. Continuing on our discussion, every car object will have the data points defined, and the designated methods that will be used to access and or change the behavior of the instantiated car object.

You declare a class using the class keyword, which use the following simplified syntax:

```
[access modifier] class class-name { /* body */ }
```

- *access-modifier*: the degree to which your class is accessible to the outside world.
- *class-name*: the name you assign to your class.
- *class-body*: the body of you class.

Classes are usually declared using the public access modifier, meaning that the class is available without restrictions. You will learn more about access modifiers later. The previous syntax has been simplified so that you are not overloaded with too much information.

Here is a simple *Car* class:

```
public class Car
{
   private string make;     // store make as string type
   private string model;    // store model as string type
   private int year;        // store year as int type
   private string color;    // store color as string type

   public Car() { /* constructor */ }

   public void Start() { /* code to start the car */ }
   public void Stop() { /* code to stop the car */ }
   public void Accelerate() { /* code for acceleration */ }

   public string GetMake() { return this.make; }
   public string GetModel() { return this.model; }
   public int GetYear() { return this.year; }
   public string GetColor() { return this.color; }

   public void SetMake(string make) { this.make = make; }
   public void SetModel(string model) { this.model = model; }
   public void SetYear(int year) { this.year = year; }
   public void SetColor(string color) { this.color = color; }
}
```

Code Block 9 - Sample Car Class

In the *Car* class, we have declared four fields: *make*, *model*, *year* and *color*. The *year* field is of type *int*, and the rest are of type *string*. The access modifier of the fields is set to *private*. This indicates that the fields are restricted, and that no one has direct access to them. To access these fields, the user would need to go through the getter and setter methods, such as the *GetMake()* method for retrieving the value of the field, or to set or modify the value through the *SetMake()* method.

As you now know, a class defines a template for creating objects. Once you've declared a class, you can then create objects of that class. The following statement creates a *Car* object:

```
Car myCar = new Car();
```

The first section, declares a reference to a *Car* object, named *my-Car*, and it is used to hold the memory location of an actual *Car* object. The second section actually creates a *Car* object in the computer's memory. The *new[1]* operator allocates the memory for the *Car* object, and the *Car()* method creates the object. The *Car()* method is known as a *constructor*. The memory location of the newly created *Car* object is assigned to *myCar*, and *myCar* is a reference through which you can access the actual *Car* object.

Encapsulation

Packaging related data and procedures together is called encapsulation. The key to object encapsulation is the message interface. The message interface serves to provide an essential barrier between the internal structure of the object and everything that lies outside the object. The message interface ensures that all interactions with the object take place through a predefined system of messages that the object is guaranteed to understand and handle correctly.

Encapsulation is essential to creating maintainable Object-Oriented Programs. When the interaction with an object uses only the publicly available interface of methods and properties, the class of the object becomes a correctly isolated unit. This unit can then be replaced independently to fix bugs, to change internal behaviors or to improve functionality or performance.

In our car analogy, the driver of a car doesn't really need to know the complex mechanics that go into turning on the car and making it accelerate or decelerate, all they need is to know what buttons to press to start the car, stop the car, and make the car move. The details are hidden! The complexity is hidden! Therefore, we can easily upgrade the internal systems of the car without changing the way drivers drive their cars!

Properties allow you to set and get fields using methods. Properties are a great feature of C# because they enable you to hide your fields from your class users by making them *private*, while still providing

---

[1] The new operator and the constructor are used to create an object. You access an object through an object reference, which holds the location of the actual object in memory.

them an easy way to get at those fields. A property is a wrapper around a private field, through which the field is accessed.

A property may define two methods, named *get* and *set*. The get method return the value of the field, and the set method sets the value of the field. Here is the Car class with properties:

```csharp
class Car
{
    private string make;    // store make as string type
    private string model;   // store model as string type
    private int year;       // store year as int type
    private string color;   // store color as string type

    public string Make
    {
        get { return this.make; }
        set { this.make = value; }
    }

    public string Model
    {
        get { return this.model; }
        set { this.model = value; }
    }

    public int Year
    {
        get { return this.year; }
        set { this.year = value; }
    }

    public string Color
    {
        get { return this.color; }
        set { this.color = value; }
    }

    public Car() { /* constructor */ }

    public void Start() { /* code to start the car */ }
    public void Stop() { /* code to stop the car */ }
    public void Accelerate() { /* code for acceleration */ }
}
```

Code Block 10 - Car class using properties

Simply put, properties make accessing data fields in C# much more elegant. On a final note, both the *set* and *get* functions of the property can have complex logic before setting or getting the data.

Message Passing

Messages, also known as interfaces, describe the communication between objects using their accessible interfaces. Message interfaces offer two important kinds of protection. First, they protect an object's internal components from being corrupted by other objects. If other objects had direct access to an object's variables and internal methods, eventually one of these other objects would handle a variable incorrectly or call the wrong method and damage the object. An object protects itself from this kind of error by hiding its variables and internal methods behind its message interface.

The second and less obvious kind of protection works in the opposite direction by hiding its variable and internal methods, an object protects other objects from depending on its internal structure. For example they are spared having to keep track of each variable's name, the type of information it contains, the amount of space it takes up in storage, and a host of other details that would complicate all their procedures for accessing and object's variables. With encapsulation, an object only needs to know how to ask another object for information. All the details about how the information is stored are neatly tucked out of sight behind the message interface.

There are three ways to pass messages in C#: *methods*, *properties* and *events*. A property can be defined in a class to allow objects of that type to advertise and allow changing of state information, such as *StartEngine* property. Methods can be provided so that other objects can request a process to be undertaken by an object, such as *Accelerate()* method. Events can be defined that an object can raise in response to an internal action. Other objects can subscribe to these so that they can react to an event occurring. One example could be for collision detection in the Unity engine framework.

Abstraction

The Car class described in our example is an example of abstraction. Abstraction is the process of representing simplified versions of real-world objects in your classes and object. The Car class does not

Vahé Karamian

describe every possible detail of a car, only the relevant parts for the system that is being developed. Modeling software around real-world objects can vastly reduce the time required to understand a solution and be able to develop and maintain the code over the lifetime of the system.

Composition

Objects can work together in many ways within a system. In some situations, classes and objects can be tightly coupled together to provide more complex functionality. This is known as composition.

Composite objects are important because they can represent far more sophisticated structures than simple objects can. For example, an aircraft consists of wings, engines, and other components that are far too complex to be represented as simple numbers or strings.

The objects contained in composite objects may themselves be composite objects, and this nesting can be carried out to infinity! The major components of an aircraft, are very complex objects in their own right. In any reasonable model of an aircraft, each of these components would be represented by a composite object that would be composed of still more composite objects, and so on.

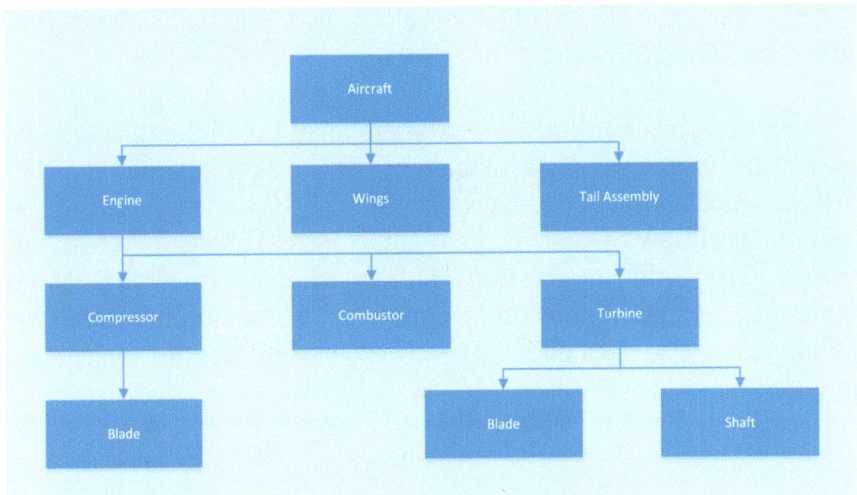

Figure 6-Airplane Composite Object

23

Because objects can be composed of other objects, we can represent real-world objects at the level we naturally think about them. Even a complex, deeply nested structure such as an aircraft can be treated as a single, unified object. And since that complex object can have its own behavior, other objects can use it with very little awareness of its internal complexity. This is a good example of how object technology can bring order to large-scale systems.

In our car example, the wheels, panels, engine and etc… can be thought of as individual classes. To create the Car class, you will need to link all of these objects together. This makes it possible to increase the complexity of your car definition over the years and introduce better features and functionality. The internal workings of each class are not important due to encapsulation as the communication between the objects is still via passing messages to their public interfaces.

Inheritance

Inheritance is an interesting object-oriented programming concept. It allows one class to be based upon another, the super-class, and inherit all of its functionality automatically. Additional code may then be written to create a more specialized version of the class. If we wanted to improve on our model and design, we would create a new class called Vehicle. This new class will be the super class, and the Car class will inherit the Vehicle class.

Inheritance is not limited to a single level but will cascade down any number of levels in a class hierarchy. This makes inheritance a very powerful mechanism because classes can be endowed with rich sets of capabilities simply by placing them in the correct branch of a class hierarchy. They will automatically pull together all the interface and implementation definitions of the classes above them in the hierarchy, defining for themselves only the additional capabilities that make them unique.

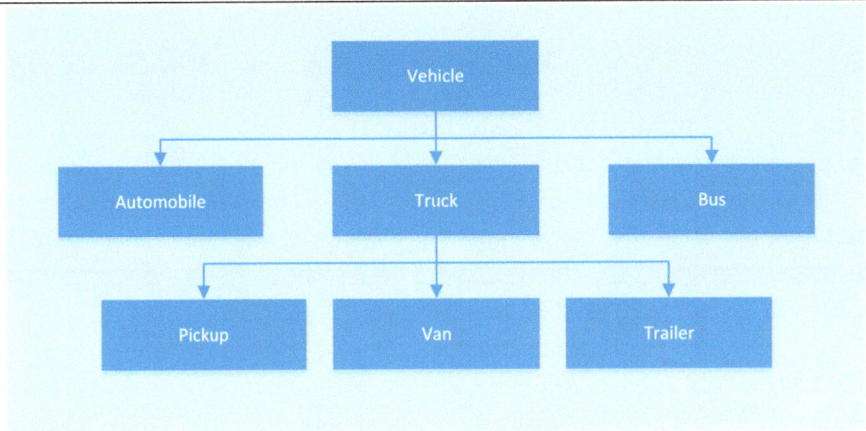

Figure 7-Inheritance Example

Consider the following, a system that represents various kinds of vehicles. This system will contain a generic class Vehicle, with sub-classes for all the specialized types. The Vehicle class will contain the methods and variables that are pertinent to all vehicles. The subclasses, in turn, will contain any additional methods and variables that were specific to the more specialized cases. This helps us to easily add other types of vehicles to the hierarchy, such as Motorcycles, Helicopters, Boats and etc…

Polymorphism

Polymorphism is the ability for an object to change its behavior according to how it is being used. Where an object's class inherits from a super-class or implements one or more interfaces, it can be referred to by those class or interface names. So if we have a method that expects an object of type 'Vehicle' to be passed as a parameter, we can pass any vehicle, car, motorcycle or airplane to that method even though the data type may be technically different.

Modularity

In addition to the concepts described so far, object-oriented programming also permits increased modularity. Individual classes or groups of classes can be thought of as a module of code that can be re-used in many software project. This reduces the need to re-develop similar functionality and therefore can lower development time and cost.

This was a quick overview of the concepts present in the object-oriented programming paradigm. We won't be able to cover every single aspect of the topic in this chapter, but I have given a fair overview of the topic and for those who are coming from a computer science background, it should be a quick review. If this is the first time you have seen or heard the terminology, then hopefully you do grasp the ideas. As I am trying to keep it as simple as possible.

Generics

Generics allow you to define type-safe data structures without committing to actual data types. This results in a significant performance boost and higher quality code, because you get to reuse data processing algorithms without duplicating type-specific code.

Generics let you reuse code and the effort you put into implementing them. The types and internal data can change without causing code bloating, regardless of whether you are using value or reference types. You can develop, test, and deploy your code once, reuse it with any type, including future types, all with compiler support and type safety. The best way to understand them is probably with a simple example.

The following is an implementation of a Stack Data Structure without Generics:

```csharp
public class MyStack
{
    private int index;
    private ArrayList stack;

    public MyStack()
    {
        this.stack = new ArrayList();
        index = -1;
    }

    public int COUNT
    {
        get { return this.stack.Count; }
    }

    public void push(object data)
    {
```

```
      this.stack.Add(data);
      this.index++;
   }

   public object pop()
   {
      object o = this.stack[index];

      this.stack.RemoveAt(index);
      this.index--;

      return o;
   }

   public void clear()
   {
      this.stack.Clear();
      this.index = -1;
   }

   public object peek()
   {
      return this.stack[this.index];
   }
}
```

Code Block 11 - MyStack Data Structure

The next implementation is using Generics:

```
public class MyStack1<T>
{
   private int index;
   private List<T> stack;

   public MyStack1()
   {
      this.stack = new List<T>();
      index = -1;
   }

   public int COUNT
   {
      get { return this.stack.Count; }
   }

   public void push(T data)
   {
      this.stack.Add(data);
      this.index++;
   }

   public T pop()
   {
      T o = this.stack[index];
```

```
        this.stack.RemoveAt(index);
        this.index--;

        return o;
    }

    public void clear()
    {
        this.stack.Clear();
        this.index = -1;
    }

    public object peek()
    {
        return this.stack[this.index];
    }

}
```

Code Block 12 - Generics Code Sample

The advantage of this programming model is that the internal algorithms and data manipulation remain the same while the actual data type can change based on the way the code is being used.

Interfaces

An *Interface* is a contract. When you are designing an interface, you're saying, "If you want to provide this capability, you must implement these methods, provide these properties and indexers, and support these events." The implementer of the interface agrees to the contract and implements the required elements. We won't get too much into the details of the definition, but here are some concepts you should understand:

The Interface:

This is the contract. By convention, interface names begin with a capital *I*, so your interface might have a name such as *IWeapon*. The *IWeapon* interface might require, among other things, an *Explode()* function. This states that any class that wants to implement *IExplosion* much implement an *Explode()* function, but it does not specify how that method works internally. This is up to you the designer.

The Implementing Class:

This is the class that agrees to the contract described in the interface. For example, a *Bomb* might be a class that implements *IWeapon* and thus implements the *Explode()* function within the class based on the *Bomb's* requirements.

The Client Class:

The client calls functions on the implementing class. For example, you might have a *Battleship* class that might have an array of *IWeapon* objects. The client can expect to be able to call *Explode()* on each object, and although each individual object may implement the method differently, each will do so appropriately and without complaint!

You might ask, what is the difference between Abstract Base Classes and an Interface? The key difference is that an abstract base class serves as the base class for a family of derived classes, and an interface is meant to be mixed in with other inheritance chains. That is, a class can inherit from only a single parent class, but it can implement multiple interfaces.

In addition, when you derive from an abstract class, you must override all the abstract methods in the abstract base class, but you don't have to override any non-abstract functions. You can simply use the implementation that the base class provides. This is called *Partial Implementation*. Interfaces don't have any implementation, so you must implement every function defined in the interface. You can't partially implement an interface.

Delegates

In programming, you are often faced with situations where you need to execute a particular action, but you don't know in advance which method, or even which object, you'll want to call upon to execute it. For example, you might want to tell an object to play a media file during runtime, but you might not know what object will be playing the file, or whether it's a video, a sound file, an animation, or something else. Rather than hardcoding a particular media player object, you would create a delegate, and then resolve that delegate to a particular method when the program executes.

A *delegate* is a reference type, like the other reference types you've seen in this book, but instead of referring to an object, a delegate refers to a method. This is called *encapsulating* the method. When you create the delegate, you specify a method signature and return type; you can encapsulate any matching method with that delegate.

For example, suppose you have a class called *MediaStorage* that you use to store and manage various media files-audio files, video files, animation files; the type of file doesn't matter to the class. Suppose further that you want this class to be able to play the files, to make sure they can be played successfully, and report on whether they played properly or not (as a way of testing whether the file is valid). The *MediaStorage* class doesn't need to know how to play the files; it just needs to receive a code indicating whether the file played successfully or not.

You could fulfill this requirement with interfaces, although it may not be worth it to you to define an entirely new interface and create an instance of it when you could use a delegate instead. In this case, we'll be testing only two types of media files, so we'll use delegates. If there were a wider range of media file types, you might want to define an appropriate interface.

Events

Events are an important part of today's programming model. A modern program presents the user interface and waits for the user to take an action. The user might take many different actions, such as choosing among menu selections, pushing buttons, updating text fields, clicking icons, and so forth. Each action causes an event to be raised.

An *event* is the encapsulation of the idea that "something happened" to which the program must respond. Events and delegates are tightly coupled concepts because flexible event handling requires that the response to the event be dispatched to the appropriate event handler. An event handler is typically implemented in C# via a delegate.

Any object can publish a set of events to which other classes can subscribe. When the publishing class raises an event, all subscribers are notified. With this mechanism, your object can say, *"I have the follow-ing things to notify you about,"* and other classes might want to sign up, saying, *"Yes, let me know when that happens."* As an example, provides an event handler for collision detection. Each time an object is colliding with another object, this even is raised.

Events in C# are implemented with delegates. The publishing class defines a delegate. The subscribing class does two things: first, it cre-ates a method that matches the signature of the delegate, and second, it creates an instance of that delegate type encapsulating that method. When the event is raised, the subscribing class's methods are invoked through the delegate.

Here is an example of an Event Handler:

```csharp
public class MyEventPublisher
{
    public event EventHandler eventHandler;

    public void Publish()
    {
        EventHandler handler = eventHandler;
        if(eventHandler != null)
        {
            handler(this, EventArgs.Empty);
        }
    }
}

public class MyEventObserver
{
    public void MyEventHandler(object sender, EventArgs args)
    {
        Console.WriteLine(string.Format("Published: {0}",
sender));
    }
}

public class TestEventHandler
{
    static void Main(string[] args)
    {

        MyEventPublisher publisher = new MyEventPublisher();
```

```
            MyEventObserver observer = new MyEventObserver();
            publisher.eventHandler += observer.MyEventHandler;

            publisher.Publish();
        }
    }
```

Code Block 13 - Simple Event Handler Example

The example above is a simplistic way of illustrating event handlers, but it does capture the necessary structure for implementation. Let's take a look at another example. Assuming our *Car* class has a property for *fuel*. If the fuel level drops to a certain level, we would like to raise an event that notifies the user that it is running low on the fuel. The *Car* class will publish this event, and the user class will subscribe to this event to update the UI and or perform other tasks.

The following code listing will illustrate the scenario:

```
public class FuelLevelChangeEventArgs : EventArgs
{
    public float FuelLevel { get; internal set; }
    public object OldValue { get; internal set; }
    public object NewValue { get; internal set; }

    public FuelLevelChangeEventArgs(float fuelLevel, object oldValue, object newValue)
    {
        this.FuelLevel = fuelLevel;
        this.OldValue = oldValue;
        this.NewValue = newValue;
    }
}

public class Car
{
    private string make;    // store make as string type
    private string model;   // store model as string type
    private int year;       // store year as int type
    private string color;   // store color as string type

    public string Make
    {
        get { return this.make; }
        set { this.make = value; }
    }

    public string Model
    {
        get { return this.model; }
```

```csharp
      set { this.model = value; }
    }

    public int Year
    {
        get { return this.year; }
        set { this.year = value; }
    }

    public string Color
    {
        get { return this.color; }
        set { this.color = value; }
    }

    private float fuelLevel;
    public float FUEL_LEVEL
    {
        get { return this.fuelLevel; }
        set
        {
            object oldValue = this.fuelLevel;
            this.fuelLevel = value;

            // we want to raise the level when the fuel
            // level drop to a certain point
            if (this.fuelLevel<0.6f)
            {
                // code here to raise the event
                FuelLevelChanged(this, new FuelLevelChangeEven-
tArgs(this.fuelLevel, oldValue, value));
            }

        }
    }

    // delegate
    public delegate void FuelLevelChangeHandler(object sender, FuelLevel-
ChangeEventArgs data);
    // event
    public event FuelLevelChangeHandler FuelLevelChanged;

    protected void OnFuelLevelChanged(object sender, FuelLevelChangeEven-
tArgs data)
    {
        // check to see if there are any subscribers
        if(FuelLevelChanged != null)
        {
            // Call the event
            FuelLevelChanged(this, data);
        }
    }


    public Car() { this.fuelLevel = 1.0f; }
```

```
        public void Start() { /* code to start the car */ }
        public void Stop() { /* code to stop the car */ }
        public void Accelerate() { /* code for acceleration */ }

        public string GetMake() { return this.make; }
        public string GetModel() { return this.model; }
        public int GetYear() { return this.year; }
        public string GetColor() { return this.color; }

        public void SetMake(string make) { this.make = make; }
        public void SetModel(string model) { this.model = model; }
        public void SetYear(int year) { this.year = year; }
        public void SetColor(string color) { this.color = color; }
    }
```

Code Block 14 - Car Class with Event handler

The delegate encapsulates any method that takes the attributes defined, this delegate must be implemented by all subscribers. The *FuelLevelChangeEventArgs* class was created to help track the old value of the property and the new value of the property.

At this point you have had a good overview of the fundamentals and also have been provided with a nice footing with object-oriented terminology. It is encouraged that the reader do their own research on the topics discussed in this chapter.

Chapter 2 – Brief Introduction to Unity IDE

Interface Overview

Before we can get started with any of the cool aspects of Unity, we would need to get ourselves familiar with the environment. At the time of writing, Unity 5.3 was the latest public release. Hence we are going to be concentrating our efforts on Unity 5.3.

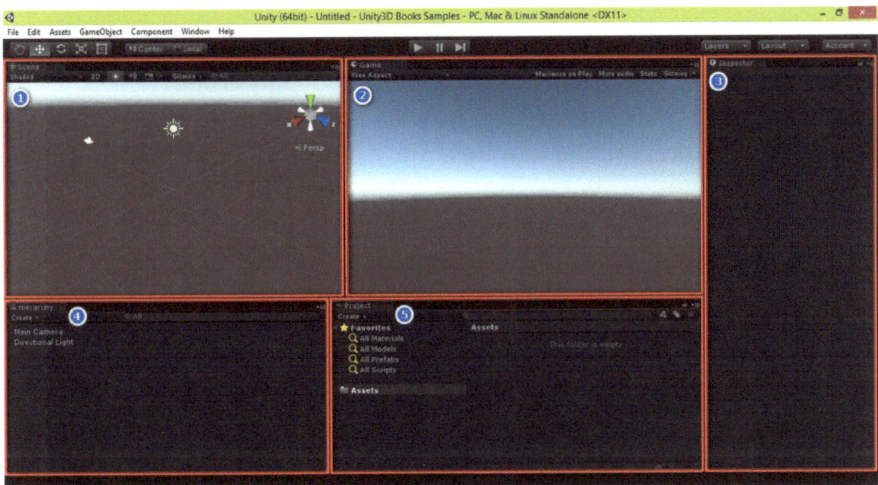

Figure 8-Unity 5 Editor

In Figure 8, you will see an empty Unity 5 project. If this is the first time you are running Unity 5, your IDE might have a slight different configuration. That is, your view might be a little different then what you see in Figure 8. I like to setup my IDE with the shown configuration because it makes it easier for me to perform the tasks which I am more interested.

Also notice, that I have broken down the IDE into five main working areas. (1) Scene Window, (2) Game Window, (3) Inspector Window, (4) Hierarchy Window, and (5) Project Window. These are the main areas of the IDE that you will be utilizing for your projects.

At the moment as you can see, the IDE is pretty uninteresting. That's because we do not have anything interesting going on in the designer, it is just a blank canvas waiting for your creative ideas! Let's get a better understanding of what each of these regions will be used for in a nut-shell:

Scene View

The Scene View is your interactive sandbox. You will use the Scene View to select and position your GameObjects. These includes the player, the camera, your enemies, and everything else that will be used to generate your level. Maneuvering and manipulating objects within the Scene View are some of the most important functions in Unity, so it is important to learn how to perform them in an efficient way. As we go along the examples, more hints will be provided to improve and increase productivity.

Game View

The Game View is rendered from the Camera(s) in your game. It is representative of your final, published game. You will need to use one or more Cameras to control what the player actually sees when they are playing your game. You can also quickly change the aspect ratio of the Game View window to quickly see how your game will look on different resolutions and screen sizes. One other great feature of the Game View window is that you can actually get the Rendering Statistics which is a great utility for checking the performance of your game. This data can then be used for optimizing graphics performance for more complex scenes.

The Inspector

The Inspector Window displays detailed information about your currently selected GameObject and all of the attached Components and their properties. Within the Inspector Window, you can modify the functionality of GameObjects in your scene. Any property that is displayed in the Inspector can be directly modified. This includes script variable. You can also use the Inspector to change properties to see the actual result during runtime! The Inspector is another part of the Unity

IDE that you need to get yourself very familiarized. You will be spending most of your time in the Scene View, the Inspector Window, and your Scripts.

Hierarchy Window

The Hierarchy contains every GameObject in the current Scene. Some of these are direct instances of asset files like 3D models and others are instances of Prefabs[2]. The Hierarchy Window will also display the parent-child relationship of all the GameObjects in the Hierarchy Window. It is basically a live view of all of the existing GameObject in your scene.

Project Window

The Project Window is where your project assets are displayed. This is a one-to-one relationship to the actual file system where the project files are being saved on your local machine. Everything from Game Objects, Scripts, Textures, Models, Audio, Video and etc… will be accessible and managed in this window. The left panel of the browser shows the folder structure of the project as a hierarchical list. Above the project structure list is a Favorites section where you can keep frequently-used items for easy access. You can drag items from the project structure list to the Favorites and also save search queries there. This will be handy on large projects with hundreds or thousands of GameObjects.

As you can see, Unity has done a wonderful job of creating an IDE that is easy to use and access by both designers and developers alike. There are other views and windows that provide more features and functions. It is just impossible to cover them all in one sitting. I have provided with the best place to get started, and each individual reader should undertake their own initiative and dive in deeper based on their interest and profession. In this book we are mostly leaning towards the programming side of game design and development. Keep in mind, that the IDE is very powerful and has more features that we will cover later on in the book. But for now, we stick with the basics.

---

[2] Custom objects that are made by the user.

Creating Our First Game Object

Unity 3D is not a 3D Modeling software, so do not expect to create sophisticated models using Unity 3D. Unity 3D is a Game Engine primarily, that also provides you with some flexibility on modifying and or creating simple 3D content! For your 3D modeling needs, you will need to work with software such as 3D Studio Max, Maya, Rhino and etc... Generally speaking, your models will be created by a 3D Modeler and Designer and you will import them and use them inside your game.

By default, there are several primitives that can be created out of the box. These are the Cube primitive, the Sphere primitive, the Capsule primitive, the Cylinder primitive, the Plane primitive and the Quad primitive. For the purpose of this demonstration we will place a Cube primitive in the scene.

NOTE: The process of creating and modifying any primitive type is the same. In fact, the modification, as far as the transform is concerned is the same for each Game Object.

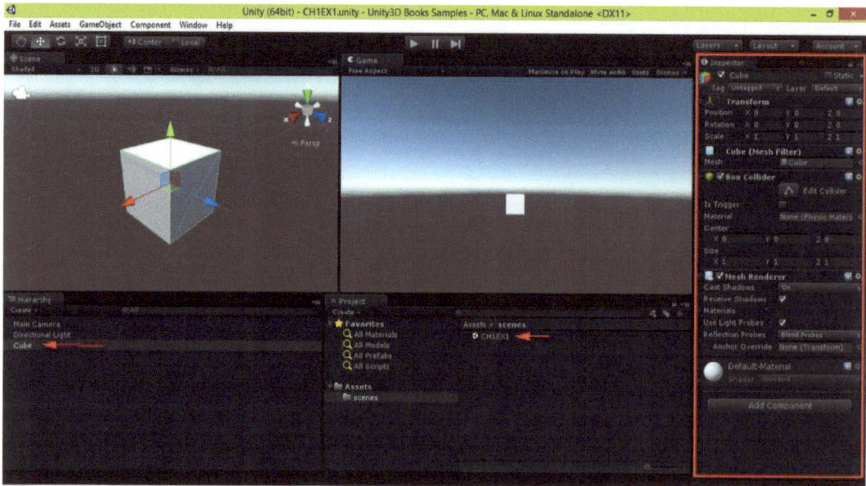

Figure 9-Cube Primitive

In order to create a Cube primitive, from the main menu select GameObject->3D Object->Cube. This action will result in placing a cube in your active scene. Before we continue further, let's go ahead and also save our scene. To save the scene, from the main menu select File->Save Scene... Unity 3D will prompt you to save your scene in the project folder under the Assets folder. Make a new folder called scenes, and then save your scene inside this folder and name it CH1EX1.

The purpose of this will be clear later on when we start to get into more complex scenarios. Just like any other project you have undertaken previously, you will need to have some sort of structure and organization, so why not start doing it from the beginning?

If you have followed the instruction you should have a similar looking IDE as in Figure 9. Notice how the Unity Editor has come to life now.

1. We have our cube primitive placed in the **Scene** window.
2. The **Hierarchy** window is displaying all of the Game Objects present in our scene.
3. The **Game** window is displaying the cube through the eyes of the camera.
4. The **Inspector** window is displaying all of the components and the properties that are attached to the Cube Game Object.
5. The **Project** window is displaying all of the assets we have in our project so far, which at the moment is just the scene that we have saved.

Take a moment to study everything you see on your screen. Looking at the Inspector window, you can see that there is a lot of information that is being displayed for the selected cube.

We have several components attached to the cube primitive by default. These are the Transform, Mesh Filter, Box Collider, Mesh Renderer and a Default Material attached to the cube GameObject.

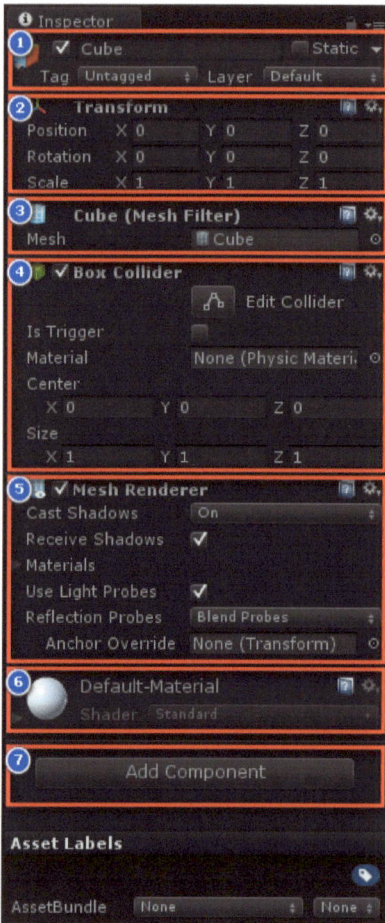

Figure 10-Inspector Window

Taking a closer look at the Inspector window in Figure 10, we can see seven different regions.

Region 1 contain the properties for the name of the GameObject, the Tag, and the Layer. We will get into the details later on.

Regions 2 through 6 are the different components that have been attached to the GameObject.

The Transform components which stores the position, rotation and scale of the GameObject.

The Mesh Filter, defining the mesh of the cube.

The Box Collider components. This is used for collision detection.

The Mesh Rendered Component detailing how the mesh should be rendered.

The Default Material component which is the material used to render our cube.

Region 7 has an Add Component function that can be used to add more components to the GameObject

Taking a look at the Transform information, we see that the cube's position, rotation and scale are represented by the transform property which is composed of three Vector3D objects. In this case the cube GameObject is placed at position (0,0,0) representing the (x,y,z) coordinates respectively. The rotation vector of the cube is at (0,0,0) on the (x,y,z) axis. And the scale vector is also set to (1,1,1) on the (x,y,z) axis.

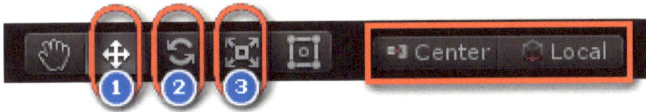

Figure 11-Transform Tools

To start making any changes to the transform property of the cube GameObject, we need to be familiar with the transform tools located at the top of the Unity 3D IDE as shown in Figure 11:

1. Gives you the ability to position the object on its x, y and z axis in the scene.
2. Gives you the ability to rotate the object on its x, y and z axis in the scene.
3. Gives you the ability to scale the object on its x, y and z axis in the scene.

When you select the cube and pick any one of the transform tools, you will get the following modifiers in the scene window:

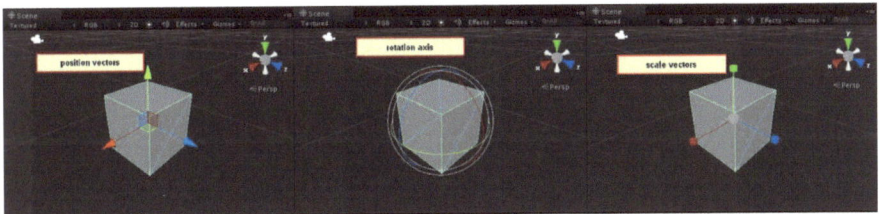

Figure 12-Position   **Figure 13-Rotation**   **Figure 14-Scale**

Using these tools, you can transform the selected GameObject in any form that will satisfy your needs. The best way to get a feel for them is by trying them out. Another way to modify the GameObject's transform properties, is by directly entering the values for each part numerically through the Inspector window. I generally find it easier to make the positioning, rotation and scale of my GameObjects through the scene view, and then fine tune them through the numerical entry fields in the Inspector window.

The next components representing the Mesh Filter and Mesh Renderer will be discussed later in the chapters. The only thing you should be aware of is that these components are the actual representation of the wireframe and the way the GameObject will be rendered on the scene. We will also discuss the Collider component in later chapters when we are building our game demos. For now you should only be aware that colliders are used for any collision detection, and they are pretty important to understand and configure properly. Especially in more complex models.

The Material component is used to define the type of material that will be applied to the selected GameObject. Materials are used in conjunction with Mesh Renderers, Particle Systems and other rendering components. They play an essential part in defining how your object is displayed. The properties that a Material's Inspector window displays are determined by the Shader that the Material uses. A shader is a specialized kind of graphics program that determines how texture and lighting information are combined to generate the pixels of the rendered object onscreen. We won't be covering shaders in this book, as it is not our primary topic and there are far better suited books to discuss and cover the topic.

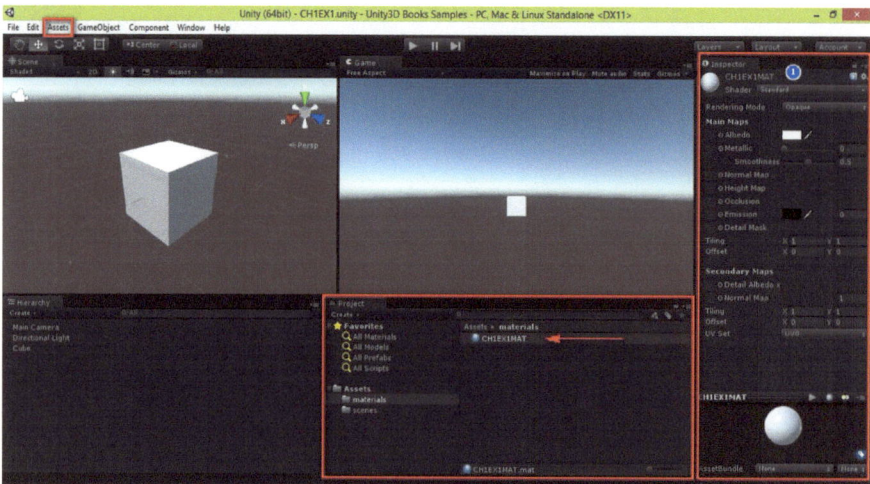

Figure 15-New Material names CH1EX1MAT

By default, every primitive that you create will have the Gray material defined by Unity assigned to it. You can easily create a new material by selecting Assets->Create->Material from the main menu, this will put a new material object in the selected folder. Alternatively, you can also create a material by right-clicking in the Project window and selecting Create->Material. In both cases, you should make sure you are in the right folder before you perform these operations.

Let's create a new folder called **materials** under the Assets, and let's create a material called **CH1EX1MAT** by right clicking on the material folder and selecting create material. Take a look at Figure 15 if you have done everything properly you should be seeing similar results.

As you can see, there is a bunch of properties associated with the materials as shown in the Inspector window. For now, we would like to just change the **Albedo** property to be of green color, to do so, select the color selector in the Inspector window for the Albedo property and select the green color. You can either select the green color by moving the mouse in the color selector window, or enter the actual numerical values in the RGB field. I have set my value to the following: R=0; G=255; B=0, and Alpha to 255 as well. To apply the newly created material to our cube, simply drag and drop it over to the cube GameObject inside our scene. Now go ahead and select the cube GameObject and you will notice the changes as shown in Figure 16.

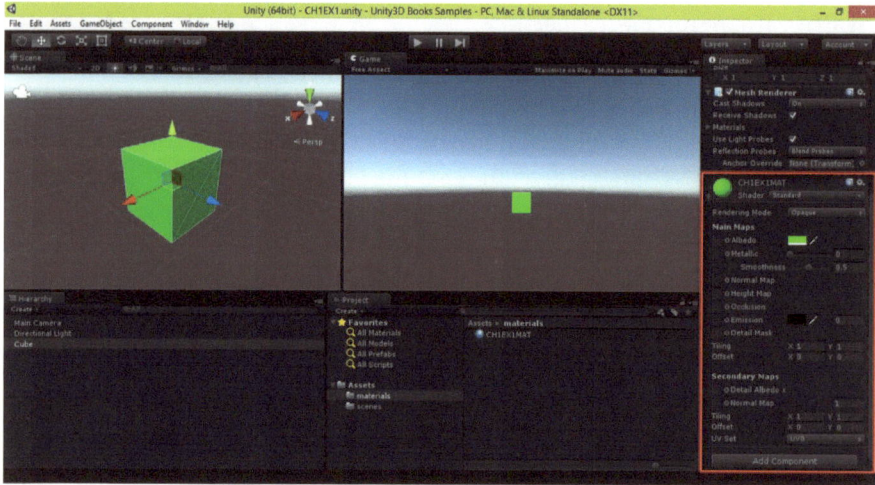

Figure 16-Applying the CH1EX1MAT material to the Cube GameObject

As mentioned earlier, this book is more concentrated on the programming portion of game development. Hence we will not delve too much into graphics related topic from a designer's perspective.

So we have looked at the most basic aspect of any GameObject's properties. Let's go ahead and create some of the other primitive types to get a feeling of them and also practice a little of design time transformation of the GameObjects. Before we move on with that excersise, there is one more important design time feature which I would like to bring to your attention.

One more important item regarding the scene window is the ability to look at the scene design or level design from different points of view. In order to achieve this, you will need to have your mouse in the scene window and while holding the Alt key[3] down, in the scene window you will notice that the icon of the mouse has changed to the eye icon, now you can left-click and move the mouse to change the view point at design time in the scene window. This will help you to rotate within the scene. To zoom in and out you can use the middle mouse button. If you have used other 3D Modeling tools, the function works similarly.

---

[3] For Mac users, you will need to use the command key.

Go ahead and zoom a little out in the scene view so you can see a larger area to play around with. Next go ahead and create another cube GameObject. By default, every GameObject will be placed at the origin (0,0,0). Let's make some modifications to the transform of the newly created cube. Also note that the new Cube GameObject is named Cube (1), in order for you to change the name of the newly created GameObject, select it and from the Inspector Window rename the object to **Cube2**. You can also rename a GameObject from the Hierarchy window by selecting it and clicking it once or pressing the F2 key. This works similar to your file system.

Let's go ahead and use the transform tools to move Cube2 to position (2,0,0) and then scale it down so that it is half its original size. You can do so by selecting the red-arrow representing the x-axis, refer to Figure 12, to drag it in the positive or negative direction. You will notice that moving objects to specific locations is not going to be as easy with the transform tool if you need to get to very specific positions such as (2.33,0,0). For these type of coordinates, it will be best to use the Inspector Window and directly input the position coordinates.

Now let's scale our GameObject to half it's size. Select the scale tool and use the indicators, refer to Figure 14, to get the size of the object down to half its size. Note that you will have to do this on all 3-axis respectively. As you can see, scaling the object to exactly 0.5 on all the three axis is hard! Make life easy and use the Inspector Window to enter in the numerical values for the scale vector to be (0.5,0.5,0.5).

One last transformation and we will be good with this exercise. Let's go ahead and rotate Cube2 by 33 degrees on the xyz-axis. Select the rotation tool and use the indicators, refer to Figure 13, to rotate the object. If you have followed the steps your screen should resemble Figure 17.

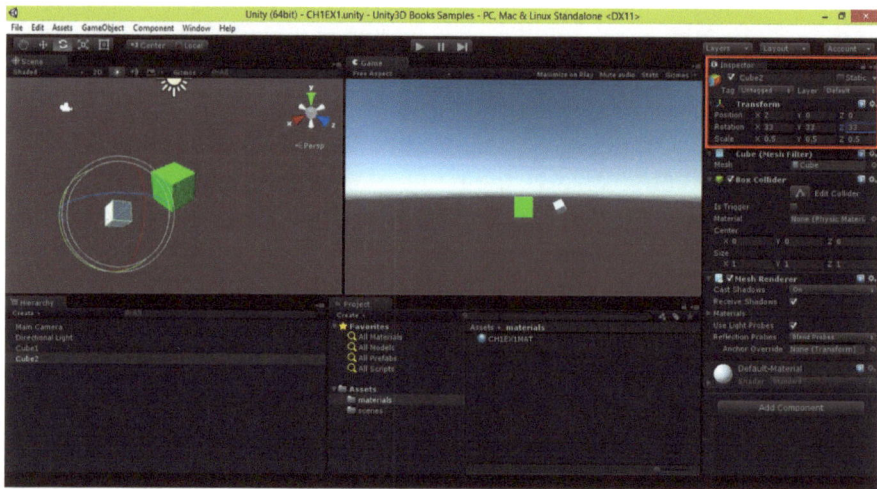

Figure 17-Cube2 Position, Rotation, Scale

There is one more view which is very important to be familiar with, and that is the Console Window. We will look at the Console window in more details when we start doing our programming. This is important for debugging purposes, it will show errors, warnings and other messages generated by Unity.

At this point you should have a fair understanding of the main regions in the Unity Editor, and their purpose. You should also have a good grasp of how to do your object transformations at design time. We will look at object transformation at runtime in later chapter.

Enter C# Programming and Unity 3D

When designing a game or a simulation, you will need to be able to manipulate your environment not just through the designer, but also at run-time, dynamically. This is where you will have to start applying your programming knowledge and skills to give LIFE to the environment. So that it is not sitting idle. Fortunately or unfortunately, there is no way to get around this!

So, to get you started, we will look at the basics of manipulation of the objects through code. Let's say we want to rotate our cube on its

Y-Axis when we build or run our application. There are several steps you will need to take:

1. You will need to create a C# script
2. In the C# script you will need to write the code which will apply the rotation to the object
3. Finally you will need to associate your script with the desired Game Object

At this point, I am not going to discuss the structure and organization of your project and file system for your project. We will discuss this in future chapters as we start building our knowledge throughout the book.

In order for you to create a C# script in your project, within the Project Window, right click to get your Context Menu, then select Create->C# Script. This action will create a C# script file in the specified location, and will ask you to name it. At this point, the name you give your script is not a big deal, but as always you should consider utilizing best practices for naming convention as defined within your organization or yourself. In any case, I call my script cubeRotate.cs. Double click the script to open it in the Mono Editor (Default Editor) you can change this to any other C# editor of your choosing. Your code should look something like this:

```csharp
using UnityEngine;
using System.Collections;

public class articleRotate : MonoBehaviour {

    // Use this for initialization
    void Start () {

    }

    // Update is called once per frame
    void Update () {
        this.transform.Rotate (new Vector3 (0, 1, 0), 1);
    }
}
```

A few things to explain before we move forward. Each script that you create will by default inherit from **MonoBehaviour**. We will discuss this class at a later point. Each script that you create will also have two functions defined as: **Start()** and **Update()**.

The **Start()** function will be run only once at the start of the program. So any logic and data initializations that you need or want to do can be placed in the Start() function.

The **Update()** function is where most of the magic happens. This is the function that gets called continuously throughout the life of your game or simulation. This is the function where you will update your game objects. In short it is the function which will be called each frame before rendering the scene.

The line this.transform.Rotate (new Vector3 (0, 1, 0), 1); will perform the desired rotation we are looking for on the given object it is applied to. Without getting too much into the details and the behind the scene complication of this function. We can utilize the Rotate function defined on the transform component of our object to pass in a Vector3 object, representing our (X,Y,Z), and the rotation angle.

Since we are planning to rotate on the Y-Axis, we have to define our Vector3 as (0,1,0). The function will do all of the necessary transformations and handle the computation for you. The next parameter is the rotation angle, which we have defined as 1.

There are several ways to apply a script to a Game Object. The simplest way would be to drag and drop your script onto the desired game object on the scene. After you have applied the script, in the Inspector Windows, you will see that the script is a component of the cube.

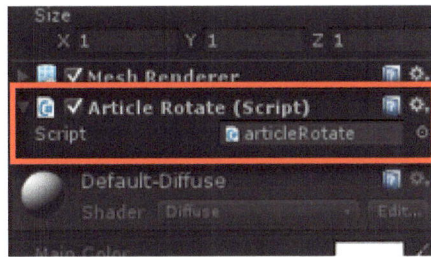

Figure 18-Script Attached to Game Object

When you apply this code to your Cube and run your program, you will notice that your Cube is now rotating on its Y-Axis, one degree continuously. This is because our rotation logic is in the Update() function which is called continuously by the game engine while the program is running. And each time, the one degree rotation is applied to the Cube's transform component! Hence you get the rotation effect.

Publishing Build and Player Settings

Once you are satisfied with your game creation, you will want to actually build it to see how it feels and looks on the intended platform. One of the main attractions and benefits of Unity is that you can target a bunch of different platform with practically the same code base. Yes, there will be some minor changes from one platform to the next, this is expected due to the different form factors between the different platforms. A PC deployment is very different then a Web deployment then a Mobile deployment. Different architecture, different amount of resources, and different resolutions and input types! For now you can just take a look at the deployment options available to you by selecting File->Build Settings… You will have different options based on your license.

Chapter 3 – Game Objects and Components

What Is a GameObject?

GameObjects are the most important concept in Unity. It is very important to understand what a GameObject is. Every object in your game is a GameObject. Think of a GameObject as an empty container that can hold different *Components*[4]. These *Components* are then used to implement the functionality of the GameObject. Depending on what kind of object you want to create, you will add different combinations of Components to the GameObject.

In Chapter 2 – Brief Introduction to Unity IDE, if you recall from the *Inspector Window*, when you created the primitive Cube GameObject, all of the predefined *Components* that make up what we see as the Cube in our *Scene View*. As a reminder we had the following Components attached to the Cube GameObject:

1. Name
2. Tag
3. Layer
4. Transform
5. Mesh Filter
6. Box Collider
7. Mesh Renderer
8. Material

Every GameObject will have the first 3 attributes and the Transform Components attached to it. This is mandatory. The Transform Component is one of the most important Components. It defines the GameObject's position, rotation, and scale in the game world.

One important note on the Tag property. You will define a Tag word to link, or more precisely identify, one or more GameObjects. For

---

[4] Components are the nuts & bolts of objects and behaviors in a game. They are the functional pieces of every GameObject.

example you will have a Tag defined that will be associated with you player character, you will have a Tag defined that will be associated with your enemies and so forth. It is another way to identify and query GameObjects in your scene during runtime.

It is important to take away from this section that a GameObject is a container for Components which in return define what that GameObject will look like and how it will behave. Jumping a little bit ahead, even the programs that we write are attached as Components to the GameObject to give it extended functions and features.

Adding and Editing Components

You can add Components to the selected GameObject through the *Components Menu* or the *Add Component* button in the *Inspector Window*. There are a bunch of predefined Components out of the box already that ship with Unity. We won't be able to get into all of the components, but we will take a look at some of the most used ones and will let the reader do their own research.

You can attach any number or combination of Components to a single GameObject. Some Components work best in combination with others. For example, the *Rigidbody* works with any *Collider*. The Rigidbody control the Transform through the NVIDIA PhysX physics engine, and the Collider allows the Rigidbody to collide and interact with other Colliders. Refer to the Unity documentation to learn more about each different type of Component that is available out of the box.

One of the great aspects of Components is flexibility. When you attach a Component to a GameObject, there are different properties in the Component that can be adjusted in the editor while designing a game, or by scripts when running the game. There are two main types of Properties:

- *Values* – value properties can be adjusted through the designer or at runtime. They can be of any data type.
- *References* – reference properties are like pointers to other GameObjects, audio, scripts, material, Prefabs, and etc…

Figure 19 - Property Types, Reference and Value

Components can include references to any other type of Component, GameObjects, or Assets. In Figure 19, you can see an example of both reference property types and value property types.

Scripts as Components

When you create a script and attach it to a GameObject, the script appears in the GameObject's Inspector Window as a Component. This is because scripts become Components when they are saved. In technical terms, a script compiles as a type of Component, and is treated like any other Component by the Unity engine.

Basically a script is a component that you create yourself. You are the author defining the members to be exposed to the inspector, and the component/script will execute the designed functionality.

In other words, each one of your scripts is a unique class, and as discussed in Object-Oriented Programming Concepts, your class definition will dictate how your component will behave at design time, and at runtime. The data fields which have a *public* access modifier will be available in the *Inspector Window* for editing.

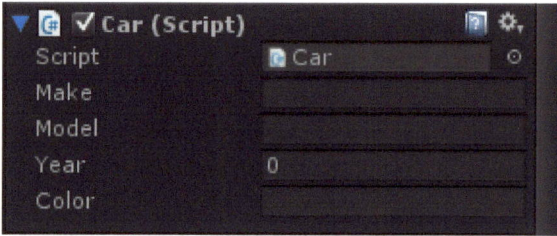

Figure 20 - Car Class Properties

However, in Unity to expose the properties, you will need to provide the following declaration on each field:

```
[SerializeField]
private string make;      // store make as string type

[SerializeField]
private string model;     // store model as string type

[SerializeField]
private int year;         // store year as int type

[SerializeField]
private string color;     // store color as string type
```

Code Block 15 - SerializeField for Inspector Window

This is the easiest way to expose the private fields of a class in the *Inspector Window*.

Static GameObjets

Many optimizations need to know if an object can move during gameplay. Information about a Static, non-moving, object can often be precomputed in the editor assuming that it will not be invalidated by a change in the object's position. This will help with the rendering and frame rate of your game. Such techniques are used for optimization and it is a good idea to learn about the benefits of them as you design and develop your game. To identify a GameObject as *Static* or *Non-Static*, there is a checkbox in the *Inspector Window*. If the checkbox is marked, then Unity will inform various internal systems that the object will not move. The whole idea here is performance enhancement! These internal systems are as follows:

1. *Global Illumination*: advanced lighting for a scene.
2. *Occluder* and *Occludee*: rendering optimization based on the visibility of objects from specific camera positions.
3. *Batching*: rendering optimization that combines several objects into one larger object.
4. *Navigation*: the system that enables characters to negotiate obstacles in the scene.
5. *Off-Mesh Links*: connections made by the Navigation system between discontinuous areas of the scene.
6. *Reflection Probe*: captures a spherical view of its surroundings in all directions.

Global Illumination

Global Illumination is a system that models how light is bounced off of surfaces onto other surfaces, indirect light, rather than being limited to just the light that hits a surface directly from a light source, direct light. Modeling indirect light allows for effects that make the virtual world seem more realistic and connected, since object's affect each other's appearance. An example would be when sunlight hits the floor at the opening of a case and bounces around inside so the inner parts of the case are illuminated as well.

Traditionally, video games and other realtime graphics applications have been limited to direct lighting, because the calculations required for indirect lighting were too slow so they could only be used in non-realtime situation such as computer generated films. A way for games to work around this limitation is to calculate indirect light only for objects and surfaces that are known ahead of time that have no motion, static object.

This will help pre-calculate the indirect lighting effect. Unity supports this technique, called *Baked Lightmaps*[5]. In addition to indirect light, Baked Lightmaps, also take advantage of the greater computation time available to generate more realistic soft shadows from area lights and indirect light than what can normally be achieved with realtime techniques.

Occlusion Culling

Occlusion Culling is a feature that disables rendering of objects when they are not currently seen by the camera because they are obscured (occluded) by other objects. This does not happen automatically, since most of the time objects farthest away from the camera are drawn first and closer objects are drawn over the top. This is different from *Frustum Culling*, as Frustum Culling only disables the renderers for objects that are outside the camera's viewing area but does not disable anything hidden from view by overdraw.

The occlusion culling process will go through the scene using a virtual camera to build a hierarchy of potentially visible sets of objects. This is the data that is used by each camera at runtime to determine what is visible and what is not. This reduces the number of draw calls and increases the performance of the game.

Batching

To draw an object on the screen, Unity engine has to issue a draw call to the graphics API[6]. Draw calls are often expensive, with the graphics API doing significant work for every draw call, causing performance overhead on the CPU side.

Unity uses static batching to address this. The goal of the static batching is to regroup as many meshes in less buffers to get better performance, rendering giant meshes instead of a lot of small meshes which is inefficient.

---

[5] The process in which the indirect light is pre-calculated and stored.
[6] OpenGL or Direct3D

Navigation

The Navigation system allows you to create characters that can intelligently move in the game world. The navigation system uses navigation meshes to reason about the environment. The navigation meshes are created automatically from your *Scene Geometry*.

Unity NavMesh system consists of the following pieces:

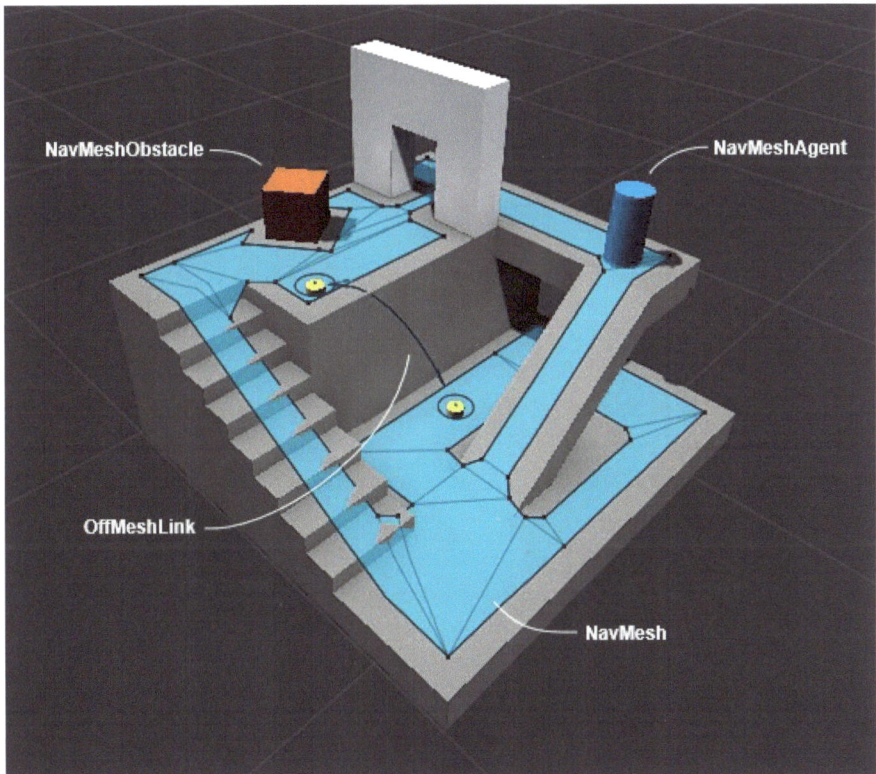

Figure 21 - NavMesh Components

1. *NavMesh*: is a data structure which describes the walkable surfaces of the game world and allows to find path from one walkable location to another in the game world. This data structure is built, automatically from the level geometry.

2. *NavMesh Agent*: is a component helping you to create characters which avoid each other while moving towards their

goal. Agents reason about the game world using the NavMesh and they know how to avoid eachother as well as moving obstacles.

3. *Off-Mesh Link*: is a component allowing you to incorporate navigation shortcuts which cannot be represented using a walkable surface. For example, jumping over a ditch or a fence, or opening a door before walking through it.

4. *NavMesh Obstacle*: is a component allowing you to describe moving obstacles the agent should avoid while navigating the world. A barrel or a crate controlled by the physics system is a good example of an obstacle.

Off-Mesh Links

The connections between the NavMesh polygons are described using links inside the pathfinding system. Sometimes it is necessary to let the agent navigate across places which are not walkable, for example, jumping over a fence, or traversing through a closed door. These cases need to know the location of the action. These actions can be annotated using Off-Mesh Links, which tell the pathfinder that a route exists through the specified link. This link can be later accessed when following the path, and the special action can be executed.

Reflection Probe

A reflection probe is like a camera that captures a spherical view of its surroundings in all directions. The captured image is then stored in a *Cubemap*[7] that can be used by objects with reflective materials. Sevral reflection probes can be used in a given scene and objects can be set to use the cubemap produced by the nearest probe.

CG films and animations commonly feature highly realistic reflections, which are important for giving a sense of connectedness among the objects in the scene. The accuracy of these reflections comes with a high cost in processor time. This is a problem as it severely limits the use of reflective objects in real-time games. Traditionally, games have

---

[7] A Cubemap is a collection of six square textures that represent the reflections on an environment.

used a technique called reflection mapping to simulate reflections from objects while keeping the processing overhead to an acceptable level.

Unity improves on basic reflection mapping through the use of Reflection Probes, which allow the visual environment to be samples at strategic points in the scene. You should generally place them at every point where the appearance of a reflective object would change noticeably. When a reflective object passes near to a probe, the reflection samples by the probe can be used for the object's reflection map. When several probes are nearby, Unity can interpolate between them to allow for gradual changes in reflection. As you observe, there are too many technical details and complexities to cover in this book, therefore, it is encouraged that the reader study the topics on their own by researching the details further.

Prefabs – Concepts and Usage

As you design and develop your game, you will be creating many GameObjects with various components and properties. Some of the GameObjects that you will be creating are going to be pretty complex. At the same time, there might be times where you will want to duplicate or replicate the same exact GameObject within the same scene or in a different scene.

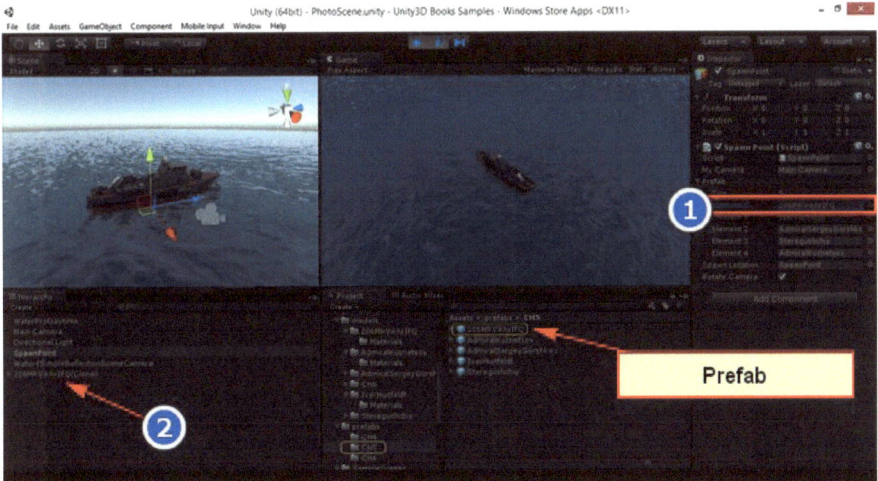

Figure 22 - Prefab Concept

A *Prefab* is a powerful feature within Unity that allows you to make a copy of your GameObject and store it for later use. The Prefab acts as a template from which you can create new object instances in the scene. Another powerful feature provided by the Prefab is the ability to edit and modify the Prefab and automatically all active instances of the Prefab will be reflected by the latest updates. You can also break a link between an instance of a Prefab and the Prefab to overwrite the properties or make special changes to that particular non-related instance. You will get a better fell of what Prefabs are and why they are so useful in later chapters.

Parent-Child Relationship

Unity uses a concept called *Parenting*. Parenting is one of the most important concepts to understand when using Unity. When a GameObject is a *Parent* to another GameObject, the *Child* GameObject will move, rotate, and scale exactly as its Parent does. You can think of parenting as being like the relationship between your arms and your body; whenever your body moves, your arms also move along with it. Child objects can also have their own children and etc[8]...

To make any GameObject the child of another, drag the desired child onto the desired parent in the *Hierarchy*. A child will inherit the movement and rotation of its parent. You can use a parent object's foldout arrow to show or hide its children as necessary. The parent-child relationship of a GameObject is visually represented in the Hierarchy Window. A GameObject can have a very complex parent-child structure.

---

[8] Any object can have multiple children, but only one parent.

Chapter 4 – Game Rules and Mechanics

Basics of Game Mechanics

The underlying activity in games is play. Play can be found in all human cultures. Play provides teaching and learning opportunities. Young children will play to assist them in practicing life skills. The key element in play is the cause-and effect nature that reinforces certain behaviors. To practice is to attempt to get better at some skill set.

When play becomes structures and goals, rules, and actions are applied they turn into games. In the playground, simple play involving chasing other children turns into a game of Tag when one child becomes "it" and the objective is to tab another child in order to make him or her "it."

These fundamental actions of human behavior found in the play and games of children are found at the very heart of computer games and make up the set of code game mechanics.

Searching

Searching is a basic human cognitive process that involves perception and scanning of an environment. In computer games, this ability is leveraged to make the player look for a specific piece of information, item, location, or character in an environment. The objective of the player's search may be to find an item needed to proceed in the game, for example, a key to open a door, or to navigate a maze to get from one place to another.

Matching

Matching is an activity that is part of the searching process. For the human brain, identifying one object as being similar to another is a simple thing. To be searching for something is to be able to identify when the mental image you have of the thing you are looking for is the same thing you are looking at; that is, they match. Many day-to-day activities involve matching, such as finding a pair of socks to putting the right PIN into an ATM.

In a game, matching is used to get players to put one or more things together because they are smaller pieces of a whole or are the same color or shape or have other similar characteristics. This common action may find players putting together parts of a machine to make it work as a whole or placing the same colored items next to each other on a grid.

Sorting

Attempting to make order out of chaos is a common human behavior. People with very extreme cases of requiring everything to be in its place may suffer from compulsive obsessive disorder. However, in many cases when things are sorted, life is much easier. When things are in order and we can rely on them being in order, it lifts some of the cognitive load off doing other tasks.

Games use this sorting desire to motivate players to arrange two or more items according to their characteristics, such as size, color, species, age or name. Sorting can also be employed in activities where performing tasks in order is necessary to complete a challenge.

Chancing

Chance devices such as die and the drawing of straws for purposes of sorting, selecting, and division are common among many cultures, and the practice is referenced in classical Greek literature as the Trojan wars and beforehand in Egyptian artifacts.

Using chance in decision making is referred to as risk. Research has shown that the types of risks people take today stem back to situations encountered by our ancestors, including competition with other individuals, competition with other cultures, mating, resource allocation, and environment.

In games, chance is used to determine the probability to future outcomes. This is one of the oldest actions used in games involving the

use of dice: rolling or coin tossing to determine an outcome based on chance. Without some element of probability in which players knew what the outcome of their actions would be before they did them, there would not be any need to take a risk. Research has shown the greater the risk, the higher the neurochemical reward.

Mixing

Mixing actions involves the combining of objects or actions to produce an outcome unachievable otherwise. In day-to-day life, people mix ingredients to make food, paint pigments to make new colors, and multi-task actions to get jobs completed more quickly.

In computer games, actions can be combined to allow characters to perform tasks they couldn't do with single actions, for example, jumping while running to leap across a crevasse in the game world or combining multiple keystrokes to perform special moves.

Combining game objects to produce other game objects is also an example of mixing.

Timing

Human society is run by time. Even before the advent of mechanical time-keeping devices, the earth's revolution around the sun meant humans were constantly on a time schedule.

The use of time in a computer game can be applied to as a game mechanic. It could involve completing a task within an allotted time, timing an action, or waiting for some event to occur. This mechanism is used to instigate urgency in situations such as racing, whether it be against the clock or an opponent or to generate anticipation when waiting for something to occur or forcing patience upon a player who has to wait for the game environment to change.

Time can be used to add respect to the long process of training one's character with new skills, acquire new set of skills and so forth. Sometimes this tends to take many hours and sometimes days. On an online game, this can be continued while the player is away from the avatar. This is another good way to keep the player engage and bring them back to the game over time for progress further.

Progressing

Life is about progressing, whether it be growing from a baby to an adult, getting a university degree, or getting a job promotion. Humans, in general, experience stages in their lives that correlate with their age and achievements.

Games employ progression scheme in which the player begins as a noob and progresses to the level of expert at the end. Along this journey, progression schemes are put in place that give the players a feeling of achievement for their efforts.

Capturing

To capture is to take something that belongs to someone else through force or your own efforts. Throughout history there is a long list of tribes capturing members of other tribes, armies capturing cities, and pirates taking ships.

Some games embed this mechanic as the primary objective of the game. Most real time strategy games require players to capture and hold resources and bases while building up their military and economics to attack and capture or destroy the opponent. Or it could be as simple as playing capture the flag.

Conquering

In a similar vein to capturing is the action of conquering. Whereas capturing is more linked to stealing, conquering is about outdoing or destroying the competition. Like capturing, human races have a long history of conquering.

Outdoing an opponent is a classic game play goal. In chess, the aim is to get your opponent into checkmate while taking pieces along the way to make them surrender.

Avoidance

One key to human survival is the avoidance of disliked and harmful things. This includes not eating poisonous substances, not playing with fire, and looking before crossing the street.

Some games incorporate such mechanics, where the player have to avoid certain situations and or objects in the game. For instance, a vehicle should avoid hitting pedestrians while going down the street. A military tank should avoid land mines while on its way to the given destination.

Instead of telling players what they can do, avoidance is all about showing them what they cannot do. This can be implemented by penalizing the player when they perform an action in a game environment where they should have avoided.

Avoidance places constraints on the actions of players such that they must keep in mind what they can't do while trying to progress throughout the game environment.

Collecting

Collecting is another natural human behavior. At the extreme, someone who cannot control collecting and letting go of their collected items might be called a junk collector.

In a game environment, items are there to be collected for a purpose or an objective. Some items can be collected and placed in an inventory to be used at a later time. The collecting mechanics is often used with searching.

For instance, some games may ask the player to collect as many gold coins as possible in a given amount of time.

Generally speaking, all games use a combination of all of the basic game mechanics we have discussed. Most of the role playing games implement all of the game mechanics to make the game play much more interesting and engaging. Obviously this leads to more complex game design and effort on the game designers and developers for implementation.

Simple Examples of the Mechanics

In this section we will look at the use and implementation of the mechanics that were discussed earlier. The examples will combine one or more of the mechanics to illustrate some basics game play concepts.

The Battle Ship game we will develop in Chapter 6 – Creating Battleship and Chapter 7 – Delving Into the Code use some of the game mechanics that we have listed and described in the previous section. The following mechanics are easy to detect in the game: searching, chancing, and conquering.

The player needs to search for the opponent's ship's to be destroyed. The player is taking a chance by placing his or her ships on to the game board, likewise, the player is taking a chance whenever he or she is picking a target to hit. Finally the objective of the game is to conquer the opponent by totally destroying all of their game pieces.

Let's quickly put together a new project to build and demonstrate the implementation of the different mechanics.

- Level 1: searching; collecting; matching and sorting.
- Level 2: chancing; mixing and timing
- Level 3: progressing; avoidance; capturing and conquering

Development of Level 1

The goal of this level is to help you understand and implement the four mechanics of searching, collecting, matching and sorting. Let us begin by addressing searching and collecting first. The initial objective of the player will be to search the game world and collect a set of objects that will be then used for matching and sorting.

- Objective 1: Search and collect objects X, Y and Z
- Objective 2: Sort the collected objects by their size.

We have just defined our objective based on the game mechanics described. Now it is time to actually put together a simple example to illustrate the concept.

Assuming you have started a new scene for the purpose of this practice, we will go ahead and create our first game object, a terrain. To create a terrain, you will need to select:

- GameObject->3D Object->Terrain

From the main menu. The default size of the Terrain will be very large, for the purpose of this practice we will need to reduce it to about 50 x 50. This is good enough for our demonstration. Also, don't forget that, this is the equivalent of a 2,500 square meters of area! Not an easy task to fill!

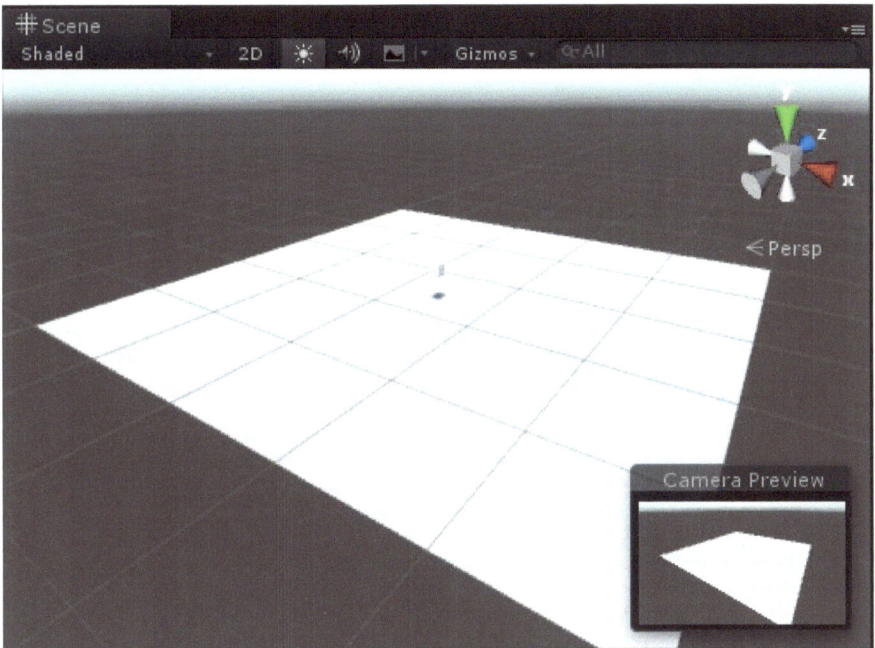

Figure 23 - Simple 50x50 Terrain

Your terrain should look similar to Figure 23. The cube was placed just for a visual clue on the size of the terrain. Using the built in terrain tool, we can give some nice contours to the surface of the terrain to make it more pleasing.

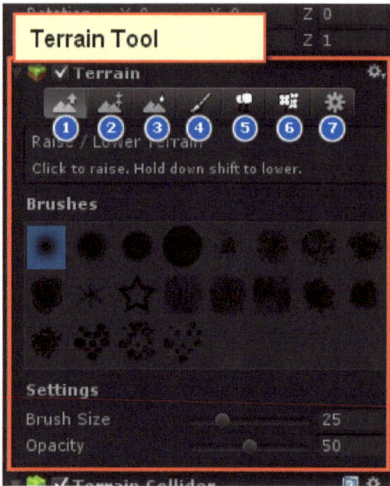

Figure 24 - Snap shot of Terrain Tool

This can be achieved within the Unity's IDE through the Inspector Window:

1. Raise/Lower Terrain
2. Paint Height
3. Smooth Height
4. Paint Texture
5. Place Trees
6. Paint Details
7. Terrain Settings

The purpose of each numbered icon has been listed above.

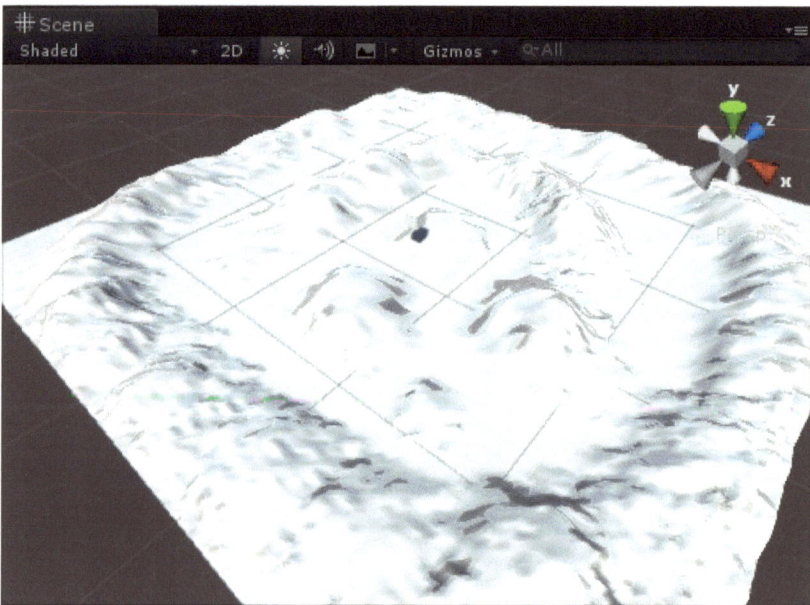

Figure 25 - Terrain Design

You can use features one through seven to modify and shape the terrain. Go ahead and play with the options and come up with a terrain model you are consent with.

Looking at Figure 25 you can see that it is very easy to create interesting terrains with the tools provided for quick prototyping. I am happy with the terrain map, now the next step would be to apply some textures, and other environmental objects such as trees and rocks. To add texture to the terrain, select Pain Texture from the Inspector Window and apply the desired texture to the terrain.

Figure 26 - Terrain with texture applied

Not bad for a programmer if you ask me. So now we have defined our terrain, and we need to place some game objects to be searched for and collected. To keep the graphics simple, we will use sphere and cube for the purpose of demonstrating the concepts. Our player will be represented as a sphere, and our game objects can be represented by any one of the primitive types.

For object search and collection, we can utilize three different sizes of cubes. For searching, the player will need to find all of the three cubes, and for sorting, the player will need to stack them on top of one another having the largest cube as the base. This will handle our Objectives one and two as listed.

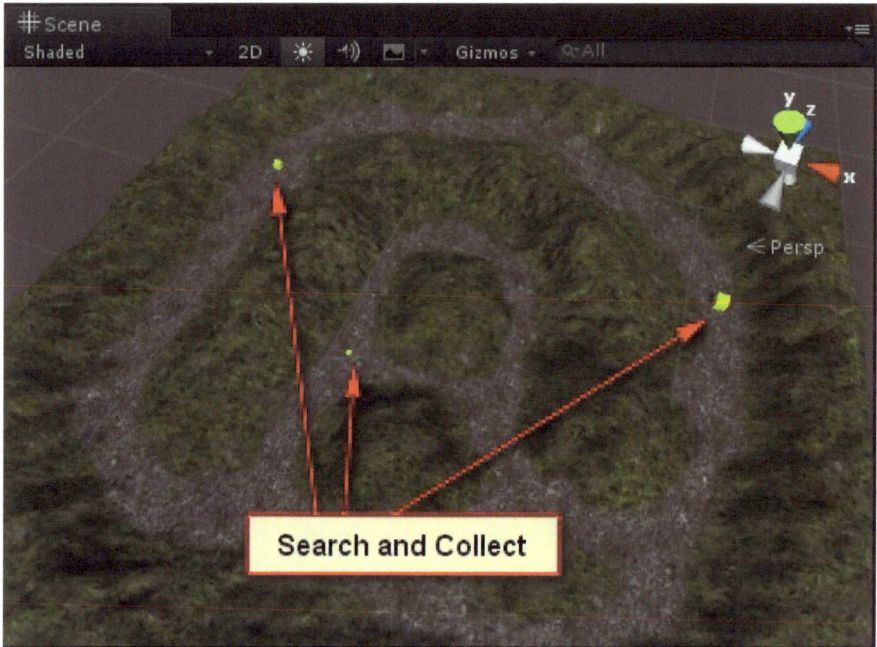

Figure 27 - Search and collect game objects

NOTE: *There are better options and tools specifically designed for building terrains and complex natural environments. In a real life scenario you will most likely use an external tool to create your terrain and then import it into Unity for programming.*

We can randomly position the three cubes of different sizes on the terrain as indicated in Figure 27. In the game we would need to be able to identify these objects as of a certain type. This will allow us to properly handle them internally through the code.

So here are a few requirements that we need to define to meet our first objectives in the game:

- Player can collect the object by going through them or by clicking on the object when they are in range.
- Player will need to move the objects to designated area so stacking.
- Player needs to identify the objects to be collected.
- Player needs to retrieve object data from the collected objects for further processing.

Before we continue on with our example, I would like to take the time and introduce some very important topics and concepts so that we have a good understanding and background regarding how Unity handles the interaction between different GameObjects.

Physics for Games

A physics engine is a computer software that provides an approximate simulation of certain physical systems, such as rigid body dynamics, collision detection, soft body dynamics, and fluid dynamics. There are generally two classes of physics engines, *real-time* and *high-precision*.

High-Precision

High-precision physics engines require more processing power to calculate very precise physics and are usually used by scientists and engineers for complex simulations.

Real-Time

Real-time physics engines are used in video games and other forms of interactive computing. They use simplified calculations and decreased accuracy to compute in time for the game to respond at an appropriate rate for gameplay.

Game Engines

In most computer games, speed of the processors and gameplay are more important than accuracy of simulation. This leads to designers for physics engines that produce results in real-time but that replicates real world physics only for simple cases and typically with some approximation.

Objects in games interact with the player, the environment, and each other. Typically, most 3D objects in games are represented by two separate meshes or shapes. One of these meshes is the highly complex and detailed shape visible to the player in the game, and a second simplified invisible mesh is used to represent the object to the physics engine so that the physics engine can interact with it.

Enter the Collider Component

Colliders are used to define the shape of an object for the purpose of physical collisions. The collider does not necessarily need to be the same shape of the game object's mesh. Usually a rough estimate is often more efficient and indistinguishable in gameplay.

The simplest colliders, which are also the least processor-intensive, are the primitive collider types: *Box Collider*, *Sphere Collider*, and the *Capsule Collider*. By combining an positioning these colliders you can pretty much create a compound collider that will satisfy most any game object for collision detection.

Colliders can be added to an object without a Rigidbody component to create floors, walls and other motionless elements of a scene. These are referred to as static[9] colliders.

Triggers

The scripting system can detect when collisions occur and initiate actions using the *OnCollisionEnter()* function. However, we can also use the physics engine simply to detect when one collider enters the space of another without creating a collision. A collider configured as a Trigger, using the *IsTrigger* property, does not behave as a solid object and will simply allow other colliders to pass through. When a

---

[9] Static colliders can interact with dynamic colliders but since they don't have Rigidbody, they will not move in response to the collisions.

collider enters its space, a trigger will call the *OnTriggerEnter()* function on the trigger object's scripts.

Script Actions on Collision

When collisions occur, the physics engine calls functions with specific names on any scripts attached to the objects involved. You will need to implement the code logic in these functions to respond to the collision event.

On the first physics update where the collision is detected, the *OnCollisionEnter()* function is called. During updates where contact is maintained, *OnCollisionStay()* function is called and finally, *OnCollisionExit()* function is called indicating that the contact has been broken. Similarly, trigger colliders call the analogous *OnTriggerEnter()* function, *OnTriggerStay()* function and the *OnTriggerExit()* functions.

Collider Interactions

Colliders interact with each other differently depending on how their Rigidbody components have been configured.

Static Collider

This is a GameObject that has a collider but no Rigidbody. Static colliders are used for level geometry which always stays at the same place and never moves around. Incoming rigidbody objects will collide with the static collider but will not move it.

Rigidbody Collider

This is a GameObject with a collider and a normal, non-kinematic Rigidbody attached. Rigidbody colliders are fully simulated by the physics engine and can react to collisions and forces applied from a script. They can collide with other objects, including static colliders, and are the most commonly used collider configuration in games that use physics.

Kinematic Rigidbody Collider

This is a GameObject with a collider and a kinematic Rigidbody attached, the *IsKinematic* property of the Rigidbody is enabled. You can move a kinematic rigidbody object from a script by modifying its

Transform component but it will not respond to collision and forces like a non-kinematic rigidbody. Kinematic rigidbodies should be used for colliders that can be moved or disabled/enabled occasionally but that should otherwise behave like static colliders. The best example to illustrate this concept would be a sliding door. The door should normally act as an immovable physical obstacle but can be opened when necessary. Unlike a static collider, a moving kinematic rigidbody will apply friction to other objects and will "wake up" other rigidbodies when they make contact.

Rigidbody

A Rigidbody is the main component that enables physical behavior for an object. With a Rigidbody attached, the object will immediately respond to gravity. If one or more Collider components are also added, then the object will be moved by incoming collisions.

Rigidbodies allow your GameObjects to act under control of the physics engine. This opens the gateway to realistic collisions, varied types of joints, and other very cool behaviours. Manipulating your GameObject by adding forces to the Rigidbody creates a very different behavior than adjusting the *Transform* component directly. As a good rule of thumb, you shouldn't manipulate the Rigidbody and the Transform of the same GameObject, only one or the other.

Joints

You can attach one rigidbody to another or to a fixed point in space using a Joint component. Generally, you want a joint to allow at least some freedom of motion. Unity provides the following Join components that enforce different restrictions: *Hinge Joint* and *Spring Joint*. Hinge Joint allows rotation around a specific point and axis, while Spring Joint keeps the object apart but lets the distance between them stretch slightly. Joints also have other options that can be enabled for specific effects.

Hinge Joint

The Hinge Joint groups two Rigidbodies together, constraining them to move like they are connected by a hinge. Best example would be a door, but can also be applied and used to model chains, and etc..

A single Hinge Joint should be applied to a GameObject. The hinge will rotate at the point specified by the *Anchor* property, moving around the specified *Axis* property.

Spring Joint

The Spring Joint joins two Rigidbody together but allows the distance between them to change as though they were connected by a spring.

The spring acts like a piece of elastic that tries to pull the two anchor points together to the exact same position. The strength of the pull is proportional to the current distance between the points with the force per unit of distance set by the *Spring* property. To prevent the spring from oscillating endlessly you can set the *Damper* value that reduces the spring force in proportion to the relative speed between the two objects. The higher the value, the more quickly the oscillation will die down.

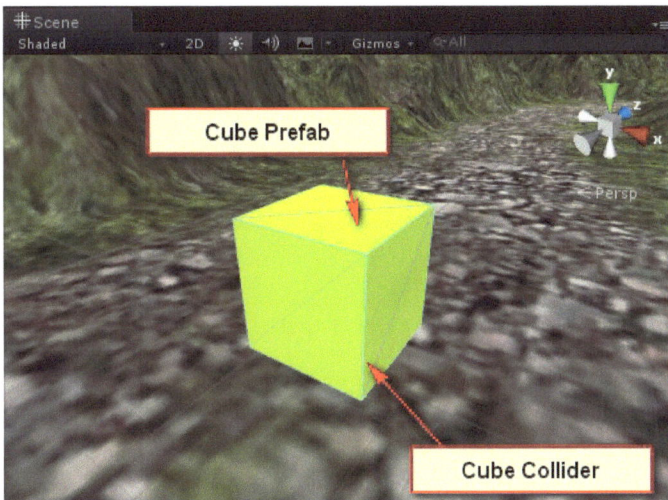

Figure 28 - Cube Prefab with Cube Collider

Now that we have a better understanding of how the system works, we can continue with the implementation of our Level 1. Notice that for each of the cube primitives we have created, a Box Collider has been automatically attached to the game object. This is shown in Figure 28.

Figure 29 - Inspector Window showing Box Collider

Taking a look at the Inspector Window, in Figure 29 for the selected cube, we get to see the details of the components attached to the cube game object.

I would like to turn your attention to the *Box Collider* component attached to the game object. Notice that by default it is exactly the same size and shape as the cube itself, and it is centered at the local origin.

These are adjustable values and you can go ahead and modify them in the editor and visually see the result.

The other main feature is the IsTrigger property indicated by the arrow. By default this is disabled, we are going to go ahead and enable the IsTrigger property so that we can use the OnTriggerEnter() function from the script to handle collision.

The next property that I would like you to pay attention to is the *Tag* property. Notice that by default all of the game objects that you create in the scene are going to be untagged. We are going to make a

76

new tag and associate our game objects with the newly created tag. This property then can be used within the script to identify what object we are interacting with.

To create a new tag, you just use the drop-down menu and select *Add Tag...* to display the user interface for entering a new tag element into the list. If a tag is already in the list, then you can simply select it without having to adding it to the list. I will use *MyCollectable* as a new tag element. Your cube prefabs should have the following configurations:

Cube 1	Cube 2	Cube 3
ID: C1	ID: C2	ID: C3
Tag: MyCollectable	Tag: MyCollectable	Tag: MyCollectable
Scale: <0.25,0.25,0.25>	Scale: <0.50,0.50,0.50>	Scale: <0.75,0.75,0.75>

I am not listing the position and orientation as that will be different for you based on the formation of your terrain and positioning of the cubes. We have configured our objects for searching and collection, now we need to work on the script. Go ahead and create a new script called *MyCollectable.cs*. At the moment we would want to implement the collision detection.

```
public class MyCollectable : MonoBehaviour {

    // Use this for initialization
    void Start () {    }

    // Update is called once per frame
    void Update () {    }

    // Function to detect if there is a collision
    // with this particular object
    void OnTriggerEnter(Collider c)
    {
        Debug.Log("You have bumped into me!!!");
    }
}
```

Code Block 16 - MyCollectable.cs listing

Go ahead and attach the script to all of the cube objects that are going to be collected. At the moment, we will not go further. The code is going to print out in the console a message indicating that we have collided with the object. Before we continue, let's go ahead and work on our player character. This will allow us to actually navigate the world and test our code and get a feel of how it will work.

Character Mechanics

Player Input

At some point in time, you will need to start getting input from the player and be able to translate the input into some sort of an action. Depending on the game and the design, this element by itself could be very complex. For the purposes of demonstration we are going to keep things simple and to the point.

So as discussed earlier, we will use a sphere primitive to represent our player. To this sphere we will need to attach some sort of a script to handle the movement. We will call this *PlayerInput.cs*. This script will handle the initial movement of our character in the world.

```
using UnityEngine;
using System.Collections;

public class PlayerInput : MonoBehaviour {

    // Use this for initialization
void Start () {   }

        // Update is called once per frame
    void Update () {

        // code for the movement of player (CP) forward
        if (Input.GetKey(KeyCode.UpArrow))
        {
            this.transform.Translate(Vector3.forward * Time.deltaTime);
        }
        // code for the movement of player (CP) backward
        if (Input.GetKey(KeyCode.DownArrow))
        {
            this.transform.Translate(Vector3.back * Time.deltaTime);
        }
        // code for the movement of player (CP) left
        if (Input.GetKey(KeyCode.LeftArrow))
        {
            this.transform.Rotate(Vector3.up, -5);
        }
        // code for the movement of player (CP) right
        if (Input.GetKey(KeyCode.RightArrow))
        {
            this.transform.Rotate(Vector3.up, 5);
```

```
        }

    }

}
```

Code Block 17 - PlayerInput() initial version

Go ahead and attach the script to the sphere[10], and use the arrow keys to move around the terrain. Notice how the physics engine interacts with the *Rigidbody* of the player. This is especially visible when you are trying to climb a hill or a mountain. You will notice that the sphere that is supposed to represent the player character is going to roll down and get affected by the forces applied to it through the interaction of the collision of the meshes between itself and the terrain by the physics engine.

To solve this issue, you will need to put some constraints on the *Rigidbody* components and the way it will react to the physics engine. The constraints would be to disable the rotation on the *X*, *Y* and the *Z-Axis* for this particular game object.

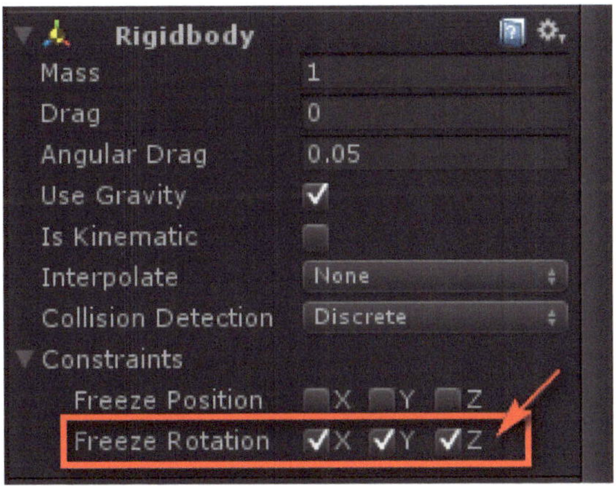

Figure 30 - Rigidbody Freeze Rotation

When you run the game now, you will notice that the player character does not go into a chaotic mode of rotation when colliding with

---

[10] The primitive game object representing your player character needs to also have a Rigidbody component attached to it. Read the Physics section to get a better understanding of how colliders work.

the terrain mesh. This is closer to the behavior we want to simulate, at this point for the demonstration purposes.

Camera Setup

One more improvement I would like to do is the positioning of the Camera object. I would like the camera to follow the player character from behind, and a little bit elevated, kind of like a third-person camera setup. It is actually very easy to setup this configuration. Here are the steps:

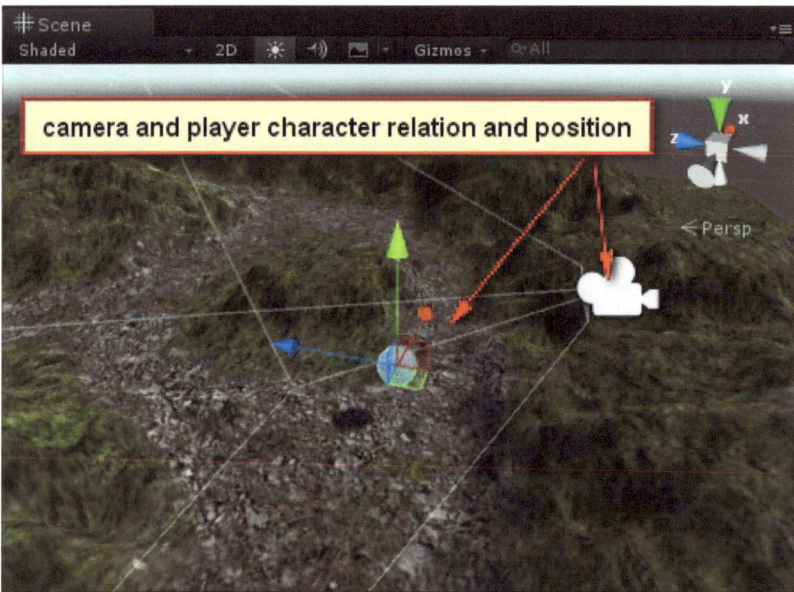

Figure 31 - Third Person Camera Setup

1. In the scene designer, orient the view so that you are behind the player character and a bit above it.
2. Select the *Main Camera* game object and from the GameObject Menu select *GameObject->Align With View* option[11].

---

[11] This will move the Main Camera game object and place it and orient the view to exactly what you see on the scene designer.

3. Make the Main Camera game object a child of the player character, by dragging it under the player character game object[12].

4. You can now use the local transform tolls available for the *Main Camera* to fine tune the angles and view port.

By the end of the steps, you should have a relationship between the player character and the camera similar to that of Figure 31. Go ahead and run the game, and you will see that we have something that is much more pleasing. Go ahead and see if you can collect the cube's we have setup in the level. You will notice that you collide with them, but nothing happens. Our debug statement is not even showing up, that is because we never enabled the *IsTrigger* property to *true* on the cube's game object. Go ahead and set them to true, and run one more time.

Figure 32 - Collider Interaction after IsTrigger is Enabled

Notice that the interaction of the two game object's colliders are handled differently by the physics engine once, we set the *IsTrigger* property on the collectable objects to true. Now, you will also notice that the console is giving us the expected output:

---

[12] This will create a parent/child relationship between the two Game Objects.

Figure 33 - Console output for collision detection

Now we can start the fun part, the magic of programming through scripting that will enable us to keep track of the collected items. We would need to expand our scripts a bit further to handle the collect of our game objects, we might also have to introduce a new script for the data node. We will start by expanding the *MyCollectable.cs* script.

```
using UnityEngine;
using System.Collections;

public class MyCollectable : MonoBehaviour {

    public int ID;
    public float size;

    // Use this for initialization
    void Start () {
        this.transform.localScale = new Vector3(size, size, size);
    }

    // Update is called once per frame
    void Update () {

    }
}
```

Code Block 18 - MyCollectable.cs ver 2

I have added two public members representing the ID and the size of the collectable object. The *Start()* function will use the size property to scale the collectable game object when the game starts. Notice that we no longer have the *OnTriggerEnter()* function listed. We will handle the collision detection in the *PlayerInput.cs* script.

In the meantime, we had to introduce a new script that is used to solely store data that will be used during the game. This new script is called *MyCollectableData.cs*. Here is the listing for it:

```
using UnityEngine;
using System.Collections;

public class MyCollectableData{

    public int ID;
    public float size;

    public MyCollectableData() { }
}
```

Code Block 19 - MyCollectableData.cs

This is a simple class that will be used to just store and retrieve the two attributes *ID* and *size*. The main script that will handle the collision and the registration of the object pick-up is implemented in the *PlayerInput.cs* script.

```
using UnityEngine;
using System.Collections.Generic;

public class PlayerInput : MonoBehaviour {

    public List<MyCollectableData> myCollection = new List<MyCollecta-
bleData>();

    void Awake()
    {
        // make sure we start clean
        this.myCollection.Clear();
    }

    // Use this for initialization
    void Start () {    }

    // Update is called once per frame
    void Update () {

        // code for the movement of player (CP) forward
        if (Input.GetKey(KeyCode.UpArrow))
        {
            this.transform.Translate(Vector3.forward * Time.deltaTime);
        }
        // code for the movement of player (CP) backward
        if (Input.GetKey(KeyCode.DownArrow))
        {
            this.transform.Translate(Vector3.back * Time.deltaTime);
        }
        // code for the movement of player (CP) left
        if (Input.GetKey(KeyCode.LeftArrow))
        {
            this.transform.Rotate(Vector3.up, -5);
        }
```

```
    // code for the movement of player (CP) right
    if (Input.GetKey(KeyCode.RightArrow))
    {
        this.transform.Rotate(Vector3.up, 5);
    }

    if (Input.GetKeyUp(KeyCode.Z))
    {
        foreach(var d in this.myCollection)
        {
            Debug.Log(d.ID);
        }
    }

}

void OnTriggerEnter(Collider c)
{
    if(c.tag.Equals("MyCollectable"))
    {
        var collect = c.gameObject.GetComponent<MyCollectable>();

        MyCollectableData data = new MyCollectableData();

        data.ID = collect.ID;
        data.size = collect.size;

        this.myCollection.Add(data);

        Destroy(c.gameObject);
    }
}
}
```

Code Block 20 - PlayerInput.cs ver. 2

You will notice a few changes from version 1 of the script. First, notice that we have a *List* for collection of type *MyCollectionData*. This is the collection that will be used to store the collectable items.

The second addition is the *OnTriggerEnter()* function. We would like to handle the collision in this particular script because it will make it easier for us to handle the data for this particular scenario. In the function, we are checking to see who we have collided with. This is done by verifying the *Tag* property of the game object that the collider belongs to. If the object is tagged as *MyCollectable*, then we extract the *MyCollectable Component* from the Game Object. This component is basically the *MyCollectable.cs* script that is attached to the cube prefab.

Once, the components is retrieved, we create a *MyCollectableData* object to copy the *ID* and the *size* retrieved from the MyCollectable Component. This object, is then stored into our collection list called *myCollection*. Once we have safely retrieved the data, we call the *Destroy()* function which will destroy the game object from the scene.

What we have done is very simple, yet very powerful once you realize how to apply it to larger projects and use cases. We are not finished yet, we need to be able to retrieve the items and re-create them in the world at another location. We now need to design and implement the mechanics to handle the next scenario.

Unloading Our Collection

We need to identify a location for our unloading of the collected object. Using a *Cylinder Primitive*, we can mark an area where after the player has collected all collectables can unload. So in the designer create a new game object of type *Cylinder* and place it somewhere that will be accessible to the player. My design looks like the following:

Figure 34 - Drop-Off Platform

So we have introduced a new game object that is a representation of a platform to be used for the drop off of the collectable items. We would also need to handle a collision detection for this object. Since we are handling the collider event in the *PlayerInput.cs* script, we can expand on the function to also handle the new game object. This would make sense, since the data that we need to access for the cubes is also stored in the same class.

So all we need to do technically is to create a unique *Tag* for the identification of the platform, and implement the code to handle the collision and the creation of the cubes in the proper location. I am going to call the tag *DropOffZone*.

Let's go ahead and put everything together and see how it will work. The following is a listing of *PlayerInput.cs* modified to meet our new criteria.

```
using UnityEngine;
using System.Collections.Generic;

public class PlayerInput : MonoBehaviour {

    public List<MyCollectableData> myCollection = new List<MyCollecta-
bleData>();

    public Material CubeMaterial;

    void Awake()
    {
        // make sure we start clean
        this.myCollection.Clear();
    }

    // Use this for initialization
    void Start () {    }

    // Update is called once per frame
    void Update () {
        // code for the movement of player (CP) forward
        if (Input.GetKey(KeyCode.UpArrow))
        {
            this.transform.Translate(Vector3.forward * Time.deltaTime);
        }
        // code for the movement of player (CP) backward
        if (Input.GetKey(KeyCode.DownArrow))
        {
            this.transform.Translate(Vector3.back * Time.deltaTime);
        }
        // code for the movement of player (CP) left
```

```
            if (Input.GetKey(KeyCode.LeftArrow))
            {
                this.transform.Rotate(Vector3.up, -5);
            }
            // code for the movement of player (CP) right
            if (Input.GetKey(KeyCode.RightArrow))
            {
                this.transform.Rotate(Vector3.up, 5);
            }

        }

        // This function handles the collision of colliders as a trigger
        void OnTriggerEnter(Collider c)
        {
            if(c.tag.Equals("MyCollectable"))
            {
                var collect = c.gameObject.GetComponent<MyCollectable>();

                MyCollectableData data = new MyCollectableData();

                data.ID = collect.ID;
                data.size = collect.size;

                this.myCollection.Add(data);

                Destroy(c.gameObject);
            }

            if(c.tag.Equals("DropOffZone"))
            {
                if(this.myCollection.Count>2)
                {
                    Vector3 center = c.transform.position;
                    int index = 1;
                    foreach (var d in this.myCollection)
                    {
                        Vector3 pos = CirclePath (center, 1.0f, index);
                        index++;

                        Quaternion rot = Quaternion.FromToRotation(Vector3.forward,
center - pos);

                        GameObject tmp = GameObject.Instantiate(GameObject.Cre-
atePrimitive(PrimitiveType.Cube),
                            pos, rot) as GameObject;

                        tmp.transform.localScale = new Vector3(d.size, d.size,
d.size);

                        tmp.GetComponent<Renderer>().material = this.CubeMaterial;
                    }
                }
            }
        }
```

```
// Function to place the calculate position of next item around
// a circular path.
Vector3 CirclePath(Vector3 center, float radius, int id)
{
   float ang = 90 * id; //Random.value * 360;
   Vector3 pos;
   pos.x = center.x + radius * Mathf.Sin(ang * Mathf.Deg2Rad);
   pos.z = center.z + radius * Mathf.Cos(ang * Mathf.Deg2Rad);
   pos.y = center.y+1;
   return pos;
}
}
```

Code Block 21 - PlayerInput.cs ver. 3

In the *OnTriggerEnter()* function, we have added a new condition for the *DropOffZone* platform. If we are on the platform, the code checks to see if we have collected all of the collectable items. Once the condition is true, then we start the process on unloading / re-creating the GameObjects in the order of collection in a circular path around the center of the platform. The function *CirclePath()* is used to calculate the position of the next collectible for unloading.

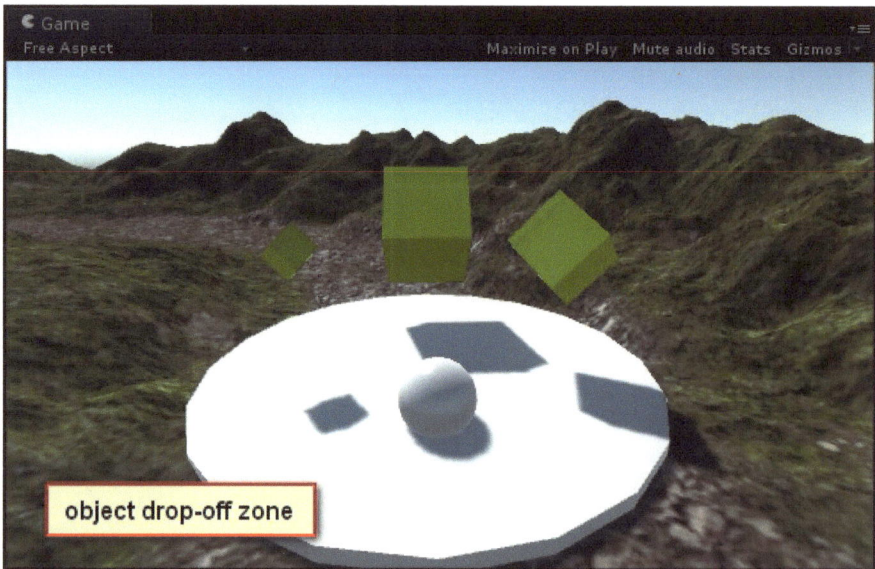

Figure 35 - Drop Off Zone in action

Notice that in the *foreach* loop, we calculate the position of the object to be placed using the *CirclePath()* function, followed by the rotation of the object. Once the cube primitive is instantiated using the position and rotation data, we use the *size* value stored in the *MyCollectableData* object.

Ordering and Matching

We have completed the implementation of searching and collecting of the game object, and hence you have been given a simple example of the two mechanics. The next step is to design matching and ordering. Keeping things simple for demonstration purposes, we can ask the player to click on the game object from smallest to the largest, this will resonate with the act of ordering without making it too complex. We can use a *Stack Data Structure*[13] to implement this feature.

The reason we are using a Stack for the data structure, is because it fits the purpose.

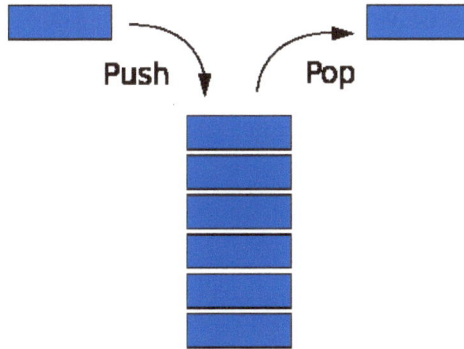

Figure 36 - Visual Representation of a Stack

We can only insert from the top, and before we insert the next value, we can peek the stack and see if the top value currently in the stack is larger than or smaller than the value to be inserted. Based on the result then we can decide what to do next. This will make more sense when we look at the code.

[13] A stack is a basic data structure that can be logically thought as linear structure represented by a real physical stack or pile, a structure where insertion and deletion of items takes place at one end called top of the stack.

The first things to do is to create a stack class. The following code is a listing of our class:

```
using UnityEngine;
using System.Collections;

public class MyStack {

    private int index;
    private ArrayList stack;

    public MyStack()
    {
        this.stack = new ArrayList();
        index = -1;
    }

    public int COUNT
    {
        get { return this.stack.Count; }
    }

    public void push(object data)
    {
        this.stack.Add(data);
        this.index++;
    }

    public object pop()
    {
        object o = this.stack[index];

        this.stack.RemoveAt(index);
        this.index--;

        return o;
    }

    public void clear()
    {
        this.stack.Clear();
        this.index = -1;
    }

    public object peek()
    {
        return this.stack[this.index];
    }
}
```

Code Block 22 - Stack Data Structure

As you can see, the implementation for a Stack data structure is pretty simple and straight forward.

Now we can go ahead and actually implement our game logic to handle matching and ordering. Here is the listing for *PlayerInput.cs* with the new updates:

```csharp
using UnityEngine;
using System.Collections.Generic;

public class PlayerInput : MonoBehaviour {

    public List<MyCollectableData> myCollection = new List<MyCollectableData>();

    public Material CubeMaterial;

    public MyStack stack = new MyStack();
    private bool MATCH = false;

    void Awake()
    {
        this.MATCH = false;

        // make sure we start clean
        this.myCollection.Clear();
    }

    // Use this for initialization
    void Start () {
        }

    // Update is called once per frame
    void Update()
    {

        if(!this.MATCH)
        {
            // code for the movement of player (CP) forward
            if (Input.GetKey(KeyCode.UpArrow))
            {
                this.transform.Translate(Vector3.forward * Time.deltaTime*10);
            }
            // code for the movement of player (CP) backward
            if (Input.GetKey(KeyCode.DownArrow))
            {
                this.transform.Translate(Vector3.back * Time.deltaTime*10);
            }
            // code for the movement of player (CP) left
            if (Input.GetKey(KeyCode.LeftArrow))
            {
                this.transform.Rotate(Vector3.up, -5);
            }
```

```
            // code for the movement of player (CP) right
            if (Input.GetKey(KeyCode.RightArrow))
            {
                this.transform.Rotate(Vector3.up, 5);
            }
        }

        if(this.MATCH)
        {
            #region MOUSE INPUT
            if (Input.mousePosition != null && Input.GetMouseButtonUp(0))
            {
                //Debug.Log("START MATCH >>>");
                RaycastHit selectedCollectable;

                // capture the mouse position and cast a ray to see what object
we hit
                Ray ray = Camera.main.ScreenPointToRay(Input.mousePosition);

                if (Physics.Raycast(ray, out selectedCollectable, 200))
                {
                    //Debug.Log("TAG="+selectedCollectable.transform.tag);

                    if (selectedCollectable.transform.tag.Equals("MyCollect-
able"))
                    {
                        var collect = selectedCollectable.transform.gameOb-
ject.GetComponent<MyCollectable>();

                        MyCollectableData data = new MyCollectableData();

                        data.ID = collect.ID;
                        data.size = collect.size;

                        MyCollectableData sd = null;

                        // check stack
                        if (stack.COUNT > 0)
                        {
                          sd = (MyCollectableData)stack.peek();
                          if (sd.size < data.size)
                           {
                              stack.push(data);
                           }
                           else
                           {
                              Debug.Log("Sorry! Try Again! ...");
                              stack.clear();
                           }
                        }
                        else
                        {
                            stack.push(data);
                        }
                    }
```

```
            }
        }

        if(stack.COUNT>=3)
        {
            for(int i=0; i<=stack.COUNT+1;i++)
            {
                MyCollectableData d = (MyCollectableData)stack.pop();
                Debug.Log(string.Format("Pop: {0}", d.size));
            }
            Debug.Log("GREAT JOB!!! Objective Completed!");
            this.MATCH = false;
        }
        #endregion
    }

}

// This function handles the collision of colliders as a trigger
void OnTriggerEnter(Collider c)
{
    if(c.tag.Equals("MyCollectable"))
    {
        var collect = c.gameObject.GetComponent<MyCollectable>();

        MyCollectableData data = new MyCollectableData();

        data.ID = collect.ID;
        data.size = collect.size;

        this.myCollection.Add(data);

        Destroy(c.gameObject);
    }

    if(c.tag.Equals("DropOffZone"))
    {
        if(this.myCollection.Count>2)
        {
            Vector3 center = c.transform.position;
            int index = 1;
            foreach (var d in this.myCollection)
            {
                Vector3 pos = CirclePath(center, 1.0f, index);
                index++;

                Quaternion rot = Quaternion.FromToRotation(Vector3.forward,
center - pos);

                GameObject tmp = GameObject.CreatePrimitive(Primitive-
Type.Cube);
                tmp.transform.position = pos;
                tmp.transform.rotation = rot;

                tmp.transform.tag = "MyCollectable";
```

```
                tmp.transform.localScale = new Vector3(d.size, d.size,
d.size);

                tmp.GetComponent<Renderer>().material = this.CubeMaterial;

                // attach collectable component, apply the data
                tmp.gameObject.AddComponent<MyCollectable>();
                tmp.gameObject.GetComponent<MyCollectable>().ID = d.ID;
                tmp.gameObject.GetComponent<MyCollectable>().size = d.size;
            }

            // everything was processed, start matching
            this.MATCH = true;
        }
    }
}

// Function to place the calculate position of next item around
// a circular path.
Vector3 CirclePath(Vector3 center, float radius, int id)
{
    float ang = 90 * id; //Random.value * 360;
    Vector3 pos;
    pos.x = center.x + radius * Mathf.Sin(ang * Mathf.Deg2Rad);
    pos.z = center.z + radius * Mathf.Cos(ang * Mathf.Deg2Rad);
    pos.y = center.y+1;
    return pos;
}
}
```

Code Block 23 - PlayerInput.cs ver. 4

You can notice quite a few changes in the code as listed in Code Block 23 - PlayerInput.cs ver. 4. First notice that in the *DropOffZone* collision detection, we are doing several new and important tasks.

1. We iterate through our collectable list.
2. For each collectable being processed, we calculate the position and rotation with the help of *CirclePath()* function.
3. Once the position, rotation and the scale have been applied, we start building the next properties, i.e., *Tag*.
4. Since this is a newly created GameObject that needs to represent the original collectable, we need to also add the *MyCollectable* components to it.
5. After attaching the component, we need to set the data values which then will be used at a later stage.
6. Finally we set a flag value *this.MATCH* to true.

The next big change is in the *Update()* function. We need a way to detect if we have successfully unloaded our collectable objects onto the *DropOffZone*. This is done by a Boolean flag names *MATCH*.

If the flag is set to true, the program goes into the second phase of the game, matching and ordering. The objective here is for the user to select the unloaded collectable boxes in the order from smallest to the largest.

We use *Camera.main.ScreenToRay()* function to convert the mouse coordinates from a 2D space to a 3D space *Ray* object. The Ray object is then used by the Physics engine to cast a ray using the *Raycase()* function. This function returns information about the first object that the ray collides with. This is stored in *selectedCollectable* variable. If we are successfully hitting the desired game object, then we start getting the data using the *GetComponent()* function to access the *MyCollectable*, and storing it into a new *MyCollectableData* object.

When we have all of the information we are looking for, we utilize the Stack data structure to start inserting our data points into it. Obviously there are a few checks and verifications that need to be done before we determine if the selected collectable is going to be pushed onto the Stack, or if we are going to have to start the selection process over again. If you have followed with the instructions thus far, you should have everything working properly. We did not implement any user interface at this point. Main reason is that we are working on the code logic and we are using the console window to output the results for feedback.

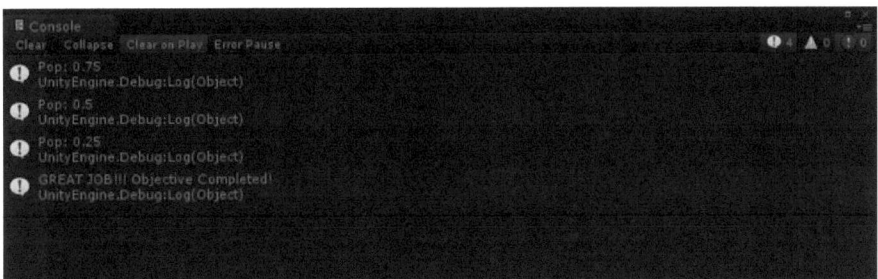

Figure 37 - Console Window Showing Stack Ouput after Successful Order

At this point we have completed the objectives we have set for ourselves for level 1. Let's start thinking about Level 2.

Development of Level 2

In Level 2 we will implement the mechanics for *timing, chancing, mixing* and *progressing*. We can create a level that will be composed of several rooms.

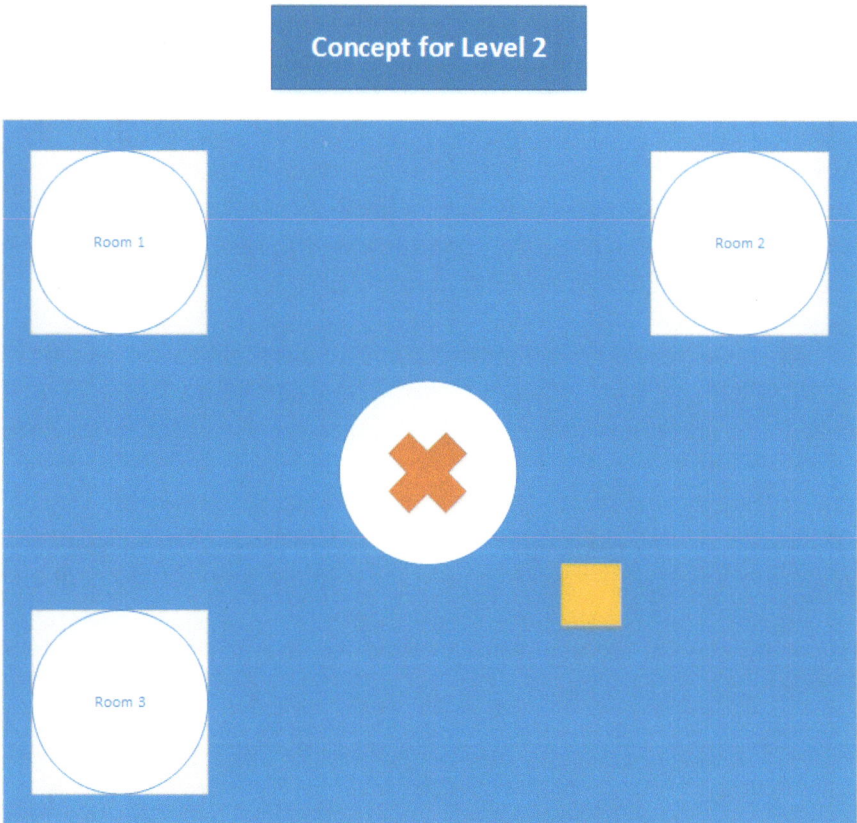

Figure 38 - Just a Concept for Level 2

The basic idea behind level 2 will be for the player to be able to complete the objectives based on some criteria. For instance, the player will need to be able to visit all three rooms within the level to complete the main objective of the level. However, he/she cannot directly access the rooms. They will first have to interact with a randomizer which will dictate which room they need to attend to.

The three rooms are going to be identified by their unique colors: Red, Green and Blue. When the player interacts with the randomizer, the randomizer will display a specific color, when the color has been selected, then the user will need to find the room in a given amount of time. Each room will have a sliding door that will open only if the conditions are met.

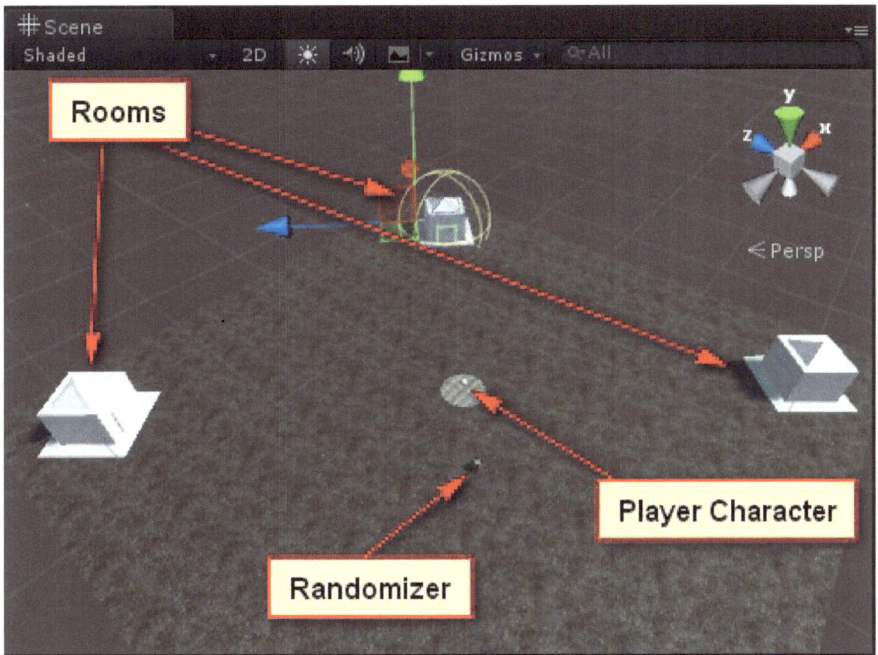

Figure 39 - Level 2 Design

To make our new level work, we need to implement a few new items. The first would be a 3D model representing our room. I have used SketchUp to model my room as it is a very easy program for non-designer to pick-up and work with. The model is displayed in Figure 40, it is a very simple room, with the following dimensions Width and Length of 4 meters, by a height of 3 meters. The opening to the room is 2 meters wide. The dimensions are important when you are designing your 3D models because they will reflect in Unity 3D based on the unit of measurement[14].

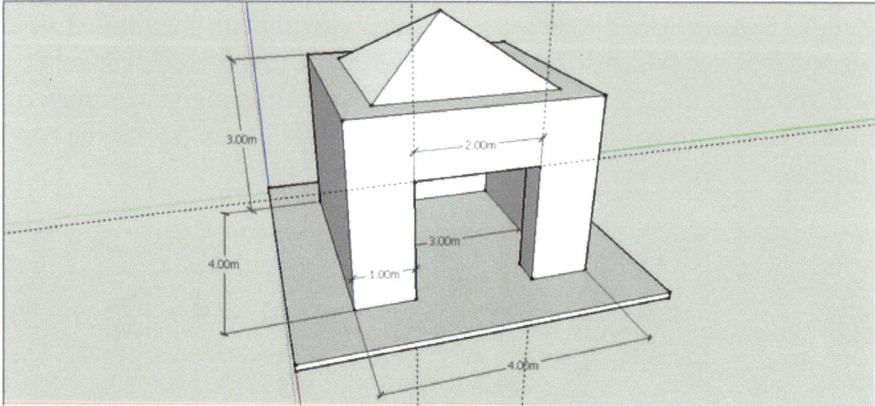

Figure 40 - 3D Room Model

Notice, that I have not applied any textures to the model. I kept things very simple as the purpose of this example is not the 3D modeling but the programming. Once we import the model into Unity, you need to make sure that the *Generate Colliders* option is checked on the model. This is important for collision detection.

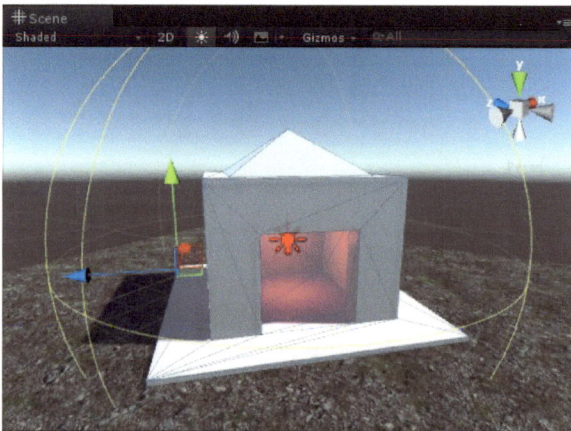

Figure 41 - 3D Model in Unity Scene

---

[14] Unity 3D uses the metric system, so it is best to make your 3D models in the metric system. This will help the importing and scaling of your models within Unity much easier.

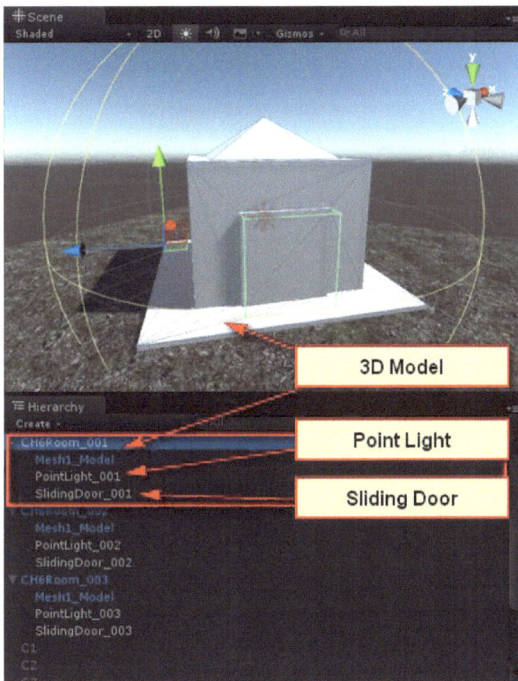

In the design view, you can go ahead and add a new *Point Light* as a child to the model, center it in the room. Each room will have one Point Light with a unique color of red, green or blue.

You will need to add another *GameObject*, a cube that will represent the sliding door.

You will need to play with the collider to make it a little larger than the actual door.

Figure 42 - Hierarchy of the Room

We are going to be also adding two new scripts to handle the randomization and selection of the room, and the sliding of the door for the room. The two scripts are called *RoomSelection.cs* and *Sliding-Door.cs*. The *RoomSelection* script is attached to the *GameObject* representing the randomizer in the scene.

Here is the listing for *RoomSelection.cs*:

```
using UnityEngine;
using System.Collections;

public class RoomSelection : MonoBehaviour
{

    public GameObject playerCharacter = null;

    // Use this for initialization
    void Start()
    {
        // if the player characte is not defined at design time
        // assign it during runtime before the game starts
        if(this.playerCharacter == null)
```

```
        {
            this.playerCharacter = GameObject.FindGameObjectWithTag("Player")
as GameObject;
        }
    }

    // Update is called once per frame
    void Update()
    {
        this.transform.Rotate(new Vector3(1, 1, 1), 1.0f);

        // check distance between this object and the player character
        float distance = Vector3.Distance(this.transform.position, this.play-
erCharacter.transform.position);
        if (distance < 2.0f)
        {
            #region MOUSE INPUT
            if (Input.mousePosition != null && Input.GetMouseButtonUp(0))
            {
                int color = Random.Range(0, 3);
                switch (color)
                {
                    case 0:
                        {
                            this.transform.GetComponent<Renderer>().material.color
= Color.blue;
                            this.playerCharacter.GetComponent<PlayerIn-
put>().ROOM_SELECTION = 0;
                            break;
                        }
                    case 1:
                        {
                            this.transform.GetComponent<Renderer>().material.color
= Color.red;
                            this.playerCharacter.GetComponent<PlayerIn-
put>().ROOM_SELECTION = 1;
                            break;
                        }
                    case 2:
                        {
                            this.transform.GetComponent<Renderer>().material.color
= Color.green;
                            this.playerCharacter.GetComponent<PlayerIn-
put>().ROOM_SELECTION = 2;
                            break;
                        }
                }
            }
            #endregion
        }
    }
}
```

Code Block 24 - Room Selection Code Listing

This script basically turns the GameObject that it is attached to into the randomizer. In our example, it is attached to a cube. It will rotate the cube on all three axis. It also checked to see if the player character is within a specified distance from itself. The threshold is set to < 2.0m. If the condition is met, then the player is allowed to click the cube. Each time the user clicks the GameObject, a new random number is generated between 0 and 3.

- 0: represents the blue room.
- 1: represents the red room.
- 2: represents the green room.

The switch statement is used to change the material color of the *GameObject* to the respective color for visual clue. Then it accesses a new variable which has been defined in the *PlayerInput.cs* script named *ROOM_SELECTION*.

The next script we are going to look at is *SlidingDoor.cs*:

```csharp
using UnityEngine;
using System.Collections;

public class SlidingDoor : MonoBehaviour
{
    public int ROOM_NUMBER;

    public Transform doorTransform;
    public float raiseHeight = 3f;
    public float speed = 3f;
    private Vector3 _closedPosition;

    // Use this for initialization
    void Start()
    {
        _closedPosition = transform.position;
    }

    void OnCollisionEnter(Collision c)
    {
        if(c.transform.tag.Equals("Player"))
        {
            if (!this.IsDoorOpen && (c.transform.GetComponent<PlayerIn-
put>().ROOM_SELECTION==this.ROOM_NUMBER))
            {
                StopCoroutine("MoveDoor");
                Vector3 endpos = _closedPosition + new Vector3(0f, raiseHeight,
0f);
```

```
            StartCoroutine("MoveDoor", endpos);
        }
    }
}

private bool IsDoorOpen = false;
IEnumerator MoveDoor(Vector3 endPos)
{
    float t = 0f;
    Vector3 startPos = doorTransform.position;
    while (t < 1f)
    {
        t += Time.deltaTime * speed;
        doorTransform.position = Vector3.Slerp(startPos, endPos, t);
        yield return null;
    }
    this.IsDoorOpen = true;
}
}
```

Code Block 25 - Sliding Door Code Listing

This code is responsible for the opening of the door based on two conditions:

1. The game object that collides with it is the Player Character.
2. The Player Character's *ROOM_SELECTION* is identical to the *ROOM_NUMBER*.

This is handled by the *OnCollisionEnter()* function. We are using this function because we actually want the GameObject that represents the door be solid, meaning, the player cannot pass through it. In other words, the *IsTrigger* feature on the *Collider Component* is false!

Notice that we are also using a co-routine that actually does the transformation on the door. Co-routines are not the same as multithreading. Normal co-routine updates are run after the *Update()* function returns. A co-routine is a function that can suspend its execution (*yield*) until the given *Yield Instruction* finishes. Here is a list:

- **yield**, the co-routine will continue after all *Update()* functions have been called on the next frame.

- **yield WaitForSeconds**, continue after a specified time delay, after all *Update()* functions have been called for the frame.
- **yield WaitForFixedUpdate**, continue after all *FixedUpdate()* has been called on all scripts.
- **yield WWW**, continue after a WWW download has completed.
- **yield StartCoroutine**, chains the co-routine, and will wait for the MyFunc co-routine to complete first.

At this point we have established our main structure for level 2. Now we need to implement the details of the game mechanics. The first of which will be a timer. The timer will be set when the player clicks on the randomizer. Here are the steps:

1. The timer will be set once the player selects the randomizer and the randomizer selects a room / color.
2. Countdown of the timer will begin immediately after the selection.
3. If the player is not able to find the room during the given time, the game will be over.
4. If they do find the room, the timer will be reset, and they will have to find the next room by going back to the randomizer.

This can be accomplished very easily by adding a few variables to keep track of the time in the *RoomSelection.cs* scrip and also updating the *PlayerInput.cs* script with its own set of variables to determine if the player failed to pass the level, as well as the *SlidingDoor.cs* script to reset the timer when the player successfully finds the selected room in the given time frame.

```
using UnityEngine;
using System.Collections;

public class RoomSelection : MonoBehaviour
{
    public GameObject playerCharacter = null;

    // Use this for initialization
    void Start()
```

```
    {
        // if the player characte is not defined at design time
        // assign it during runtime before the game starts
        if(this.playerCharacter == null)
        {
            this.playerCharacter = GameObject.FindGameObjectWithTag("Player")
as GameObject;
        }
    }

    // myTime will be used to give the amount of time in seconds
    // for the player to find the room!!!
    public float myTime = 33.0f;
    private float endTime = 0.0f;

    // Update is called once per frame
    void Update()
    {
        this.transform.Rotate(new Vector3(1, 1, 1), 1.0f);

        if(this.endTime>Time.time)
        {
            Debug.Log("Timer Started!!! " + Mathf.CeilToInt(this.endTime -
Time.time).ToString());
        }
        else if(this.endTime==0.0f)
        {
            ; // do nothing
        }
        else
        {
            Debug.Log("Time Ended!!!");
            this.playerCharacter.GetComponent<PlayerInput>().GAME_OVER = true;
        }

        // check distance between this object and the player character
        float distance = Vector3.Distance(this.transform.position, this.play-
erCharacter.transform.position);
        if (distance < 2.0f)
        {
            #region MOUSE INPUT
            if (Input.mousePosition != null && Input.GetMouseButtonUp(0))
            {
                int color = Random.Range(0, 3);
                switch (color)
                {
                    case 0:
                        {
                            this.transform.GetComponent<Renderer>().material.color
= Color.blue;
                            this.playerCharacter.GetComponent<PlayerIn-
put>().ROOM_SELECTION = 0;
                            break;
                        }
                    case 1:
```

```
                    {
                        this.transform.GetComponent<Renderer>().material.color
= Color.red;
                        this.playerCharacter.GetComponent<PlayerIn-
put>().ROOM_SELECTION = 1;
                        break;
                    }
                case 2:
                    {
                        this.transform.GetComponent<Renderer>().material.color
= Color.green;
                        this.playerCharacter.GetComponent<PlayerIn-
put>().ROOM_SELECTION = 2;
                        break;
                    }
                }

            // start timer
            this.endTime = this.myTime + Time.time;
        }
        #endregion
    }

    }

    public void ResetTimer()
    {
        this.endTime = 0.0f;
    }
}
```

Code Block 26 - RoomSelection Script Update to Include Timer

Notice that we introduced two variables in the script, *endTime* and *myTime*. The variable *myTime* is used as the amount of time in seconds the player has to perform a specific tasks. The variable *endTime* is set as a combination of the runtime of the game, taken from *Time.time*[15] added with the *myTime* value. This is set, when the user selects the randomizer.

In the *Update()* function, there is a conditional block checking to see if the variable *endTime* is larger than *Time.time*. If that condition is met, then we are still within the timeframe and the player can do as he or she pleases in the level. Once that condition is no longer valid, then we use the *PlayerCharacter* object to extract the *PlayerInput* object and set the *GAME_OVER* variable to true. This indicates that the player

---

[15] This is the time in seconds since the start of the game.

has failed to complete his or her task properly. The following is a snippet of the changes/modification done to the *PlayerInput.cs* script:

```csharp
using UnityEngine;
using System.Collections.Generic;

public class PlayerInput : MonoBehaviour {

    public List<MyCollectableData> myCollection = new List<MyCollecta-
bleData>();

    public Material CubeMaterial;

    public MyStack stack = new MyStack();
    private bool MATCH = false;

    #region variables for level 2
    public int ROOM_SELECTION;
    public bool GAME_OVER;
    #endregion

    void Awake()
    {

        this.ROOM_SELECTION = -1;
        this.GAME_OVER = false;

        this.MATCH = false;

        // make sure we start clean
        this.myCollection.Clear();
    }

    // Use this for initialization
    void Start () {
        }

    private float SPEED = 2.0f;

    // Update is called once per frame
    void Update()
    {
        if(!this.GAME_OVER)
        {
            if (!this.MATCH)
            {
...
            }

            if (this.MATCH)
            {
                #region MOUSE INPUT
                if (Input.mousePosition != null && Input.GetMouseButtonUp(0))
                {
```

106

```
                //Debug.Log("START MATCH >>>");
                RaycastHit selectedCollectable;
...
            if (stack.COUNT >= 3)
            {
                for (int i = 0; i <= stack.COUNT + 1; i++)
                {
                    MyCollectableData d = (MyCollectableData)stack.pop();
                    Debug.Log(string.Format("Pop: {0}", d.size));
                }
                Debug.Log("GREAT JOB!!! Objective Completed!");
                this.MATCH = false;
            }
            #endregion
        }

    }
}

    // This function handles the collision of colliders as a trigger
    void OnTriggerEnter(Collider c)
    {
        if(c.tag.Equals("MyCollectable"))
        {
...
        }
    }

    // Function to place the calculate position of next item around
    // a circular path.
    Vector3 CirclePath(Vector3 center, float radius, int id)
    {
        float ang = 90 * id; //Random.value * 360;
        Vector3 pos;
        pos.x = center.x + radius * Mathf.Sin(ang * Mathf.Deg2Rad);
        pos.z = center.z + radius * Mathf.Cos(ang * Mathf.Deg2Rad);
        pos.y = center.y+1;
        return pos;
    }

}
```

Code Block 27 - PlayerInput.cs Update to include Timer Condition

I did not provide the whole listing of the script as we have already done so in the previous sections of the book. The key updates / modifications we did to the script has been **bold** faced. Two variables, *ROOM_SELECTION* and *GAME_OVER*. It is clear what they are used for. *ROOM_SELECTION* is used to store which room the player needs to find, and *GAME_OVER* dictates if the player has timed out and hence lost the game.

The next script we should take a look at is the *SlidingDoor.cs* script. This script is actually used to reset the timer if the player finds the correct room and enters into it. As the previous code listing, I will only do partial listing of the code to demonstrate the modifications.

```csharp
using UnityEngine;
using System.Collections;

public class SlidingDoor : MonoBehaviour
{
    public int ROOM_NUMBER;

    public Transform doorTransform;
    public float raiseHeight = 3f;
    public float speed = 3f;
    private Vector3 _closedPosition;

    public GameObject roomSelection;

    // Use this for initialization
    void Start()
    {
        if(this.roomSelection== null)
        {
            this.roomSelection = GameObject.Find("RoomSelection") as GameObject;
        }

        _closedPosition = transform.position;
    }

    void OnCollisionEnter(Collision c)
    {
        if(c.transform.tag.Equals("Player"))
        {
...
            // reset the timer once the player is in the room
            this.roomSelection.GetComponent<RoomSelection>().ResetTimer();

            Debug.Log("Timer has been reset!");
        }
    }
}

    private bool IsDoorOpen = false;
    IEnumerator MoveDoor(Vector3 endPos)
    {
...
    }
}
```

Code Block 28 - SlidingDoor.cs Script update for Timer function

There are two new tasks that are being performed in the updated script, the first one is in the *Start()* function. We identify and find the GameObject with the name or id of *RoomSelection*, and store a reference to the GameObject for using it at a later time. The second addition in this script is the calling of the *ResetTimer()* function through the *RoomSelection* GameObject *RoomSelection* object in the *OnCollisionEnter()* function.

At this point we have implemented the fundamentals, but we need to somehow keep score for the player. In other words, we need a way to identify which rooms the player has visited, and when all the rooms have been visited by the player, they would have completed the level. We can utilize our Stack data structure to overcome this obstacle. We can push each room onto the stack when the player visits them and when all three rooms have been visited then the player wins the level.

This scenario and data updates would be handled by the *SlidingDoor.cs* script and the *PlayerInput.cs* script. The *SlidingDoor* class will call the method defined in the *PlayerInput* class to push the room data onto the stack.

The code segment that needs to be changed in *SlidingDoor.cs* is listed below:

```
void OnCollisionEnter(Collision c)
{
    if(c.transform.tag.Equals("Player"))
    {
        if (!this.IsDoorOpen && (c.transform.GetComponent<PlayerIn-
put>().ROOM_SELECTION==this.ROOM_NUMBER))
        {
...
            // reset the timer once the player is in the room
            this.roomSelection.GetComponent<RoomSelection>().ResetTimer();

            // push the room data onto the stack
            c.gameObject.GetComponent<PlayerInput>().RoomVisited(this);

            Debug.Log("Timer has been reset!");
        }
    }
}
```

Code Block 29 - Room Visited addition to SlidingDorr.cs script

The changes we need to make in the *PlayerInput.cs* script are listed below:

```
public void RoomVisited(SlidingDoor room)
{
    if(room != null)
    {
        this.stack.push(room);

        string msg = string.Format("Room #{0} inserted, stack count={1}",
room.ROOM_NUMBER, this.stack.COUNT);
        Debug.Log(msg);

        if(this.stack.COUNT>=3)
        {
            Debug.Log("YOU WIN!!!");
            this.GAME_OVER = true;
        }
    }
}
```

Code Block 30 - Addition to PlayerInput.cs script to handle rooms visited

So now we have seen a few different types of game mechanic implementations. Albeit the examples provided are very simplistic, on purpose, they do demonstrate the main concepts and ideas of the individual mechanics.

Development of Level 3

In Level 3, we are going to illustrate progressing, capturing/conquering and advancing game mechanics. We would also probably combine a few of the other game mechanics we have seen so far in combination to create a level that is a little more sophisticated and involved.

One of my favorite game genera is Real Time Strategy. Two of my favorites were *Age of Empires I, II, III,* and *Command and Conquer*. One of the main reasons I love RTS games is the fact that you really have to think and use a lot of logistics to plan out your strategy and be able to defeat the opponent. I always draw a line between the game of Chess and RTS, the difference being that in a Chess game the players take turns to make their moves, so they have time to think ahead a few steps. In an RTS, your opponent can attack you at any time and from any direction, and with superior weapons and resources!!!

In a nut-shell, each of these games, the player is required to collect resources, build an army, build their base and required structures, progress through the different stages of upgrading their structures and units, and at the same time maintaining their base. On top of these actions, there is a time element for the collection and creation of the resources and units. As you can tell by now, the game design and mechanics are pretty involved and need to be planned out really well.

We do not have the time nor the resources to undertake such a task for level 3. Therefore, we are going to make a simplified version of an RTS type game. To perform our objectives, we can draw an outline of the tasks the user will need to complete in level 3.

Here is a brief outline:

1. The player will start with a set amount of resources when the game starts.
2. The player will need to build a collection facility.
3. The player will need to create a collector unit.
4. The player will need to identify the location of resources to be collected.
5. The player will need to assign the collector to the resource to be collected.
6. While the collector unit(s) are collecting, the player will need to explore the terrain to identify the enemy and kill it.
7. The player will need to avoid being killed by the enemy and or other objects harmful to the player.

To keep things simple, both the player and the enemy will start off with the same amount of resources. In this particular case, there will be two types of resources, one of them would be mining for gold, and the other would be bullets. However, the catch here is that, in order for the player / enemy accumulate bullets, they will need to continuously collect gold.

The collection of the gold will also be based on a specific time. This will force the player to be more cautious on how they utilize their bullets, too many shots with no hit will put the player at risk of being killed by the enemy.

In order for us to accomplish this, we would need to create some new scripts. We would need a script to represent the storage unit, we would need a script to represent the collector unit, and we would need a script to represent the resource unit. We also need to create two simple prefabs to represent our *Storage Unit* and *Collector Unit*.

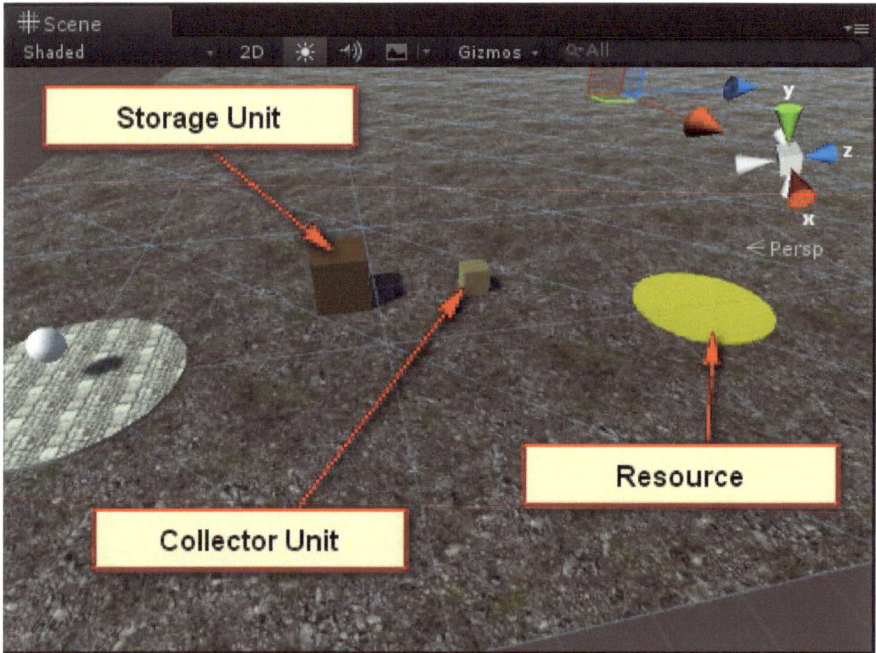

Figure 43 - Design Sample of Storage and Collector Units

I will not get into the details of how to create the Storage and Collector Units, as they should be very elementary for you by now. Likewise, the character player and resource game object. The key is the connection between the GameObjects and their interaction through the scripts.

Let's start looking at the storage unit first. The function of a storage unit is to store resources for the purposes of the game. It could be used to store any type of resource, however, usually there are different types of storage units for different types of resources. In our case, we are keeping things very simple, therefore, the storage unit will be storing only one type of resource, since we only have one type of resource to store to begin with!

Secondly, the storage unit will automatically create the first Collector Unit once it has been placed within the 3D world. Therefore, the Storage Unit is responsible to keep track of the Collector Unit as well as making sure the Collector Unit knows which Storage Unit it belongs to! Finally, the Storage Unit will also need to have a reference to the player character so that it can update statistics on the player.

The code that helps us achieve these results is listed below:

```csharp
using UnityEngine;
using System.Collections;

public class MyStorage : MonoBehaviour
{

    public GameObject myCollector;
    private GameObject collectorObj;

    private GameObject playerCharacter;

    // variables for timer
    public float myTime = 3.0f;
    private float endTime = 0.0f;

    // Use this for initialization
    void Start()
    {
        Vector3 pos = new Vector3(this.transform.position.x + 1, 2,
this.transform.position.z + 1);
        this.collectorObj = GameObject.Instantiate(this.myCollector, pos,
this.transform.rotation) as GameObject;
        this.collectorObj.GetComponent<MyCollector>().myStorage = this.gameOb-
ject;

        this.playerCharacter = GameObject.FindGameObjectWithTag("Player") as
GameObject;
    }

    // Update is called once per frame
    void Update()
    {
        if (this.endTime > Time.time)
        {
            // we will put some code here for visually display loading
        }
```

```
        else if (this.endTime == 0.0f)
        {
            ; // do nothing
        }
        else
        {
            this.endTime = 0.0f;
            this.collectorObj.GetComponent<MyCollector>().GOTO_RESOURCE = true;

            // add bullet to player character
            this.playerCharacter.GetComponent<PlayerInput>().NUM_BULLETS += 1;
        }
    }

    // This function handles the collision of colliders as a trigger
    void OnCollisionEnter(Collision c)
    {
        if (c.transform.tag.Equals("CollectorUnit"))
        {
            c.transform.GetComponent<MyCollector>().GOTO_STORAGE = false;

            // start timer
            this.endTime = this.myTime + Time.time;
        }
    }

}
```

Code Block 31 - MyStorage.cs initial version

When you read the code, you will notice that in that *Start()* function we instantiate a *CollectorUnit* object and assign the *StorageUnit* object as a reference so that it know where to come back to after it has collected the resources. The next thing we do is have a reference to the player character.

The *Update()* function defined in *MyStorage* class is utilized only when the Collector Unit returns back to it. It is triggered by the *OnCollissionEnter()* function where the timer for unloading the resources get set. The timer is then checked in the *Update()* function for the unloading and re-routing of the Collector Unit back to the resource location.

This makes us to take a look at the next item of interest, the Collector Unit. The Collector Unit in this scenario is only concerned about knowing where the resource is located so that it can go and collect the resources, and which Storage Unit it belongs to so that it can safely return and unload the resources. It also needs to know how much resources it has collected, this variable is defined, but is not used at this point. Also, there are two critical flags that define the state of the collector, it is either going to the resource location for loading, or it is going to the storage unit for unloading.

The listing for the *MyCollector.cs* is below:

```csharp
using UnityEngine;
using System.Collections;

public class MyCollector : MonoBehaviour
{
    public GameObject myResource;
    public GameObject myStorage;

    public bool GOTO_RESOURCE;
    public bool GOTO_STORAGE;

    public int UNINTS_COLLECTED;

    // Use this for initialization
    void Start()
    {
        this.myResource = GameObject.FindGameObjectWithTag("ResourcePlayer")
as GameObject;

        this.GOTO_RESOURCE = true;
        this.GOTO_STORAGE = false;

        this.UNINTS_COLLECTED = 0;
    }

    // Update is called once per frame
    void Update()
    {
        if(this.GOTO_RESOURCE)
        {
            // goto the resource location for collection
            Vector3 refillHeading = this.myResource.transform.position -
this.transform.position;
            refillHeading.Normalize();

            // use Quaternion Slerp function to make smooth transition ...
            this.transform.rotation =
            Quaternion.Slerp(transform.rotation,
                Quaternion.LookRotation(refillHeading), 10 * Time.deltaTime);

            this.transform.Translate(Vector3.forward * Time.deltaTime);
        }

        if(this.GOTO_STORAGE)
```

```
    {
        Vector3 refillHeading = this.myStorage.transform.position -
this.transform.position;
        refillHeading.Normalize();

        // use Quaternion Slerp function to make smooth transition ...
        this.transform.rotation =
            Quaternion.Slerp(transform.rotation,
                        Quaternion.LookRotation(refillHeading), 10 *
Time.deltaTime);

        this.transform.Translate(Vector3.forward * Time.deltaTime);
    }
  }
}
```

Code Block 32 - MyCollector.cs version 1

Observing the code, you will notice that the Collector Unit finds where the resource for player is, and it stores that in its memory. Since it has been just initialized by the Storage Unit, its initial state would be to go and collect resources. This is defined in the *Start()* function.

The *Update()* function is just responsible to make sure that the collector is properly driven to either the resource location, or to the storage unit. Very simple and very straight forward. The key here is to notice that the state of the collector is changed by outside forces!

The next piece of the puzzle to complete the cycle is the resource. As it is designed, the resource object is stationary and cannot be moved or relocated. It also does not create anything from within, although this can be something you may want to do at a later time. So the main tasks of the resource object it to know when the collector has arrived to collect, and how to change the state of the collector when the time has come to return to base!

Here is a listing for *MyResource.cs* script:

```
using UnityEngine;
using System.Collections;

public class MyResource : MonoBehaviour
{
    public GameObject collectorUnit;

    // variables for timer
```

```csharp
    public float myTime = 3.0f;
    private float endTime = 0.0f;

    // Use this for initialization
    void Start()
    {

    }

    // Update is called once per frame
    void Update()
    {
        if (this.endTime > Time.time)
        {
            // we will put some code here for visually display loading
        }
        else if (this.endTime == 0.0f)
        {
            ; // do nothing
        }
        else
        {
            this.endTime = 0.0f;
            this.collectorUnit.GetComponent<MyCollector>().GOTO_STORAGE = true;
        }
    }

    // This function handles the collision of colliders as a trigger
    void OnTriggerEnter(Collider c)
    {
        if (c.tag.Equals("CollectorUnit"))
        {
            c.GetComponent<MyCollector>().GOTO_RESOURCE = false;
            this.collectorUnit = c.gameObject;

            // start timer
            this.endTime = this.myTime + Time.time;
        }
    }
}
```

Code Block 33 - MyResource.cs version 1

The code I have shown you so far is very simple and straight forward. But the concept is very powerful if you start building on top of it and creating larger systems. Again, one of the keys of this book is to demonstrate you some basics ideas and for those who grasp it, they can build far more interesting and complex scenarios and environment or simulations.

Now it is time to build the components for the opponent. Let's start by outlining the items we would need to properly define a simple opponent for the purposes of the demonstration.

Here is a brief outline:

1. The enemy will start with a set amount of resources when the game starts.
2. The enemy will need to build a collection facility.
3. The enemy will need to create a collector unit.
4. The enemy will need to identify the location of resources to be collected.
5. The enemy will need to assign the collector to the resource to be collected.
6. While the collector unit(s) are collecting, the enemy will need to explore the terrain to identify the player and kill it.
7. The enemy will need to avoid being killed by the player and or other objects harmful to the enemy.

Pretty much it is exactly the same as that of the player. But it is worth mentioning again to give us a concrete idea. You might want to use the same scripts to handle both the player's logic and the enemy's logic, but as time goes by and your code becomes more complex you will see that this strategy is not sustainable. In fact, it might become tedious to maintain and expand over the long run. Therefore, it would be better to create separate classes to handle the player's logic and units from that of the enemy's.

So just like the player we would need to create three scripts to handle the enemy's Storage Unit, Collector Unit, and Resource Unit. These scripts are going to be exactly identical to the player's script, with the exception that they will be addressing the enemy's objects.

The main new addition to our scripts is going to be, the script that will drive our enemy. We will call this *MyEnemy.cs*. It will be responsible to give the enemy some intelligence, albeit not much, just for the sake of the demonstration of this level. The objective of the script would be to allow the enemy to roam around the terrain and be able to place its Storage Unit for resource collection, and also be able to defend its base and attack the player if necessary.

The script will start out by placing a Storage Unit at a random location based on the enemy's movement and an interval of time. Once the Storage Unit is placed, the Storage Unit will start automating its collector unit mechanism and this will go on until the game is over. In the meantime, the logic for the enemy character is to go into scout mode until it has enough ammunition / resources to be able to attack the player. During this time, it will iterate through a set of specified point in the world until it is ready for attacking. When it is ready to attack, it will locate the player's position and head straight towards the player for a kill.

Here is the initial listing of *MyEnemy.cs* script:

```csharp
using UnityEngine;
using System.Collections;

public class MyEnemy : MonoBehaviour
{
    public GameObject myBase;

    public GameObject myStorage;
    private GameObject myStorageObj;

    public GameObject myEnemy;

    public int NUM_BULLETS;

    // variables for timer
    public float myTime = 5.0f;
    private float endTime = 0.0f;

    public bool ATTACK;
    public bool SCOUT;

    public Transform[] scoutPoints;
    private int nextPointIndex;

    // Use this for initialization
    void Start()
    {
        this.NUM_BULLETS = 1;
        this.ATTACK = true;
```

```
        this.myEnemy = GameObject.FindGameObjectWithTag("Player") as GameOb-
ject;

    // start timer
    this.endTime = this.myTime + Time.time;

    this.nextPointIndex = 0;
    }

    // Update is called once per frame
    void Update()
    {
        if(this.myStorageObj== null)
        {
            if(this.endTime<Time.time)
            {
                // drop the storage
                Vector3 pos = new Vector3(this.transform.position.x + 1, 2,
this.transform.position.z + 1);
                this.myStorageObj = GameObject.Instantiate(this.myStorage, pos,
this.myStorage.transform.rotation) as GameObject;

                this.endTime = 0.0f;
            }
        }

        if(this.NUM_BULLETS>1)
        {
            this.ATTACK = true;
        }
        else
        {
            this.ATTACK = false;
        }

        // seek the player to attack
        if (this.ATTACK)
        {
            Vector3 refillHeading = this.myEnemy.transform.position -
this.transform.position;
            refillHeading.Normalize();

            // use Quaternion Slerp function to make smooth transition ...
            this.transform.rotation =
                Quaternion.Slerp(transform.rotation,
                            Quaternion.LookRotation(refillHeading), 10 *
Time.deltaTime);

            this.transform.Translate(Vector3.forward * Time.deltaTime);
        }
        else
        {
            if(this.scoutPoints.Length>0)
            {
```

```
            Vector3 refillHeading = this.scoutPoints[nextPointIndex].posi-
tion - this.transform.position;
            refillHeading.Normalize();

            // use Quaternion Slerp function to make smooth transition ...
            this.transform.rotation =
                Quaternion.Slerp(transform.rotation,
                                Quaternion.LookRotation(refillHeading), 10 *
Time.deltaTime);

            this.transform.Translate(Vector3.forward * Time.deltaTime);

            if (Vector3.Distance(this.transform.position,this.scout-
Points[nextPointIndex].position)<0.25f)
            {
                this.nextPointIndex += 1;
                if(this.nextPointIndex>=this.scoutPoints.Length)
                {
                    this.nextPointIndex = 0;
                }
            }
        }
    }
}
```

Code Block 34 - MyEnemy.cs version 1

Putting the pieces together and running the program, you see how the environment comes to life. The graphics we have used and the 3D models we have used are very primitive, but this books is not for 3D Modeling, it is for programming. So, we use primitive placeholder that can very easily be substituted when we get better models!

The only aspect which we have not implemented yet, is the ability to attack. This is the case for both the player and the enemy. We can start by first implementing the player's attack feature and then we can implement the enemy's attack feature.

To implement the attack feature we would need to adjust a few items. First we would need to have a physical representation of how and where the attack initiation will take place. The next task is to identify how powerful the actual attack will be. Finally, we need to determine what the range for the attack is.

The last condition is more for the enemy player character rather than the actual player. The player can attack anytime and anywhere he or she desires, as long as there are resources available! The same principle applies to the enemy, but, it would be aimless to design an enemy to attack for no reason, as it would be the same for the player to attack aimlessly and losing their resources without any real effect.

Here is the new listing for the *PlayerInput.cs* script:

```csharp
using UnityEngine;
using System.Collections.Generic;

public class PlayerInput : MonoBehaviour {

    public List<MyCollectableData> myCollection = new List<MyCollectableData>();

    public Material CubeMaterial;

    public MyStack stack = new MyStack();
    private bool MATCH = false;

    #region variables for level 2
    public int ROOM_SELECTION;
    public bool GAME_OVER;
    #endregion

    #region variables for level 3
    public GameObject myStorageUnit;
    public GameObject myBullet;
    public GameObject myGun;

    public int NUM_BULLETS;

    public GameObject myEnemy;
    #endregion

    void Awake()
    {
        this.stack.clear();

        this.ROOM_SELECTION = -1;
        this.GAME_OVER = false;

        this.MATCH = false;

        this.NUM_BULLETS = 1;

        // make sure we start clean
        this.myCollection.Clear();
    }

    // Use this for initialization
    void Start () {
```

```
        if(this.myEnemy== null)
        {
            this.myEnemy = GameObject.FindGameObjectWithTag("Enemy") as GameOb-
ject;
        }
      }

    private float SPEED = 2.0f;

    // Update is called once per frame
    void Update()
    {
        if(!this.GAME_OVER)
        {
            if (!this.MATCH)
            {
                // code for the movement of player (CP) forward
                if (Input.GetKey(KeyCode.UpArrow))
                {
                    this.transform.Translate(Vector3.forward * Time.deltaTime *
this.SPEED);
                }
                // code for the movement of player (CP) backward
                if (Input.GetKey(KeyCode.DownArrow))
                {
                    this.transform.Translate(Vector3.back * Time.deltaTime *
this.SPEED);
                }
                // code for the movement of player (CP) left
                if (Input.GetKey(KeyCode.LeftArrow))
                {
                    this.transform.Rotate(Vector3.up, -5);
                }
                // code for the movement of player (CP) right
                if (Input.GetKey(KeyCode.RightArrow))
                {
                    this.transform.Rotate(Vector3.up, 5);
                }

                // go ahead and place our storage structure at the position
where the player is at
                if(Input.GetKeyUp(KeyCode.Space))
                {
                    Vector3 pos = new Vector3(this.transform.position.x + 1, 2,
this.transform.position.z + 1);
                    GameObject storageObj = GameObject.Instantiate(this.myStor-
ageUnit, pos, this.transform.rotation) as GameObject;
                    storageObj.name = string.Format("StorageUnit{0}", Time.time);
                }

                // fire
                if(Input.GetKeyUp(KeyCode.F))
                {
                    if(this.NUM_BULLETS>0)
                    {
                        GameObject bullet = GameObject.Instantiate(this.myBullet,
```

```
                    this.myGun.transform.position, this.myGun.transform.ro-
tation) as GameObject;

                bullet.GetComponent<Rigidbody>().velocity = trans-
form.TransformDirection(new Vector3(0, 0, 10.0f));

                GameObject.Destroy(bullet, 3.0f);

                this.NUM_BULLETS--;

            }
          }
        }

        if (this.MATCH)
        {
            #region MOUSE INPUT
            if (Input.mousePosition != null && Input.GetMouseButtonUp(0))
            {
                RaycastHit selectedCollectable;

                // capture the mouse position and cast a ray to see what ob-
ject we hit
                Ray ray = Camera.main.ScreenPointToRay(Input.mousePosition);

                if (Physics.Raycast(ray, out selectedCollectable, 200))
                {
                    if (selectedCollectable.transform.tag.Equals("MyCollect-
able"))
                    {
                        var collect = selectedCollectable.transform.gameOb-
ject.GetComponent<MyCollectable>();

                        MyCollectableData data = new MyCollectableData();

                        data.ID = collect.ID;
                        data.size = collect.size;

                        MyCollectableData sd = null;

                        // check stack
                        if (stack.COUNT > 0)
                        {
                            sd = (MyCollectableData)stack.peek();
                            if (sd.size < data.size)
                            {
                                stack.push(data);
                            }
                            else
                            {
                                Debug.Log("Sorry! Try Again! ...");
                                stack.clear();
                            }
                        }
                        else
```

```
                    {
                        stack.push(data);
                    }
                }
            }
        }

        if (stack.COUNT >= 3)
        {
            for (int i = 0; i <= stack.COUNT + 1; i++)
            {
                MyCollectableData d = (MyCollectableData)stack.pop();
                Debug.Log(string.Format("Pop: {0}", d.size));
            }
            Debug.Log("GREAT JOB!!! Objective Completed!");
            this.MATCH = false;
        }
        #endregion
    }

    }
}

// This function handles the collision of colliders as a trigger
void OnTriggerEnter(Collider c)
{
    if(c.tag.Equals("MyCollectable"))
    {
        var collect = c.gameObject.GetComponent<MyCollectable>();

        MyCollectableData data = new MyCollectableData();

        data.ID = collect.ID;
        data.size = collect.size;

        this.myCollection.Add(data);

        Destroy(c.gameObject);
    }

    if(c.tag.Equals("DropOffZone"))
    {
        if(this.myCollection.Count>2)
        {
            Vector3 center = c.transform.position;
            int index = 1;
            foreach (var d in this.myCollection)
            {
                Vector3 pos = CirclePath(center, 1.0f, index);
                index++;

                Quaternion rot = Quaternion.FromToRotation(Vector3.forward,
center - pos);

                GameObject tmp = GameObject.CreatePrimitive(Primitive-
Type.Cube);
```

```
            tmp.transform.position = pos;
            tmp.transform.rotation = rot;

            tmp.transform.tag = "MyCollectable";
            tmp.transform.localScale = new Vector3(d.size, d.size,
d.size);

            tmp.GetComponent<Renderer>().material = this.CubeMaterial;

            // attach collectable component, apply the data
            tmp.gameObject.AddComponent<MyCollectable>();
            tmp.gameObject.GetComponent<MyCollectable>().ID = d.ID;
            tmp.gameObject.GetComponent<MyCollectable>().size = d.size;
        }

        // everything was processed, start matching
        this.MATCH = true;
      }
    }
  }

  // Function to place the calculate position of next item around
  // a circular path.
  Vector3 CirclePath(Vector3 center, float radius, int id)
  {
    float ang = 90 * id; //Random.value * 360;
    Vector3 pos;
    pos.x = center.x + radius * Mathf.Sin(ang * Mathf.Deg2Rad);
    pos.z = center.z + radius * Mathf.Cos(ang * Mathf.Deg2Rad);
    pos.y = center.y+1;
    return pos;
  }

  public void RoomVisited(SlidingDoor room)
  {
    if(room != null)
    {
      this.stack.push(room);

      string msg = string.Format("Room #{0} inserted, stack count={1}",
room.ROOM_NUMBER, this.stack.COUNT);
      Debug.Log(msg);

      if(this.stack.COUNT>=3)
      {
        Debug.Log("YOU WIN!!!");
        this.GAME_OVER = true;
      }
    }
  }
}
```

Code Block 35 - PlayerInput.cs with Attack Enemy function

Looking at the code you see that we have used the Key 'F' on the keyboard to start firing the bullets at the enemy.

This is done by checking and making sure that there are bullets in the inventory. Once the bullet is initialized, it is given a velocity that will use the physics engine for its trajectory. Finally, we auto destroy the game object after a certain timeframe, which happens to be 3 seconds.

Now we can take a look at the enemy script and study the structure of the code. Here is the listing for *MyEnemy.cs* with the attack feature implemented:

```csharp
using UnityEngine;
using System.Collections;

public class MyEnemy : MonoBehaviour
{
    public GameObject myBase;

    public GameObject myStorage;
    private GameObject myStorageObj;

    public GameObject myEnemy;

    public GameObject myBullet;
    public GameObject myGun;

    public int NUM_BULLETS;

    // variables for timer
    public float myTime = 5.0f;
    private float endTime = 0.0f;

    public bool ATTACK;
    public bool SCOUT;

    public Transform[] scoutPoints;
    private int nextPointIndex;

    // Use this for initialization
    void Start()
    {
        this.NUM_BULLETS = 1;
        this.ATTACK = true;

        this.myEnemy = GameObject.FindGameObjectWithTag("Player") as GameObject;

        // start timer
```

```
            this.endTime = this.myTime + Time.time;

        this.nextPointIndex = 0;
    }

    private float SPEED = 2.0f;

    // Update is called once per frame
    void Update()
    {
        if(this.myStorageObj == null)
        {
            if(this.endTime<Time.time)
            {
                // drop the storage
                Vector3 pos = new Vector3(this.transform.position.x + 1, 2,
this.transform.position.z + 1);
                this.myStorageObj = GameObject.Instantiate(this.myStorage, pos,
this.myStorage.transform.rotation) as GameObject;

                this.endTime = 0.0f;
            }
        }

        if(this.NUM_BULLETS>1)
        {
            this.ATTACK = true;
        }
        else
        {
            this.ATTACK = false;
        }

        // seek the player to attack
        if (this.ATTACK)
        {
            Vector3 refillHeading = this.myEnemy.transform.position -
this.transform.position;
            refillHeading.Normalize();

            // use Quaternion Slerp function to make smooth transition ...
            this.transform.rotation =
                Quaternion.Slerp(transform.rotation,
                            Quaternion.LookRotation(refillHeading), 10 *
Time.deltaTime);

            this.transform.Translate(Vector3.forward * Time.deltaTime *
this.SPEED);

            if(Vector3.Distance(this.myEnemy.transform.position, this.trans-
form.position)<5.0f)
            {
                if (this.NUM_BULLETS > 0)
                {
                    if(this.endTime<Time.time)
```

```
                {
                    GameObject bullet = GameObject.Instantiate(this.myBullet,
                        this.myGun.transform.position, this.myGun.transform.ro-
tation) as GameObject;

                    bullet.GetComponent<Rigidbody>().velocity = trans-
form.TransformDirection(new Vector3(0, 0, 10.0f));

                    GameObject.Destroy(bullet, 3.0f);

                    // decrease inventory
                    this.NUM_BULLETS--;

                    // set timer before next shot
                    this.endTime = this.myTime + Time.time;
                }

            }
        }
    }
    else
    {
        if(this.scoutPoints.Length>0)
        {
            Vector3 refillHeading = this.scoutPoints[nextPointIndex].posi-
tion - this.transform.position;
            refillHeading.Normalize();

            // use Quaternion Slerp function to make smooth transition ...
            this.transform.rotation =
                Quaternion.Slerp(transform.rotation,
                            Quaternion.LookRotation(refillHeading), 10 *
Time.deltaTime);

            this.transform.Translate(Vector3.forward * Time.deltaTime);

            if (Vector3.Distance(this.transform.position,this.scout-
Points[nextPointIndex].position)<0.25f)
            {
                this.nextPointIndex += 1;
                if(this.nextPointIndex>=this.scoutPoints.Length)
                {
                    this.nextPointIndex = 0;
                }
            }
        }
    }
}
```

Code Block 36 - MyEnemy.cs with Attack Function

If you notice the modification to the attack feature is similar to how we have implemented for the player, but there is one big difference, we have integrated a timer in the logic so that the computer does not shoot continuously. The timer will allow the player to make a move and also for the enemy itself not to drain all of its resources in a short amount of time.

The logic we have implemented is not very sophisticated and can be improved quite a bit. At this point I want you to take the opportunity and see how you can improve the logic one step further. I will give you a hint, if you play the level and pay attention the details you will notice that the enemy will shoot if the player is within two meters of it, even though the enemy is not facing the player. This is a drawback that the current logic does not take into consideration, so an improvement would be to make sure the enemy is always facing the player before it fires. This is something that can be implemented easily and I would have you do that part on your own.

Chapter 5 – Creating the User Interface

User Interface (UI) design is a very important aspect of any software system. After all, this is how your users are going to be able to interact with your applications, games and environments. In this chapter we are going to take a look at the new UI architecture available with Unity 5. If you have done any development in older versions of Unity, you will appreciate the new enhancement that are made in the new release of Unity 5.

User Interface design and development is an art by itself. Just like anything else, it takes years of practice and hands on experience to really fine-tune your UI designs. There is no science in the design of a UI per-se, however, good UI designers tap into other human sciences and art sciences to bring about something unique.

Figure 44 - User Interface Sample 1

Since each UI is going to be unique to the environment you are designing for, it will be very important for the UI designer to understand the system inside and out. I am not talking about the technical details of how things might work internally, but, you should be aware of all of the specifications for the inputs and the outputs of the system.

This will lead to a better decision making when you are designing the layout of your UI and the features and functions available at a given time.

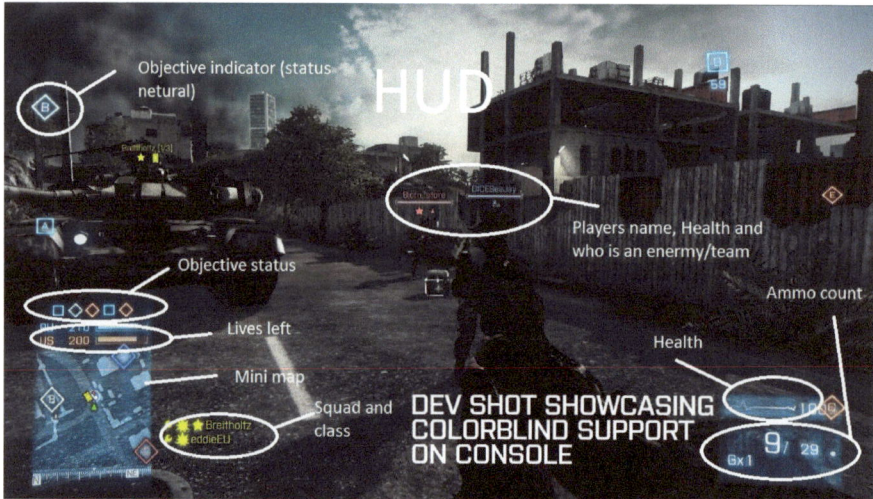

Figure 45 - User Interface Sample 2

User Interfaces come in many shapes and forms. As mentioned before, it really comes down to what type of information you want to share with the player, and what type of functionality, if any, you would like to provide to the player.

The Basics of User Interface Design in Unity 5

If you have experience with creating user interfaces with previous versions of Unity, you know that it was extremely tedious and limited. With the introduction of Unity 5, the underlying UI engine has been improved tenfold.

The Canvas

A little bit of background and fun. What is a Canvas?

"Canvas is an extremely durable plain-woven fabric used for making sails, tents, marquees, backpacks, and other items for which sturdiness is required. It is also popularly used by artists as a painting surface, typically stretched across a wooden frame."

In computer science and visualization, a canvas is a container that holds various drawing elements (lines, shapes, text, frames containing other elements, etc.). It takes its name from the canvas used in visual arts. It is sometimes called a scene graph because it arranges the logical representation of a user interface or graphical scene. Some implementations also define the spatial representation and allow the user to interact with the elements via a graphical user interface.

In Unity 3D, the canvas is the area that all UI elements should be inside. It is a GameObject with a Canvas Component attached to it, and all UI elements must be children of such a Canvas.

Draw Order and Render Modes:

UI elements in the Canvas are drawn in the same order they appear in the Hierarchy. The first child is drawn first, the second child next, and etc... If two UI elements overlap, the later one will appear on top of the earlier one.

Render Modes:

There are three render modes available for the Canvas:

- *Screen Space – Overlay:* This render mode places UI elements on the screen rendered on top of the scene. If the screen is resized or changes resolution, the Canvas will automatically change size to match it.

- *Screen Space – Camera:* Similar to Screen Space – Overlay, but in this render mode, the Canvas is placed a given distance in front of a specified Camera. The UI elements are rendered by the Camera, which indicates that the Camera settings will have an effect on the appearance of the UI elements.

- *World Space:* In this render mode, the Canvas will behave as any other object in the scene. The size of the Canvas can be set manually using its Rect Transform, and UI elements will render in front of or behind other objects in the scene based on 3D placement. This is useful for UIs that are meant to be a part of the world. This is also known as a "diegetic interface".

Basic Layout

Every UI element is represented as a rectangle for layout purposes. This rectangle can be manipulated in the Scene View using the Rect Tool in the toolbar. The Rect Tool is used both for Unity's 2D features and for UI, and in fact can be used even for 3D objects as well.

Figure 46 - Rect Tool Toolbar Buttons

The Rect Tool can be used to move, resize and rotate UI elements. Once you have selected a UI element, you can move it by clicking anywhere inside the rectangle and dragging. You can resize it by clicking on the edges or corners and dragging.

The element can be rotated by hovering the cursor slightly away from the corners until the mouse cursor looks like a rotation symbol. You can then click and drag in either direction to rotate.

Just like the other tools, the Rect Tool uses the current pivot mode and space, set in the toolbar. When working with UI it's usually a good idea to keep those set to Pivot and Local.

Rect Transform:

The Rect Transform is a new transform component that is used for all UI elements instead of the regular Transform component.

Rect Transforms have position, rotation, and scale just like regular Transforms, but it also has a width and height, used to specify the dimensions of the rectangle.

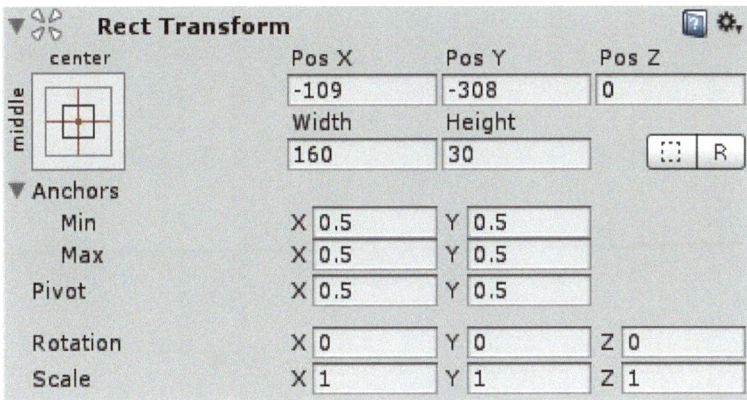

Figure 47 - Rect Transform Component

Pivot:

Rotations, size, and scale modifications occur around the pivot so the position of the pivot affects the outcome of a rotation, resizing, or scaling. When the toolbar Pivot button is set to Pivot mode, the pivot of a Rect Transform can be moved in the Scene View.

Figure 48 - Pivot Interface

Anchors and Anchor Presets:

Rect Transforms include a layout concept called anchors. Anchors are shown as four small triangular handles in the Scene View and anchor information is also shown in the Inspector. If the parent of a Rect Transform is also a Rect Transform, the child Rect Transform can be anchored to the parent Rect Transform in various ways. For example, the child can be anchored to the center of the parent, or to one of the corners.

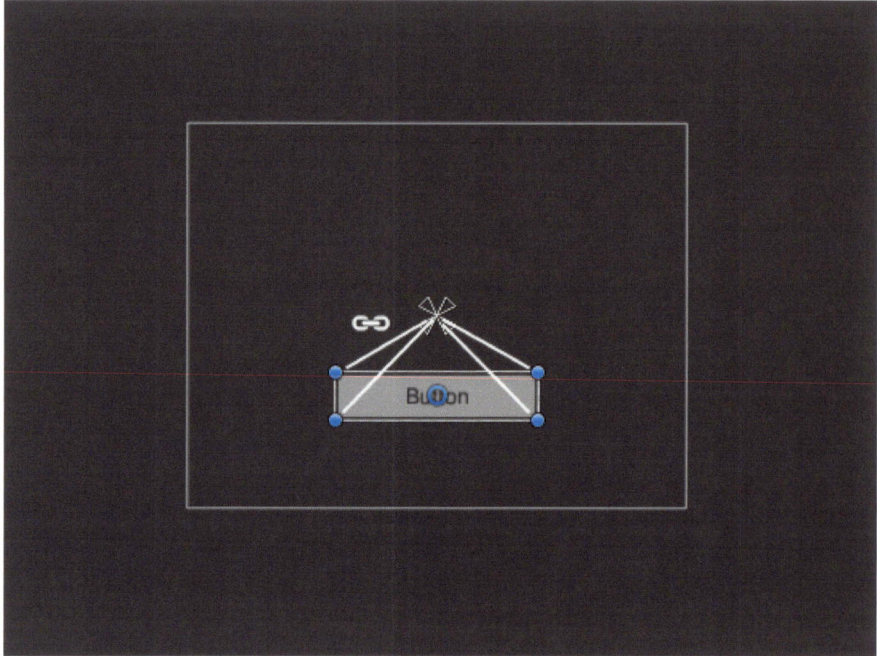

Figure 49 - Anchor UI Elements

The anchoring also allows the child to stretch together with the width or height of the parent. Each corner of the rectangle has a fixed offset to its corresponding anchor, i.e. the top left corner of the rectangle has a fixed offset to the top left anchor, etc. This way the different corners of the rectangle can be anchored to different points in the parent rectangle.

In the Inspector, the Anchor Preset button can be found in the upper left corner of the Rect Transform component. Clicking the button brings up the Anchor Presets dropdown. From here you can quickly select from some of the most common anchoring options. You can anchor the UI element to the sides or middle of the parent, or stretch together with the parent size. The horizontal and vertical anchoring is independent.

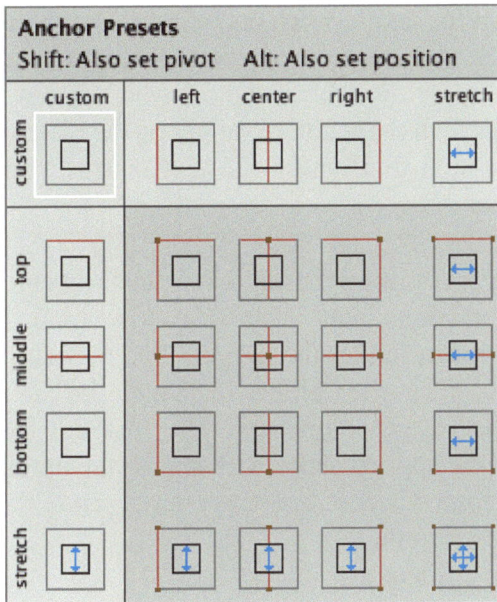

Figure 50 - Preset Anchor Component

The Anchor Presets buttons displays the currently selected preset option if there is one. If the anchors on either the horizontal or vertical axis are set to different positions than any of the presets, the custom options is shown.

Unity 5 User Interface Components

There are two types of UI components in Unity. There are *Visual Components* and *Interactive Components*. We will start by looking at the Visual Components first, and then the Interactive Components.

Visual Components:

These are the UI elements that are used to display information back to the user. I will be giving you just the overview and have you dig deeper into them on your own.

- *Text:* The Text component, which is also known as a Label, has a Text area for entering the text that will be displayed. It is possible to set the font, font style, font size and whether or not the text has rich text capability. There are options to set the alignment of the text, settings for horizontal and vertical overflow which control what happens if the text is larger than the width or height of the rectangle, and a Best Fit option that makes the text resize to fit the available space.

- *Image:* An Image has a Rect Transform component and an Image component. A sprite can be applied to the Image component under the Target Graphic field, and its colour can be set in the Color field. A material can also be applied to the Image component. The Image Type field defines how the applied sprite will appear, the options are:

    o Simple
    o Sliced
    o Tiled
    o Filled

Images can be imported as UI sprites by selecting Sprite(2D / UI) from the 'Texture Type' settings. Sprites have extra import settings compared to the old GUI sprites, the biggest difference is the addition of the sprite editor. The sprite editor provides the option of 9-slicing the image, this splits the image into 9 areas so that if the sprite is resized the corners are not stretched or distorted.

- *Raw Image:* The Image component takes a sprite but Raw Image takes a texture (no borders etc). Raw Image should only be used if necessary otherwise Image will be suitable in the majority of cases.

- *Mask:* A Mask is not a visible UI control but rather a way to modify the appearance of a control's child elements. The mask restricts (ie, "masks") the child elements to the shape of the parent. So, if the child is larger than the parent then only the part of the child that fits within the parent will be visible.

- *Effects:* Visual components can also have various simple effects applied, such as a simple drop shadow or outline.

Interactive Components:

Every UI needs to have some sort of an intractable element to it. That is the user needs to be able to select something. These are UI elements that the user can interact with, such as a:

- *Button:* The button is designed to initiate an action when the user clicks and releases it. If the mouse is moved off the button control before the click is released, the action does not take place. The button has a single event called On Click that responds when the user completes a click.

- *Toggle:* The Toggle control allows the user to switch an option on or off. You can also combine several toggles into a Toggle Group in cases where only one of a set of options should be on at once. The Toggle has a single event called On Value Changed that responds when the user changes the current value. The new value is passed to the event function as a Boolean parameter.

- *Toggle Group:* The Toggle Group is setup by dragging the Toggle Group object to the Group property of each of the Toggles in the group. Toggle Groups are useful anywhere the user must make a choice from a mutually exclusive set of options. Common examples include selecting player character types, speed settings (slow, medium, fast, etc), preset colors and days of the week. You can have more than one Toggle Group object in the scene at a time, so you can create several separate groups if necessary.

- *Slider:* The value of a Slider is determined by the position of the handle along its length. The value increases from the

Min Value up to the Max Value in proportion to the distance the handle is dragged. The default behavior is for the slider to increase from left to right but it is also possible to reverse this behavior using the Direction property.

You can also set the slider to increase vertically by selecting Bottom to Top or Top to Bottom for the Direction property. The slider has a single event called On Value Changed that responds as the user drags the handle. The current numeric value of the slider is passed to the function as a float parameter.

- *Scrollbar:* The value of a Scrollbar is determined by the position of the handle along its length with the value being reported as a fraction between the extreme ends. For example, the default left-to-right bar has a value of 0.0 at the left end, 1.0 at the right end and 0.5 indicates the halfway point. A scrollbar can be oriented vertically by choosing Top to Bottom or Bottom to Top for the Direction property.

  A significant difference between the Scrollbar and the similar Slider control is that the Scrollbar's handle can change in size to represent the distance of scrolling available; when the view can scroll only a short way, the handle will fill up most of the bar and only allow a slight shift either direction. The Scrollbar has a single event called On Value Changed that responds as the user drags the handle. The current value is passed to the even function as a float parameter.

- *Dropdown:* The Dropdown[16] can be used to let the user choose a single option from a list of options. The control shows the currently chosen option. Once clicked, it opens up the list of options so a new option can be chosen. Upon choosing a new option, the list of closed again, and the control shows the new selected option. The list is also closed

---

[16] Look at the online documentation for all of the options and configurations available.

if the user clicks on the control itself, or anywhere else inside the Canvas.

- *Input Field:* An Input Field is a way to make the text of a Text Control editable. Like the other interaction controls, it's not a visible UI element in itself and must be combined with one or more visual UI elements in order to be visible.

  The Input Field script can be added to any existing Text control object from the menu (Component > UI > Input Field). Having done this, you should also drag the object to the Input Field's Text property to enable editing.

  The Text property of the Text control itself will change as the user types and the value can be retrieved from a script after editing. Note that Rich Text is intentionally not supported for editable Text controls; the field will apply any Rich Text markup instantly when typed but the markup essentially "disappears" and there is no subsequent way to change or remove the styling.

- *Scroll Rect:* A Scroll Rect can be used when content that takes up a lot of space needs to be displayed in a small area. The Scroll Rect provides functionality to scroll over this content. Usually a Scroll Rect is combined with a Mask in order to create a scroll view, where only the scrollable content inside the Scroll Rect is visible. It can also additionally be combined with one or two Scrollbars that can be dragged to scroll horizontally or vertically.

Creating Our First User Interface

Now that you have an understanding of the Canvas and the different User Interface elements available to you, we can go ahead and get hands on practice by creating our first UI.

We will use the levels we have developed in the previous chapter to demonstrate the concepts and also give an overview of the UI system in Unity 5. We have created tree levels for the demonstration of the game mechanics concepts. Let's go ahead and list them here, and also the objectives for each. This is important, because you need to understand the objectives of the level to be able to design your UI to support your game environment.

If you recall these were the levels we discussed:

- Level 1: searching; collecting; matching and sorting.
- Level 2: chancing; mixing and timing
- Level 3: progressing; avoidance; capturing and conquering

To design the UI for level 1, we would need to display some information to the user regarding the status of the game. In the previous chapter we used *Debug.Log()* as a way to test and debug our logic. In a way giving us an update on the state of the environment. This however, is not visible to the player and we would need to create something that will be more appealing to them.

Level 1 – UI Design

To start creating our UI, we need to introduce a Canvas Game Object into our scene. The easiest way to do so is by right-clicking in the *Hierarchy Window* and from the *Context Menu* select (*UI->Canvas*). This will place a Canvas Game Object into your scene. We want to set the *Render Mode* to *Screen Space – Overlay*[17] if this is not the value set already.

There are two main information we need to communicate to the player: (1) how many collectables items there are in the scene, (2) how many items the player has collected. We can combine two UI elements to display this information to the player:

- Panel
- Text

---

[17] This render mode places UI elements on the screen rendered on top of the scene.

To add a Panel UI Element, you will right-click in the *Hierarchy Window* on the Canvas Game Object, and select (*UI->Panel*). This will add a Panel element as a child to the Canvas Game Object. By default, the Panel will fill the whole Canvas.

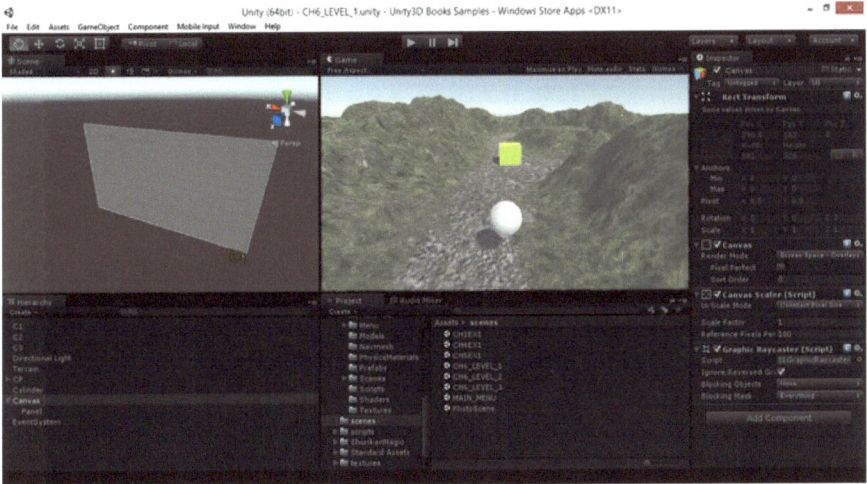

Figure 51 - Canvas with Panel Attached

Notice how the Game Window has changed with the screen overlay from the Canvas Game Object. We want to make sure that the Panel UI element does not take up the whole space. Selecting the Panel UI element, we can use the Inspector Window to adjust the properties.

The first thing we would like to do is to change the Anchors of the Panel. We can use the Preset configuration to anchor the control to the top left corner of the screen. When you make the change, notice that the Rect Transform updated its PosX/PosY and Width/Height values. We will be adjusting these values to our linking. I have done ahead and updated my values to the following:

- Pos X: *50*
- Pos Y: *-25*
- Width: *100*
- Height: *50*

The width and the height, define the actual width and the height of the panel in pixels, and the position values are displacement relative to the anchor point.

Let's go ahead and add out Text UI element, to do this, you will again right-click in the *Hierarchy Window* on the Panel element, and select (*UI->Text*). This action will create a Text element and make it a child of the Panel. Also notice that in the Inspector Window, by default, the Text element is anchored at the center with the default width and height.

There are a few properties that I have changed on the Text element.

In the *Rect Transform*, I have updated the Width and the Height to be 80 and 40 respectively.

In the Text Script Component, I have changed the Alignment to be Horizontally centered, and Vertically also centered.

Lastly, I have checked the *Best Fit* checkbox to auto-fix the text in the provided area.

Notice, that you can also change the font and the font size, as well as the color of the Text, or even apply Material to be used for rendering.

We have now composed a simple UI that can be used to give some feedback to the player. As far as the UI design is concerned, we are done at this point. But, we need to be able to update the Text element somehow from within our game! In order for us to be able to achieve this, we would need to do some minor coding.

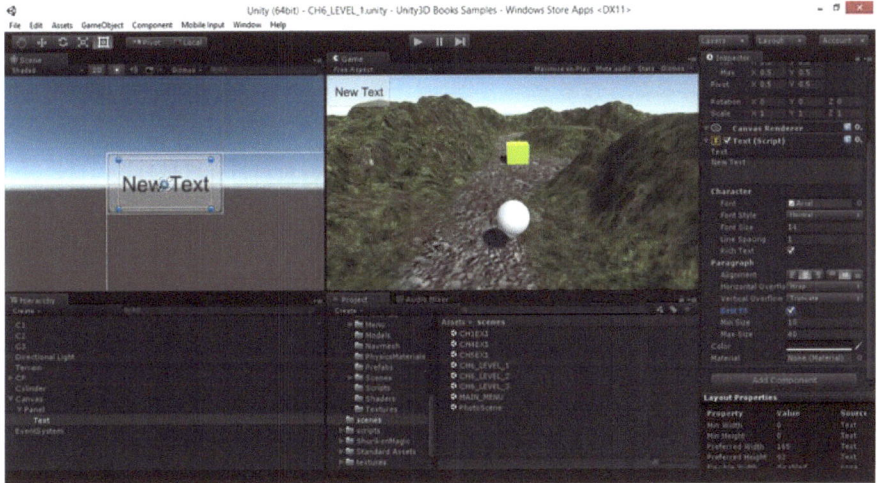

Figure 52 - UI Panel and Text Element

We need to be able to reference the Text UI element from our code, and once we have a reference, we can update the Text property of the Text UI element.

Since the *PlayerInput.cs* script is in charge of keeping track of the status for the game, we will create a new public variable of type Text that will be used to refer to the Text UI element.

We would update the class adding the following two variables:

```
public Text lblCollectables;
private int collectables = 0;
```

And we would change our *Start()* function be something like the following:

```
void Start ()
{
    if(this.myEnemy== null)
    {
        this.myEnemy = GameObject.FindGameObjectWithTag("Enemy") as GameOb-
ject;
    }
```

```
    if(this.lblCollectables!= null)
    {
        GameObject[] collectables = GameObject.FindGameObjectsWithTag("MyCol-
lectable");
        this.collectables = collectables.Length;
        this.lblCollectables.text = string.Format("{0}/{1}", this.myCollec-
tion.Count, this.collectables);
    }
}
```

Finally, we would need to update the information during game time, therefore, we will also include the following segment in the *Update()* function.

```
if (this.lblCollectables != null)
{
    this.lblCollectables.text = string.Format("{0}/{1}", this.myCollec-
tion.Count, this.collectables);
}
```

The resulting interface would be something like this:

Figure 53 - Collectables UI Implemented

So we have created one aspect of our UI, but we have more work to do. Once we collect all of our collectables, we need to find the Drop-Zone and be able to match the collectables based on their size. We

146

would need to implement an interface that can properly identify this process for the player in a nice way.

Since, we are using a Stack data structure to maintain the order of selection performed by the player, we can create our UI for this task in a similar fashion. Also, we would like to display this specific UI portion once the user has collected all of the collectables and is at the *Drop-Zone*. Hence, when that triggers, we will also display the UI specific for matching. For this to work properly, we would need to create a new Canvas Object. Remember, that we can have multiple Canvas object in the scene, and each canvas can be used for a different purpose within the scene and enabled or disabled as needed.

To create a second Canvas, you will right-click in the *Hierarchy Window* and from the Context Menu select (*UI->Canvas*). You would want to add a new Panel element and also three Button element objects to the Panel. The process is the same for add any UI element, so we are not going to list that any more.

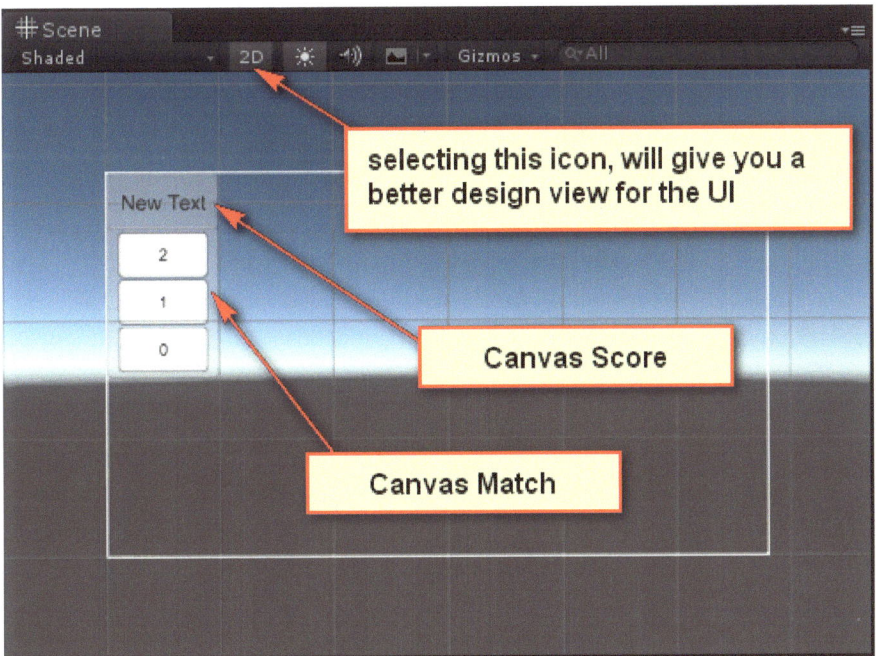

Figure 54 - Additional UI for Matching

Once you have designed the UI in the Scene View, we would need to create the code to access and control it. At the minimum, we need to be able to enable and disable the Canvas object based on some criteria. We also need to update the caption of the Button elements based on the user selection at the *Drop-Zone*.

```
public Canvas canvasMatching;
public Text lblStackTop;
public Text lblStackMiddle;
public Text lblStackBottom;
```

Code Block 37 - Level 1 Match Canvas Variables

We can easily setup some variables to reference the needed UI object as shown in Code Block 37. But look at the code we have previously written, we aren't really handling it properly. To make the process and the UI a little more intuitive, we should probably add two more buttons to the UI, giving the player the ability to either Reset the whole game, or in the case of matching, be able to try the challenge again. Taking this two new addition into consideration, our UI will be updated to look like the following:

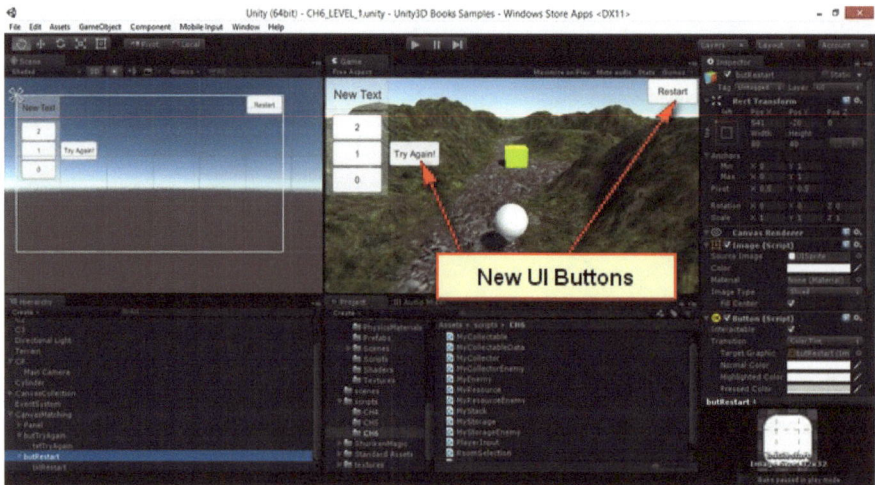

Figure 55 - Additional UI Elements for Level 1

Since we have enhanced our UI, we need to revisit our logic for the matchmaking and also update it properly to reflect the new changes. The first task we should do is to create the button trigger functions, at least the placeholder. We would introduce two new functions to handle the button click events for the newly created buttons: *butRestartClick()* and *butTryAgainClick()*.

```
public void butRestartClick()
{
    Application.LoadLevel("CH6_LEVEL_1");
}

public void butTryAgainClick()
{
    // handle the try again event
}
```

Code Block 38 - Button triggers for Level 1

The functions listed above will handle the *OnClick* event for each button respectively. We still need to hook these functions with the *On-Click* event. In order to do this, you will need to select the desired button from the *Hierarchy Window*, and from the *Inspector Window*, you will need to add a new event on the *OnClick()* property.

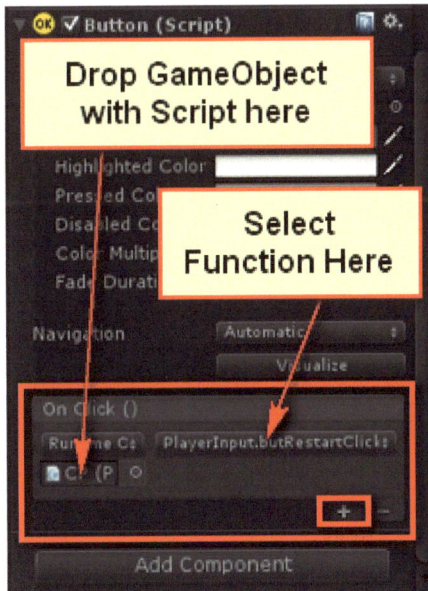

Figure 56 - Button OnClick Event

So from the *Inspector Window*, you will go to the *Button Script Component* and add an event handler by clicking the *(+)* button. This will create an empty drop slot for you.

You will need to drag and drop the GameObject that the Event Handler is attached to, in our case it is the CP GameObject.

Once that is placed in the empty slot, you will use the DropDown list to select the Script->Function() which will handle the OnClick event.

This happens to be *PlayerInput.butRestartClick()* for our code. That is it! You have just created your first button event handler. At the time of this writing, Unity Event function can only receive one parameter, hence, if there is a need to pass several parameters, one way around this limitation, is to create multiple functions and multiple events handler and attach them just like we did. At this point each time the button is clicked at runtime, we are re-loading the whole level.

Here are the code snippets for the additions and also modification that have been applied to the *PlayerInput.cs* script:

```
public void butRestartClick()
{
    Application.LoadLevel("CH6_LEVEL_1");
}

public void butTryAgainClick()
{
    // handle the try again event
    this.stack.clear();
    this.lblStackBottom.text = "0";
    this.lblStackMiddle.text = "0";
    this.lblStackTop.text = "0";
}
```

The two functions that handle the Button OnClick event for the Restart button and the Try Again button are listed above. The *Awake()* function has been removed, and the *Start()* function has been modified to call a new function to Reset all variables called *ResetGame()*. Here is the listing:

```
private void ResetGame()
{
    this.stack.clear();

    this.ROOM_SELECTION = -1;
    this.GAME_OVER = false;

    this.MATCH = false;

    this.NUM_BULLETS = 1;

    // make sure we start clean
    this.myCollection.Clear();
}

// Use this for initialization
void Start () {
```

```
    this.ResetGame();

    if(this.myEnemy== null)
    {
        this.myEnemy = GameObject.FindGameObjectWithTag("Enemy") as GameOb-
ject;
    }

    #region code for UI elements - Level 1
    if(this.lblCollectables!= null)
    {
        GameObject[] collectables = GameObject.FindGameObjectsWithTag("My-
Collectable");
        this.collectables = collectables.Length;
        this.lblCollectables.text = string.Format("{0}/{1}", this.myCollec-
tion.Count, this.collectables);
    }

    if(this.canvasMatching != null)
    {
        this.canvasMatching.enabled = false;

        if(this.lblStackTop != null)
        {
            this.lblStackTop.text = "0";
        }
        if (this.lblStackMiddle != null)
        {
            this.lblStackMiddle.text = "0";
        }
        if (this.lblStackBottom != null)
        {
            this.lblStackBottom.text = "0";
        }

        this.butTryAgain.gameObject.SetActive(false);
    }
    #endregion
}
```

Basically the *ResetGame()* function is doing what the *Awake()* function used to do, however, since we have the ability to re-start the game during gameplay, and the restart feature basically loads the level again, we are using the *Start()* function to call the *ResetGame()* function to reset all of the variables in the level.

The *Update()* function also has been modified to accommodate the new changes we have made through the UI. You will notice that now, when the player selects three matching items, if they are not ordered properly, a button will display to give them the chance to try again.

Here is the listing for the new logic handling the mouse input in the *Update()* function:

```
        if (this.MATCH)
        {
            #region MOUSE INPUT
            if (Input.mousePosition != null && Input.GetMouseButtonUp(0))
            {
                //Debug.Log("START MATCH >>>");
                RaycastHit selectedCollectable;

                // capture the mouse position and cast a ray to see what ob-
ject we hit
                Ray ray = Camera.main.ScreenPointToRay(Input.mousePosition);

                if (Physics.Raycast(ray, out selectedCollectable, 200))
                {
                    //Debug.Log("TAG="+selectedCollectable.transform.tag);

                    if (selectedCollectable.transform.tag.Equals("MyCollect-
able"))
                    {
                        //Debug.Log("YOU CLICKED ME >>>");
                        var collect = selectedCollectable.transform.gameOb-
ject.GetComponent<MyCollectable>();

                        MyCollectableData data = new MyCollectableData();

                        data.ID = collect.ID;
                        data.size = collect.size;

                        MyCollectableData sd = null;

                        if(this.stack.COUNT<3)
                            this.stack.push(data);

                        Debug.Log("STACK COUNT = " +
stack.COUNT.ToString());

                        switch (stack.COUNT)
                        {
                            case 1:
                                this.lblStackBottom.text = data.size.ToString();
                                break;
                            case 2:
                                this.lblStackMiddle.text =
data.size.ToString();
                                break;
                            case 3:
                                this.lblStackTop.text = data.size.ToString();
                                break;
                        }
                    }
                }
            }
```

```
            }

         if (stack.COUNT >= 3)
         {
            bool WIN = false;
            ArrayList tmp = new ArrayList();

            for (int i = 0; i <= stack.COUNT + 1; i++)
            {
               MyCollectableData d = (MyCollectableData)stack.pop();
               Debug.Log(string.Format("Pop: {0}", d.size));
               tmp.Add(d);
            }

            if((((MyCollectableData)tmp[0]).size > ((MyCollecta-
bleData)tmp[1]).size) && (((MyCollectableData)tmp[1]).size >
((MyCollectableData)tmp[2]).size))
            {
               Debug.Log("GREAT JOB!!! Objective Completed!");
               this.MATCH = false;
            }
            else
            {
               this.butTryAgain.gameObject.SetActive(true);
            }
         }
         #endregion
      }
```

We have completed our initial UI design for Level 1. Now let's take a look at how to implement the UI for level 2.

Level 2 – UI Design

For Level 2, the player had to select a randomizer which would indicate what room he or she had to visit. After the selection was done, the player was given a specific set of time to be able to visit the room. Upon the visit, the timer would be rest, and the room would be marked as visited.

Our UI should be designed in a way to capture the status of the environment at any given moment. So we need a way to display the timer. It would also be nice to display the objective for the player; that is which room he or she has to visit. And finally, there should be a way to indicate if the player has won the game or not, and as always a way for them to replay the game, like a restart.

Since there are some similarities between the UI for Level 2 and the UI for Level 1, we can make life easier by copying the *Canvas Gamebjects* we have defined in Level 1 and paste them into Level 2. Obviously we will make some changed, but overall it will give us a good base to start from.

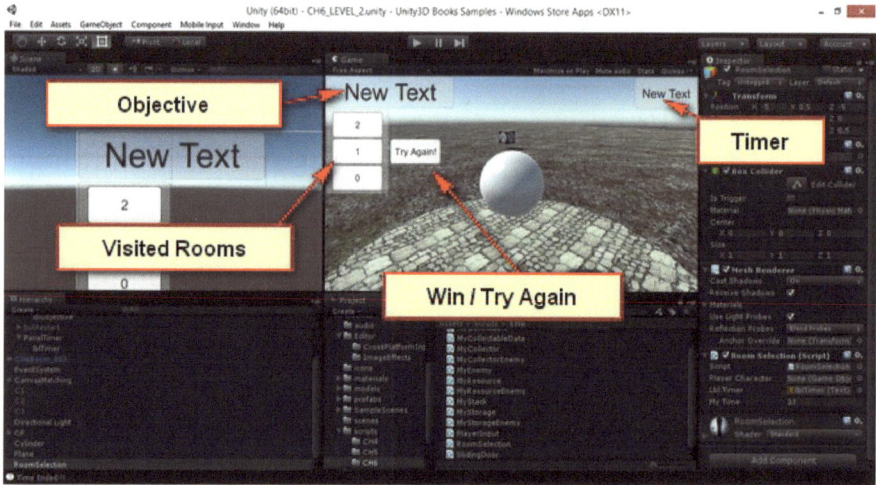

Figure 57 - Level 2 Level Concept

Let's start by implementing the Timer UI first. We want to basically create a new Panel element with an associated Text element and anchor it to the top-right corner of the screen. If you recall, the script that handles the timer is attached to the *RoomSelection GameObject* and the script itself is called *RoomSelection.cs*. To display the timer, we will need to create a reference to the label and basically make sure that it is displaying the proper value during the update cycle.

As it happens, we can also set the objective for the player in the same script. We would need to create a new variable to reference the Objective Text and basically update the content based on the player's selection during the game. Here is the code listing for the new script:

```
using UnityEngine;
using UnityEngine.UI;

using System.Collections;

public class RoomSelection : MonoBehaviour
```

```
{
    public GameObject playerCharacter = null;

    #region UI Variables
    public Text lblTimer;
    public Text lblObjective;
    #endregion

    // Use this for initialization
    void Start()
    {
        if(this.lblTimer != null)
        {
            this.lblTimer.text = "0";
        }

        if(this.lblObjective != null)
        {
            this.lblObjective.text = string.Format("Select Randomizer!");
        }

        // if the player characte is not defined at design time
        // assign it during runtime before the game starts
        if(this.playerCharacter == null)
        {
            this.playerCharacter = GameObject.FindGameObjectWithTag("Player")
as GameObject;
        }
    }

    // myTime will be used to give the amount of time in seconds
    // for the player to find the room!!!
    public float myTime = 33.0f;
    private float endTime = 0.0f;

    // Update is called once per frame
    void Update()
    {
        this.transform.Rotate(new Vector3(1, 1, 1), 1.0f);


        if (this.endTime>Time.time)
        {
            this.lblTimer.text = Mathf.CeilToInt(this.endTime -
Time.time).ToString();
            Debug.Log("Timer Started!!! " + Mathf.CeilToInt(this.endTime -
Time.time).ToString());
        }
        else if(this.endTime==0.0f)
        {
            this.lblTimer.text = "0";
            ; // do nothing
        }
        else
        {
            Debug.Log("Time Ended!!!");
```

```
                this.playerCharacter.GetComponent<PlayerInput>().GAME_OVER = true;
        }

        // check distance between this object and the player character
        float distance = Vector3.Distance(this.transform.position, this.play-
erCharacter.transform.position);
        if (distance < 2.0f)
        {
            #region MOUSE INPUT
            if (Input.mousePosition != null && Input.GetMouseButtonUp(0))
            {
                int color = Random.Range(0, 3);
                switch (color)
                {
                    case 0:
                        {
                            this.transform.GetComponent<Renderer>().material.color
= Color.blue;
                            this.playerCharacter.GetComponent<PlayerIn-
put>().ROOM_SELECTION = 0;
                            this.lblObjective.text = string.Format("Find Blue
Room");
                            break;
                        }
                    case 1:
                        {
                            this.transform.GetComponent<Renderer>().material.color
= Color.red;
                            this.playerCharacter.GetComponent<PlayerIn-
put>().ROOM_SELECTION = 1;
                            this.lblObjective.text = string.Format("Find Red
Room");
                            break;
                        }
                    case 2:
                        {
                            this.transform.GetComponent<Renderer>().material.color
= Color.green;
                            this.playerCharacter.GetComponent<PlayerIn-
put>().ROOM_SELECTION = 2;
                            this.lblObjective.text = string.Format("Find Green
Room");
                            break;
                        }
                }

                // start timer
                this.endTime = this.myTime + Time.time;
            }
            #endregion
        }

    }

    public void ResetTimer()
```

```
    {
        this.endTime = 0.0f;
        this.lblObjective.text = string.Format("Select Randomizer");
    }
}
```

Code Block 39 - Level 2 Timer and Objective UI Code

When you run the scene now, you will see a screen similar to the following:

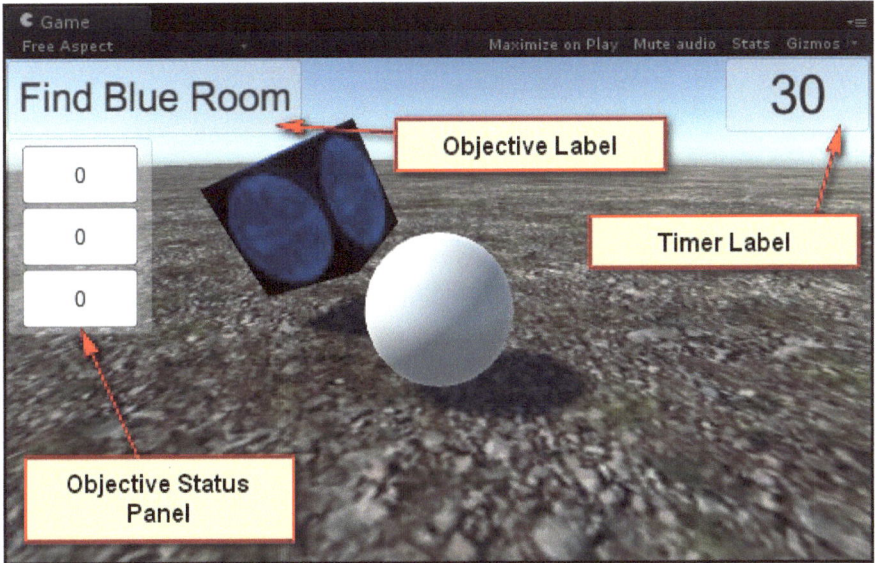

The next UI element we want to implement is when the player visits the room they are supposed to find. Since we have three rooms we can reuse our existing Match Panel from Level 1. We would just have to write a new piece of code to update the caption according to the objectives for Level 2.

To achieve this, we are going to have to update several script files. If you recall we have three scripts that are specifically dealing with Level 2: *RoomSelection.cs*, *SlidingDoor.cs* and *PlayerInput.cs*.

If you look at the scripts, the main updates are actually happening in the *RoomSelection.cs* script and the *PlayerInput.cs* script. *SlidingDoor.cs* is triggering a function in the *PlayerInput.cs* script to indicate which room was visited.

On the *OnCollisionEnter()* function within the *SlidingDoor.cs* script, if the right conditions are met, the *RoomVisited()* function is called on the *PlayerInput.cs* script. So we would need to update that scrip to reflect the correct information on the Objective Status Panel display.

Here is the listing for the revised *RoomVisited()* function in the *PlayerInput.cs* scripts:

```csharp
public void RoomVisited(SlidingDoor room)
{
    if(room != null)
    {
        this.stack.push(room);

        string msg = string.Format("Room #{0} inserted, stack count={1}",
room.ROOM_NUMBER, this.stack.COUNT);
        Debug.Log(msg);

        #region used for UI element
        switch(room.ROOM_NUMBER)
        {
            case 0:
            {
                this.lblStackTop.text = "Blue";
                break;
            }
            case 1:
            {
                this.lblStackBottom.text = "Red";
                break;
            }
            case 2:
            {
                this.lblStackMiddle.text = "Green";
                break;
            }
        }
        #endregion

        if (this.stack.COUNT>=3)
        {
            Debug.Log("YOU WIN!!!");
            this.lblObjective.text = "YOU WIN!!!";
            this.GAME_OVER = true;

            this.butTryAgain.gameObject.SetActive(true);
        }
    }
}
```

```
    }
```

Code Block 40 - Revised RoomVisited() function for Level 2

Notice we have added a switch statement to determine which room was visited and update the button captions in the panel accordingly. Since this function also determines if the player has completed the level successfully, we have also included a line to enable the Try Again button which will be used to replay the game.

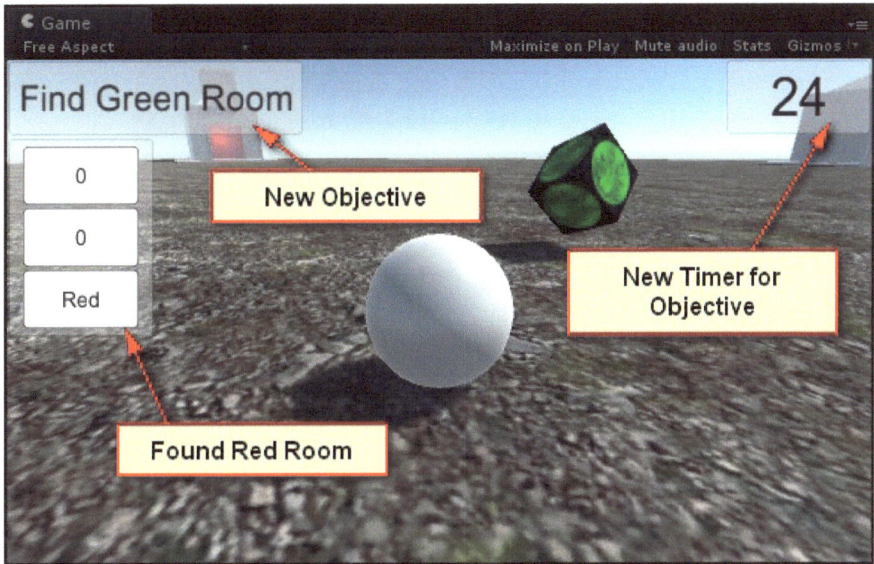

Now we also need to make some changes in the *RoomSelection.cs* script. Here is the snippet for the updates we had to make to that script:

```
    if (this.endTime>Time.time)
    {
        this.lblTimer.text = Mathf.CeilToInt(this.endTime -
Time.time).ToString();
        Debug.Log("Timer Started!!! " + Mathf.CeilToInt(this.endTime -
Time.time).ToString());
    }
    else if(this.endTime==0.0f)
    {
        this.lblTimer.text = "0";
        ; // do nothing
    }
    else
    {
        Debug.Log("Time Ended!!!");
```

```
        this.playerCharacter.GetComponent<PlayerInput>().GAME_OVER = true;
        this.lblObjective.text = "YOU LOSE!!!";
        this.lblTimer.text = "0";
        this.playerCharacter.GetComponent<PlayerInput>().butT-
ryAgain.gameObject.SetActive(true);
    }
```

We have now completed the UI implementation for *Level 1* and *Level 2*. Let's take a look at the UI implementation of *Level 3*.

Level 3 – UI Design

For Level 3, we would need to create a totally different type of a UI. In Level 3, our objective is to create a Storage Facility which will collect and store resources for us. The objective of the level is for the player to kill the opponent and for the opponent to kill the player. Whoever accomplishes this first is the winner.

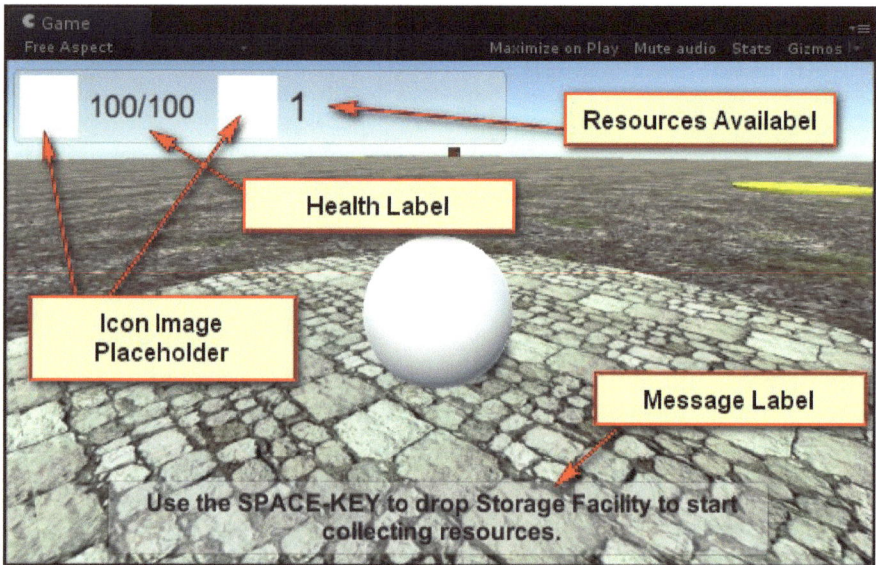

Figure 58 - Level 3 UI Concept

Our UI will need to be designed in a way to give us information regarding the status of our resources, our health and also the next collectable resource. It would be nice to also have a way to display relevant messages to the player. For instance, making sure they know they need to create a Storage Facility to collect resources.

We would also like to show the health of our opponent, but not necessarily their resources. Even though this is very well possible to do if we choose to include it in the design.

The main update code for the health, inventory and messages will be taking place in the *PlayerInput.cs* script file. Here is a code snippet of the supporting code necessary for the initial setup of the labels upon startup of the level:

```
// variables for Level 3 UI
public Text lblHealth;
public Text lblResources;
public Text lblMessages;
#endregion

...

private void ResetLevel3UI()
{
    if(this.lblHealth != null)
        this.lblHealth.text = string.Format("{0}/100", this.HEALTH);
    if(this.lblResources != null)
        this.lblResources.text = this.NUM_BULLETS.ToString();
    if(this.lblMessages != null)
        this.lblMessages.text = "Use the SPACE-KEY to drop Storage Facility
to start collecting resources.";
}
```

Once we drop the Storage Facility, we can use the Message Panel to display the status of the Resource Collector. In order to perform this task, we would need to perform several key steps.

We would need to update the Message Panel each time when one of this actions happen:

1. Storage Facility is Dropped
2. Collector Unit is traveling to the Resource Area
3. Collector Unit is traveling to the Storage Facility
4. Collector Unit is loading resources.
5. Collector Unit is unloading resources.

The scripts that will handle the UI updates are: *MyStorage.cs*, *My-Collector.cs*, *MyResource.cs* and of course *PlayerInput.cs* scripts. The following code listing will display the full script for *MyStorage.cs*, *My-Collector.cs* and *MyResource.cs* scripts:

```csharp
using UnityEngine;
using System.Collections;

public class MyStorage : MonoBehaviour
{

    public GameObject myCollector;
    private GameObject collectorObj;

    private GameObject playerCharacter;

    // variables for timer
    public float myTime = 3.0f;
    private float endTime = 0.0f;

    // Use this for initialization
    void Start()
    {
        Vector3 pos = new Vector3(this.transform.position.x + 1, 2,
this.transform.position.z + 1);
        this.collectorObj = GameObject.Instantiate(this.myCollector, pos,
this.transform.rotation) as GameObject;
        this.collectorObj.GetComponent<MyCollector>().myStorage = this.gameOb-
ject;

        this.playerCharacter = GameObject.FindGameObjectWithTag("Player") as
GameObject;

        this.playerCharacter.GetComponent<PlayerInput>().lblMessages.text =
"Storage Facility Created!";
    }

    // Update is called once per frame
    void Update()
    {
        if (this.endTime > Time.time)
        {
            string msg = string.Format("Unloading Resources: {0}",
Mathf.CeilToInt(this.endTime - Time.time));
            this.collectorObj.GetComponent<MyCollector>().UpdateMessage(msg);
        }
        else if (this.endTime == 0.0f)
        {
            ; // do nothing
        }
        else
        {
            this.endTime = 0.0f;
```

```
            this.collectorObj.GetComponent<MyCollector>().GOTO_RESOURCE = true;
            int collectedResources = this.collectorObj.GetComponent<MyCollec-
tor>().UNINTS_COLLECTED;

            // add bullet to player character
            this.playerCharacter.GetComponent<PlayerInput>().NUM_BULLETS +=
collectedResources;
            this.playerCharacter.GetComponent<PlayerInput>().UpdateResources();

        }
    }

    // This function handles the collision of colliders as a trigger
    void OnCollisionEnter(Collision c)
    {
        if (c.transform.tag.Equals("CollectorUnit"))
        {
            c.transform.GetComponent<MyCollector>().GOTO_STORAGE = false;

            // start timer
            this.endTime = this.myTime + Time.time;

            string msg = string.Format("Unloading Resources: {0}",
Mathf.CeilToInt(this.endTime - Time.time));
            c.transform.GetComponent<MyCollector>().UpdateMessage(msg);
        }
    }

}
```

Code Block 41 - MyStorage.cs Listing for UI Design

```
using UnityEngine;
using UnityEngine.UI;

using System.Collections;

public class MyCollector : MonoBehaviour
{
    public GameObject myResource;
    public GameObject myStorage;

    public bool GOTO_RESOURCE;
    public bool GOTO_STORAGE;

    public int UNINTS_COLLECTED;

    private GameObject playerCharacter;

    // Use this for initialization
    void Start()
    {
        this.myResource = GameObject.FindGameObjectWithTag("ResourcePlayer")
as GameObject;

        this.GOTO_RESOURCE = true;
        this.GOTO_STORAGE = false;
```

```
        this.UNINTS_COLLECTED = 0;

        this.playerCharacter = GameObject.FindGameObjectWithTag("Player") as
GameObject;
    }

    // Update is called once per frame
    void Update()
    {

        if (this.GOTO_RESOURCE)
        {
            // goto the resource location for collection
            Vector3 refillHeading = this.myResource.transform.position -
this.transform.position;
            refillHeading.Normalize();

            // use Quaternion Slerp function to make smooth transition ...
            this.transform.rotation =
                Quaternion.Slerp(transform.rotation,
                            Quaternion.LookRotation(refillHeading), 10 *
Time.deltaTime);

            this.transform.Translate(Vector3.forward * Time.deltaTime);

            int distance = Mathf.CeilToInt(Vector3.Distance(this.transform.po-
sition, this.myResource.transform.position));
            this.playerCharacter.GetComponent<PlayerInput>().lblMessages.text =
string.Format("Distance to Resource {0}", distance);
        }

        if (this.GOTO_STORAGE)
        {
            Vector3 refillHeading = this.myStorage.transform.position -
this.transform.position;
            refillHeading.Normalize();

            // use Quaternion Slerp function to make smooth transition ...
            this.transform.rotation =
                Quaternion.Slerp(transform.rotation,
                            Quaternion.LookRotation(refillHeading), 10 *
Time.deltaTime);

            this.transform.Translate(Vector3.forward * Time.deltaTime);

            int distance = Mathf.CeilToInt(Vector3.Distance(this.transform.po-
sition, this.myResource.transform.position));
            this.playerCharacter.GetComponent<PlayerInput>().lblMessages.text =
string.Format("Distance to Storage {0}", distance);

        }
    }

    public void UpdateMessage(string message)
```

```
    {
        this.playerCharacter.GetComponent<PlayerInput>().lblMessages.text =
message;
    }
}
```

Code Block 42 - MyCollector.cs Listing for UI Design

```csharp
using UnityEngine;
using System.Collections;

public class MyResource : MonoBehaviour
{
    public GameObject collectorUnit;

    // variables for timer
    public float myTime = 3.0f;
    private float endTime = 0.0f;

    // Use this for initialization
    void Start()
    {

    }

    // Update is called once per frame
    void Update()
    {
        if (this.endTime > Time.time)
        {
            string msg = string.Format("Collecting Resources: {0}",
Mathf.CeilToInt(this.endTime - Time.time));
            this.collectorUnit.GetComponent<MyCollector>().UpdateMessage(msg);
        }
        else if (this.endTime == 0.0f)
        {
            ; // do nothing
        }
        else
        {
            this.endTime = 0.0f;
            this.collectorUnit.GetComponent<MyCollector>().GOTO_STORAGE = true;
            this.collectorUnit.GetComponent<MyCollector>().UNINTS_COLLECTED =
1;
        }
    }

    // This function handles the collision of colliders as a trigger
    void OnTriggerEnter(Collider c)
    {
        if (c.tag.Equals("CollectorUnit"))
        {
            c.GetComponent<MyCollector>().GOTO_RESOURCE = false;
            this.collectorUnit = c.gameObject;

            // start timer
            this.endTime = this.myTime + Time.time;
```

```
        string msg = string.Format("Collecting Resources: {0}",
Mathf.CeilToInt(this.endTime - Time.time));
        this.collectorUnit.GetComponent<MyCollector>().UpdateMessage(msg);
    }
  }

}
```

Code Block 43 - MyResource.cs Listing for UI Design

We would need to update the Resource Label and the Health Label each time when one of this actions happen:

1. Resource is loaded at the Storage Facility.
2. Player is hit by the enemy.

If you have been paying attention and testing out the code while discussing it in the book, you might have noticed that there are a few minor bugs in Level 3. First, we never implemented a way to capture the HEALTH of the player or the enemy. Second, when the resources were collected and brought back to the Storage Facility, you might have noticed that the increments of the resources was not performed correctly after the first collection. This is because we never reset the variable in the Collector Unit back to 0 after the unloading.

Another issue here is that we have not implemented a way to stop the game! We need to make sure that when the player or the enemy dies, we stop all moving objects inside the game and display the proper message. The following listings put everything together to make Level 3 complete both from the UI side of the development and also the Game Mechanics side of the development.

Complete listing for *MyStorage.cs*:

```
using UnityEngine;
using System.Collections;

public class MyStorage : MonoBehaviour
{
    public GameObject myCollector;
    private GameObject collectorObj;

    private GameObject playerCharacter;
```

```
    // variables for timer
    public float myTime = 3.0f;
    private float endTime = 0.0f;

    // Use this for initialization
    void Start()
    {
        Vector3 pos = new Vector3(this.transform.position.x + 1, 2,
this.transform.position.z + 1);
        this.collectorObj = GameObject.Instantiate(this.myCollector, pos,
this.transform.rotation) as GameObject;
        this.collectorObj.GetComponent<MyCollector>().myStorage = this.gameOb-
ject;

        this.playerCharacter = GameObject.FindGameObjectWithTag("Player") as
GameObject;

        this.playerCharacter.GetComponent<PlayerInput>().lblMessages.text =
"Storage Facility Created!";
    }

    // Update is called once per frame
    void Update()
    {
        if(!this.playerCharacter.GetComponent<PlayerInput>().GAME_OVER)
        {
            if (this.endTime > Time.time)
            {
                string msg = string.Format("Unloading Resources: {0}",
Mathf.CeilToInt(this.endTime - Time.time));
                this.collectorObj.GetComponent<MyCollector>().UpdateMes-
sage(msg);
            }
            else if (this.endTime == 0.0f)
            {
                ; // do nothing
            }
            else
            {
                this.endTime = 0.0f;
                this.collectorObj.GetComponent<MyCollector>().GOTO_RESOURCE =
true;
                int collectedResources = this.collectorObj.GetComponent<MyCol-
lector>().UNINTS_COLLECTED;
                this.collectorObj.GetComponent<MyCollector>().UNINTS_COLLECTED =
0;

                // add bullet to player character
                this.playerCharacter.GetComponent<PlayerInput>().NUM_BULLETS +=
collectedResources;
                this.playerCharacter.GetComponent<PlayerInput>().Up-
dateResources();

            }
        }
```

```
    }

    // This function handles the collision of colliders as a trigger
    void OnCollisionEnter(Collision c)
    {
        if (c.transform.tag.Equals("CollectorUnit"))
        {
            c.transform.GetComponent<MyCollector>().GOTO_STORAGE = false;

            // start timer
            this.endTime = this.myTime + Time.time;

            string msg = string.Format("Unloading Resources: {0}",
Mathf.CeilToInt(this.endTime - Time.time));
            c.transform.GetComponent<MyCollector>().UpdateMessage(msg);
        }
    }
}
```

Complete Listing for *MyCollector.cs*:

```
using UnityEngine;
using UnityEngine.UI;

using System.Collections;

public class MyCollector : MonoBehaviour
{
    public GameObject myResource;
    public GameObject myStorage;

    public bool GOTO_RESOURCE;
    public bool GOTO_STORAGE;

    public int UNINTS_COLLECTED;

    private GameObject playerCharacter;

    // Use this for initialization
    void Start()
    {
        this.myResource = GameObject.FindGameObjectWithTag("ResourcePlayer")
as GameObject;

        this.GOTO_RESOURCE = true;
        this.GOTO_STORAGE = false;

        this.UNINTS_COLLECTED = 0;

        this.playerCharacter = GameObject.FindGameObjectWithTag("Player") as
GameObject;
    }
```

```csharp
    // Update is called once per frame
    void Update()
    {
        if(!this.playerCharacter.GetComponent<PlayerInput>().GAME_OVER)
        {
            if (this.GOTO_RESOURCE)
            {
                // goto the resource location for collection
                Vector3 refillHeading = this.myResource.transform.position -
this.transform.position;
                refillHeading.Normalize();

                // use Quaternion Slerp function to make smooth transition ...
                this.transform.rotation =
                    Quaternion.Slerp(transform.rotation,
                                    Quaternion.LookRotation(refillHeading), 10 *
Time.deltaTime);

                this.transform.Translate(Vector3.forward * Time.deltaTime);

                int distance = Mathf.CeilToInt(Vector3.Distance(this.trans-
form.position, this.myResource.transform.position));
                this.playerCharacter.GetComponent<PlayerInput>().lblMes-
sages.text = string.Format("Distance to Resource {0}", distance);
            }

            if (this.GOTO_STORAGE)
            {
                Vector3 refillHeading = this.myStorage.transform.position -
this.transform.position;
                refillHeading.Normalize();

                // use Quaternion Slerp function to make smooth transition ...
                this.transform.rotation =
                    Quaternion.Slerp(transform.rotation,
                                    Quaternion.LookRotation(refillHeading), 10 *
Time.deltaTime);

                this.transform.Translate(Vector3.forward * Time.deltaTime);

                int distance = Mathf.CeilToInt(Vector3.Distance(this.trans-
form.position, this.myResource.transform.position));
                this.playerCharacter.GetComponent<PlayerInput>().lblMes-
sages.text = string.Format("Distance to Storage {0}", distance);
            }
        }
    }

    public void UpdateMessage(string message)
    {
        this.playerCharacter.GetComponent<PlayerInput>().lblMessages.text =
message;
    }
}
```

Complete listing of *MyResource.cs*:

```
using UnityEngine;
using System.Collections;

public class MyResource : MonoBehaviour
{
    public GameObject collectorUnit;

    // variables for timer
    public float myTime = 3.0f;
    private float endTime = 0.0f;

    // Use this for initialization
    void Start()
    {

    }

    // Update is called once per frame
    void Update()
    {
        if (this.endTime > Time.time)
        {
            string msg = string.Format("Collecting Resources: {0}",
Mathf.CeilToInt(this.endTime - Time.time));
            this.collectorUnit.GetComponent<MyCollector>().UpdateMessage(msg);
        }
        else if (this.endTime == 0.0f)
        {
            ; // do nothing
        }
        else
        {
            this.endTime = 0.0f;
            this.collectorUnit.GetComponent<MyCollector>().GOTO_STORAGE = true;
            this.collectorUnit.GetComponent<MyCollector>().UNINTS_COLLECTED =
1;
        }
    }

    // This function handles the collision of colliders as a trigger
    void OnTriggerEnter(Collider c)
    {
        if (c.tag.Equals("CollectorUnit"))
        {
            c.GetComponent<MyCollector>().GOTO_RESOURCE = false;
            this.collectorUnit = c.gameObject;

            // start timer
            this.endTime = this.myTime + Time.time;
            string msg = string.Format("Collecting Resources: {0}",
Mathf.CeilToInt(this.endTime - Time.time));
            this.collectorUnit.GetComponent<MyCollector>().UpdateMessage(msg);
```

```
        }
    }
}
```

For the Enemy scripts, *MyStorageEnemy.cs*, *MyCollectorEnemy.cs* and *MyResourceEnemy.cs* are all similar to the player's scripts, only the references have to be updated to point to the enemy scripts and or prefabs.

However, here is the *MyEnemy.cs* script which is unique:

```csharp
using UnityEngine;
using UnityEngine.UI;

using System.Collections;

public class MyEnemy : MonoBehaviour
{
    public GameObject myBase;

    public GameObject myStorage;
    private GameObject myStorageObj;

    public GameObject myEnemy;

    public GameObject myBullet;
    public GameObject myGun;

    public int NUM_BULLETS;

    // variables for timer
    public float myTime = 5.0f;
    private float endTime = 0.0f;

    public bool ATTACK;
    public bool SCOUT;

    public Transform[] scoutPoints;
    private int nextPointIndex;

    public bool GAME_OVER;
    private int HEALTH;

    public Text lblHealth;

    // Use this for initialization
    void Start()
    {
        this.NUM_BULLETS = 1;
        this.ATTACK = true;
```

```
    this.myEnemy = GameObject.FindGameObjectWithTag("Player") as GameOb-
ject;

    // start timer
    this.endTime = this.myTime + Time.time;

    this.nextPointIndex = 0;
    this.GAME_OVER = false;
    this.HEALTH = 100;

    if (this.lblHealth != null)
        this.lblHealth.text = string.Format("{0}/100", this.HEALTH);
}

private float SPEED = 2.0f;

// Update is called once per frame
void Update()
{
    if(!this.GAME_OVER)
    {
        if (this.myStorageObj == null)
        {
            if (this.endTime < Time.time)
            {
                // drop the storage
                Vector3 pos = new Vector3(this.transform.position.x + 1, 2,
this.transform.position.z + 1);
                this.myStorageObj = GameObject.Instantiate(this.myStorage,
pos, this.myStorage.transform.rotation) as GameObject;

                this.endTime = 0.0f;
            }
        }

        if (this.NUM_BULLETS > 1)
        {
            this.ATTACK = true;
        }
        else
        {
            this.ATTACK = false;
        }

        // seek the player to attack
        if (this.ATTACK)
        {
            Vector3 refillHeading = this.myEnemy.transform.position -
this.transform.position;
            refillHeading.Normalize();

            // use Quaternion Slerp function to make smooth transition ...
            this.transform.rotation =
                Quaternion.Slerp(transform.rotation,
```

```
                              Quaternion.LookRotation(refillHeading), 10 *
Time.deltaTime);

            this.transform.Translate(Vector3.forward * Time.deltaTime *
this.SPEED);

            if (Vector3.Distance(this.myEnemy.transform.position,
this.transform.position) < 5.0f)
            {
                if (this.NUM_BULLETS > 0)
                {
                    if (this.endTime < Time.time)
                    {
                        GameObject bullet = GameObject.Instantiate(this.myBul-
let,
                            this.myGun.transform.position, this.myGun.trans-
form.rotation) as GameObject;

                        bullet.GetComponent<Rigidbody>().velocity = trans-
form.TransformDirection(new Vector3(0, 0, 10.0f));

                        GameObject.Destroy(bullet, 3.0f);

                        // decrease inventory
                        this.NUM_BULLETS--;

                        // set timer before next shot
                        this.endTime = this.myTime + Time.time;
                    }

                }
            }
        }
        else
        {
            if (this.scoutPoints.Length > 0)
            {
                Vector3 refillHeading = this.scoutPoints[nextPointIndex].po-
sition - this.transform.position;
                refillHeading.Normalize();

                // use Quaternion Slerp function to make smooth transition
...
                this.transform.rotation =
                    Quaternion.Slerp(transform.rotation,
                                Quaternion.LookRotation(refillHeading),
10 * Time.deltaTime);

                this.transform.Translate(Vector3.forward * Time.deltaTime);

                if (Vector3.Distance(this.transform.position, this.scout-
Points[nextPointIndex].position) < 0.25f)
                {
                    this.nextPointIndex += 1;
                    if (this.nextPointIndex >= this.scoutPoints.Length)
                    {
```

```csharp
                    this.nextPointIndex = 0;
                }
            }
        }
    }
}

void OnCollisionEnter(Collision c)
{
    if (c.transform.tag.Equals("bullet"))
    {
        Destroy(c.gameObject);

        this.HEALTH -= 25;
        this.lblHealth.text = string.Format("{0}/100", this.HEALTH);

        if (this.HEALTH <= 0)
        {
            this.GAME_OVER = true;
            this.myEnemy.GetComponent<PlayerInput>().GAME_OVER =
this.GAME_OVER;
        }
    }
}
}
```

We have now seen the implementation of a few game mechanics we have discussed in the Game Mechanics chapter and in this chapter we have seen how to create related User Interface elements that will support the game mechanics.

While you were studying this chapter and going over the UI designs, you might have thought to yourself about the plainness of them. This is intentional as this book is geared towards game programmers / developers. There is more emphasis on the coding and scripting and less on the graphics. Having said that, for those who are more creative, you can take what you have learned in this book and apply your own creative touch.

There are some minor enhancements we can do improve our user interface design further. This is covered in the next section.

Enhancing the User Interface

In this section we will take Level 3 and make a few additions to the UI design. The main layout will not be changing, but what I would like to demonstrate is the easiness of how to use textures to enhance the look and feel of the UI elements.

Figure 59 - Another UI Sample

Now that you are familiar with the basics of UI design and the UI Architecture in Unity, we can take it a little further. Generally speaking, when you are designing and developing your game, you will have a team of people dedicated only for creating graphics content and models for the purposes of the project. You will be working with them hand in hand to incorporate their elegant design into the game environment.

Most of the UI will have highly polished 2D texture graphics that can be used to provide visually appealing themes for the player. I want to show you how easy it is to incorporate such textures in the new UI Architecture in Unity 5.

Consider our UI design for Level 3:

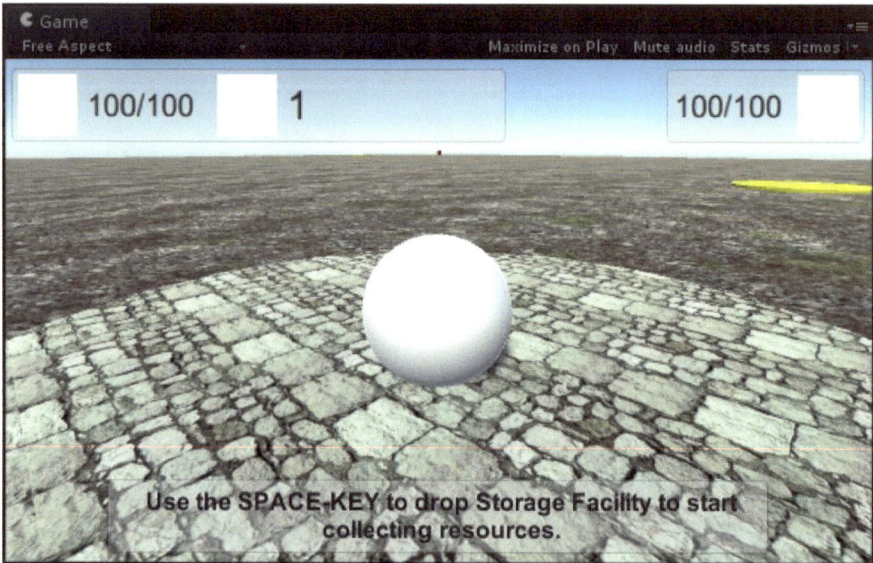

The layout of the UI is pretty good for the purposes of this demonstration. What we can improve is the visual aspect of the UI. One of the big changes we can apply is a texture to the Panel UI element. At the moment we are using all of the default textures that come with Unity and they work fine for prototyping, which we did. Now, let's apply some more interesting textures.

For this part to work properly, you will have to really have a good grasp of how the dimensions of your UI and textures. This will help in making finer textures. In our case we have three panels we would like to apply a texture to:

- Status Panel – (333px X 50px)
- Messaging Panel – (444px X 50px)
- Enemy Health Panel – (135px X 50px)

The dimensions of each panel is listed next to the item. We will use these dimensions to create our textures. As you know by now, my creative skills are not going to be as pleasing as yours. Having said that, here are the textures I have come up with for each Panel:

Figure 60 - Status Panel Background

Figure 61 - Message Panel Background

Figure 62 - Enemy Panel Background

Once you create your desired texture, you will need to import it into Unity. You can simply use the File System on your Operating System to copy and paste the files into the Assets Folder within your Project Folder. I have placed my textures in the following directory:

<Project Folder>/Assets/Textures/CH5/

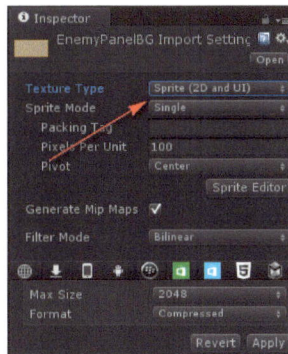

After you import your textures, you will need to perform a few configurations on the textures. Since these are going to be UI textures, we need to change the *Texture Type* from *Texture* to *Sprite (2D and UI)*. After you select the proper Texture Type, you will need to click the *Apply* button for the changes to take effect. Perform this for all of your UI Textures.

NOTE: You will notice there are more properties and options available. I will let you study these on your own. These properties will come in handier in 2D Sprite based games.

Now is time for us to apply our first texture. Go ahead and select the *Status Panel* UI element from the *Hierarchy Window* in *Level 3*. Take a look at the *Inspector Window*, and you will notice that there is an *Image Components* and that is has a property to set the *Image Source*. Drag and Drop the texture designed for the Status Panel into this property. Perform the same for each of the other panel we have defined in the scene. Your UI should look something like the following now:

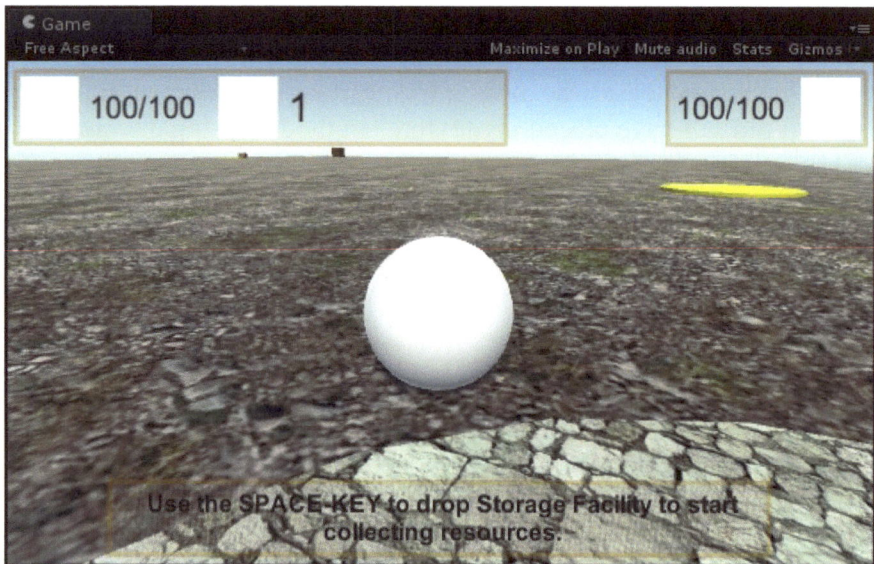

Figure 63 - Panel Textures Applied to Level 3

So this looks nicer then the plain default textures we had previously. The next thing I would like to do is provide some icons for the images we have placed as placeholder. If you recall, our images have a dimension of 40x40 pixels. We technically need to icons, one will be used for both the player's health and the enemy's health, and the other will be used for the player's inventory.

The process to apply the icons are going to be similar, first you will need to create the desired icons, then you will need to import them into your project, and then configure them to be of type *Sprite*, and finally, you will need to select the UI element, in this case the Image UI element for the Player's health and the Image UI element for the Enemy's health from the *Hierarchy Window*, and in the *Image Component*, apply the texture to the Source Image property. The result is:

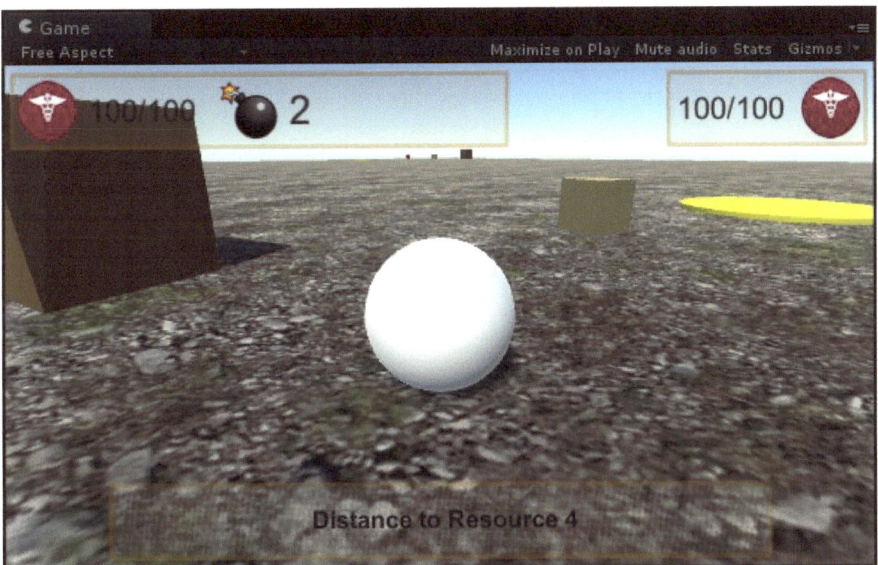

Figure 64 - Level 3 UI Enhancement

As you can see, even a simple enhancement on the UI will have a big impact on the overall look and feel of the game.

One last improvement I would like to illustrate for the UI is the ability to display information in the *World Space*. Some of the information you might want to consider for a World Space display would be UI elements for specific GameObjects.

For instance, it would be nice to display a health bar on the player characters, this includes both the player and also the enemy. This is actually very easily achievable in the new UI architecture within Unity. Let's take a look at how we can implement such a feature for our player.

Obviously we need to have a new set of Canvas Object. The newly created Canvas object will be attached to our Player Character GameObject, a child of the Player Character (PC). It will also have its *Render Mode* set to *World Space*. The simplest way to create this new Canvas is to *right-click* on the PC and select (*UI->Canvas*). Once the canvas is created, you will need to modify several properties, the first is the *Render Mode*, go ahead and set it to *World Space*. The next modification will be on the *Rect Transform* Component. You want to make sure the canvas is relative to the PC at all times, and the best way to do so it to make sure that it is positioned correctly.

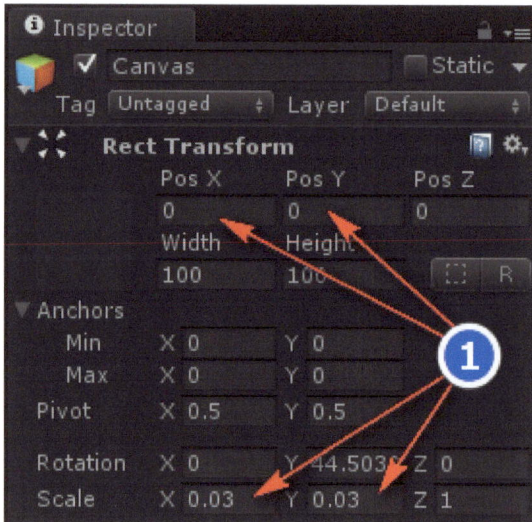

Figure 65 - World Space Canvas Properties

First, change the *Pos X* and *Pos Y* properties for the *Rect Transform* to *0* and *0* respectively. This will make sure you are aligned with the Center of the PC. The next property to change would be the *Width* and the *Height* of the Canvas. This will depend on the GameObject you are attaching the Canvas to and also the purpose of your World Space Canvas. In this case, we would like to display only a Health Bar, therefore we don't need much space. We will also take a look at the Scale property and use it to scale the Canvas without losing quality.

Take a look at Figure 65 to see the properties I have set for my project. The result is the following screen capture:

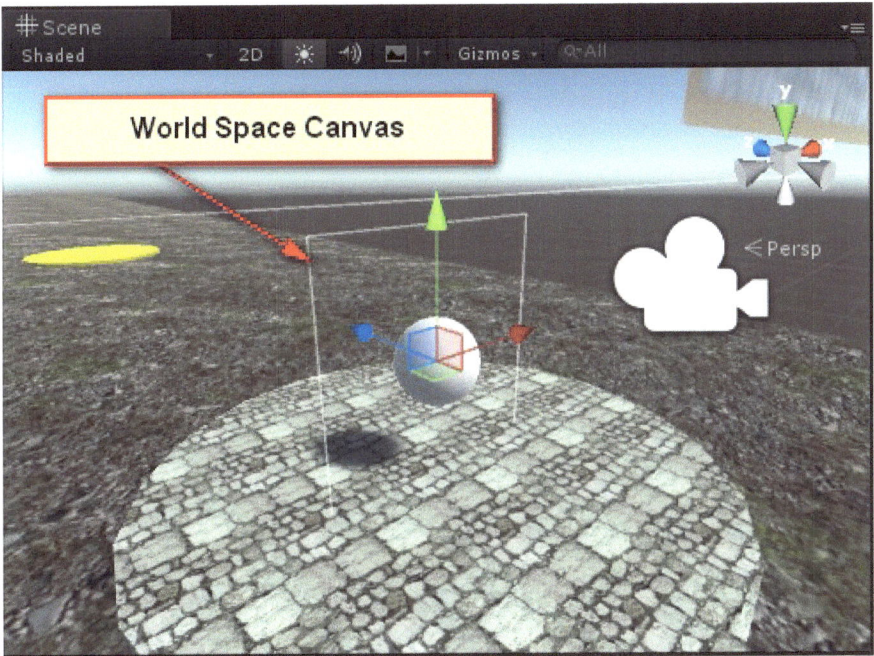

The rest is as before, we need a way to create a health bar. The easiest way is to represent the health bar is with three images.

One of the images will represent the border, and the other two images will represent the actual health.

Keeping things simple, here is how I want my health bar to look like:

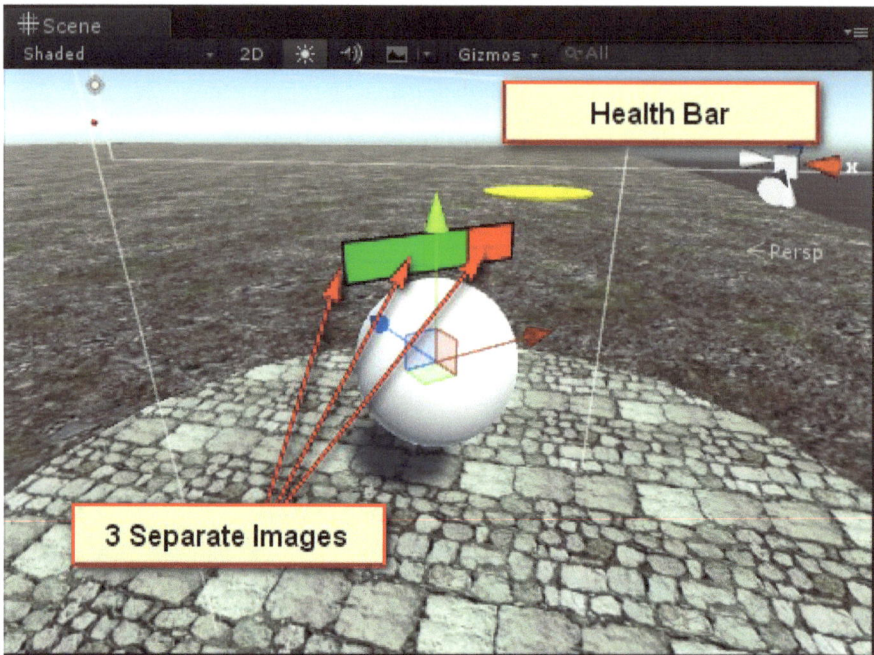

Figure 66 - UI Concept for Health Bar

The hierarchy for the PC and Canvas are shown in the following figure:

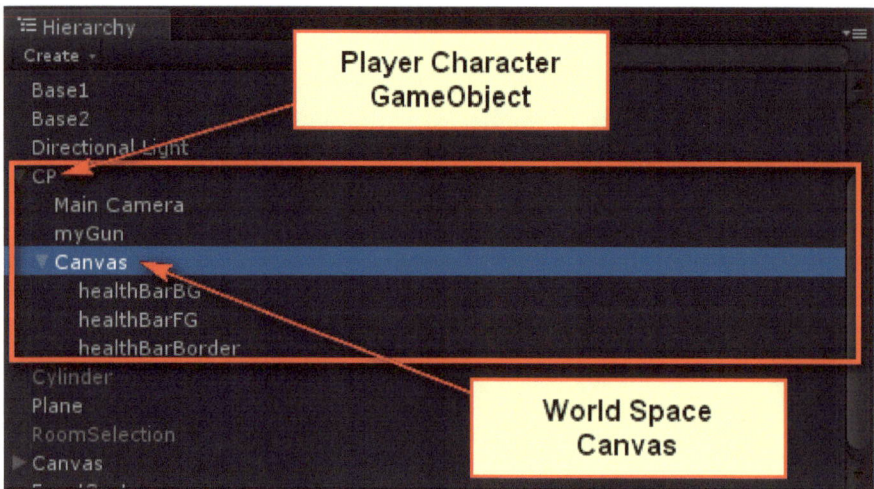

Figure 67 - World Space Canvas Hierarchy

The next step is to create the code to manage the health bar. We would need a reference to the *healthBarFG* Image UI element. We would need to modify the PlayerInput.cs script to properly update the Health Bar. Here is the partial code listing dealing with the update of the Health Bar UI element:

```csharp
private void ResetLevel3UI()
{
    if (this.lblHealth != null)
        this.lblHealth.text = string.Format("{0}/100", this.HEALTH);
    if (this.lblResources != null)
        this.lblResources.text = this.NUM_BULLETS.ToString();
    if (this.lblMessages != null)
        this.lblMessages.text = "Use the SPACE-KEY to drop Storage Facility
to start collecting resources.";

    if (this.imgHealthBar != null)
    {
        this.imgHealthBar.fillAmount = (this.HEALTH / 100.0f);
    }
}
```

Updated *OnCollisionEnter()* function:

```csharp
void OnCollisionEnter(Collision c)
{
    if (c.transform.tag.Equals("bullet"))
    {
        Destroy(c.gameObject);

        this.HEALTH -= 25;
        this.lblHealth.text = string.Format("{0}/100", this.HEALTH);

        if (this.imgHealthBar != null)
        {
            this.imgHealthBar.fillAmount = (this.HEALTH / 100.0f);
        }

        if (this.HEALTH <= 0)
        {
            this.GAME_OVER = true;
            this.myEnemy.GetComponent<MyEnemy>().GAME_OVER = this.GAME_OVER;

            if (this.imgHealthBar != null)
            {
                this.imgHealthBar.fillAmount = 0.0f;
            }
        }
    }
}
```

You have now seen a good portion of how to incorporate UI elements within your game environment. The tools are basic but the ability to create and enhance on the building blocks are great. With some creativity and imagination you can achieve more sophisticated user interfaces.

One other modification I would do on the health bar is to make it semi-transparent. At the moment it is blocking the GameObjects right in front of the Main Camera, and this is annoying. To apply transparency to the health bar simply select the UI element and from the *Color Picker* reduce the Alpha channel for all images to 100. You can also apply the transparency before importing the images into Unity.

As a challenge see if you can create a visual loading and unloading UI element for the Collector.

Chapter 6 – Creating Battleship

Historical Background

The game of Battleship is thought to have its origins in the French game L'Attaque played during World War I. The game is said to have been played by Russian officers before World War I. The first commercial version of the game was Salvo, published in 1931 in the United States by the Starex company. Other versions of the game were printed in the 1930s and 1940s, including the Strathmore Company's Combat: The Battleship Game, Milton Bradley's Broadsides: A Game of Naval Strategy and Maurice L. Freedman's Warfare Naval Combat.

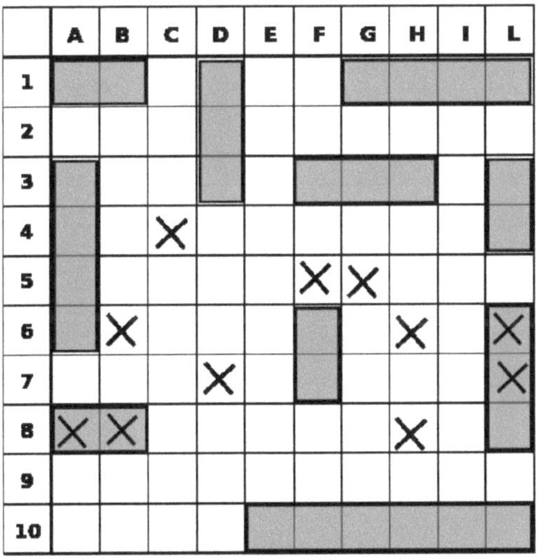

Figure 68-Grid Sample Layout

Battleship was one of the earliest games to be produced as a computer game, with a version being released for the Z80 Compucolor in 1979. Many computer editions of the game have been produced since. In Clubhouse Games for the Nintendo DS, Battleship is known as Grid Attack. It is played on an 8×8 grid, and includes slight variations, such as 4-player gameplay, various ship sizes and shapes, as well as the option to make the ships touch each other.

Game Play

The game is played on four grids, two for each player. The grids are typically square – usually 10×10 – and the individual squares in the grid are identified by letter and number. On one grid the player arranges ships and records the shots by the opponent. On the other grid the player records his/her own shots.

Before play begins, each player secretly arranges their ships on their primary grid. Each ship occupies a number of consecutive squares on the grid, arranged either horizontally or vertically. The number of squares for each ship is determined by the type of the ship. The ships cannot overlap (i.e., only one ship can occupy any given square in the grid). The types and numbers of ships allowed are the same for each player. These may vary depending on the rules.

Type of Ship	Size
Aircraft Carrier	5
Battleship	4
Submarine	3
Destroyer	3
Patrol Boat	2

After the ships have been positioned, the game proceeds in a series of rounds. In each round, each player takes a turn to announce a target square in the opponent's grid which is to be shot at. The opponent announces whether or not the square is occupied by a ship, and if it is a "miss", the player marks their primary grid with a white peg; if a "hit" they mark this on their own primary grid with a red peg. The attacking player notes the hit or miss on their own "tracking" grid with the appropriate color peg (red for "hit", white for "miss"), in order to build up a picture of the opponent's fleet.

The player who successfully locates all their opponent's ships first by hitting each square they occupy is the winner as all ships have been destroyed.

Game Plan for Implementation

Since we have a good understanding of the game and the game rules, we can start thinking about how to implement our version of the Battleship board game.

The first thing we should concentrate on is creating the board on which we are going to play our game. Representing the board digitally in the computer memory is going to be simple based on the rules that we have. There are two items we need to think about (1) representing the board visually (2) keeping track of board data.

Let's take a look and see how we are going to represent our board visually. We know that the board is going to be of size N x N. In this case we have decided to make it a 10 x 10 board. The next step is to determine how we are going to represent each single unit on the board.

To make it easier, we can use a cube with the following scale vector: <1,0.1,1> in the <x,y,z> coordinates. This will give us a nice unit base for the board.

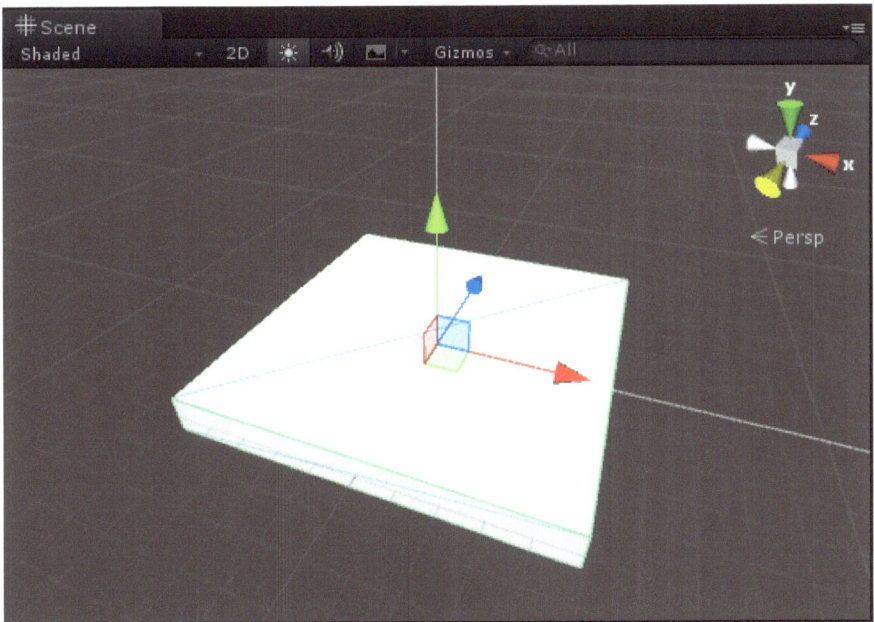

Figure 69-Base Board Unit

The next thing I would like to do, is to give the unit some texture that will resemble a boarder. To do this, we need to create a new material and apply a texture that will resemble our desired look. The next step is to somehow identify the actual unit by its location on the board! To do this, we will create an UI object and attach it to the board unity to display the location of the unit on the board. The final board unit will look something like this:

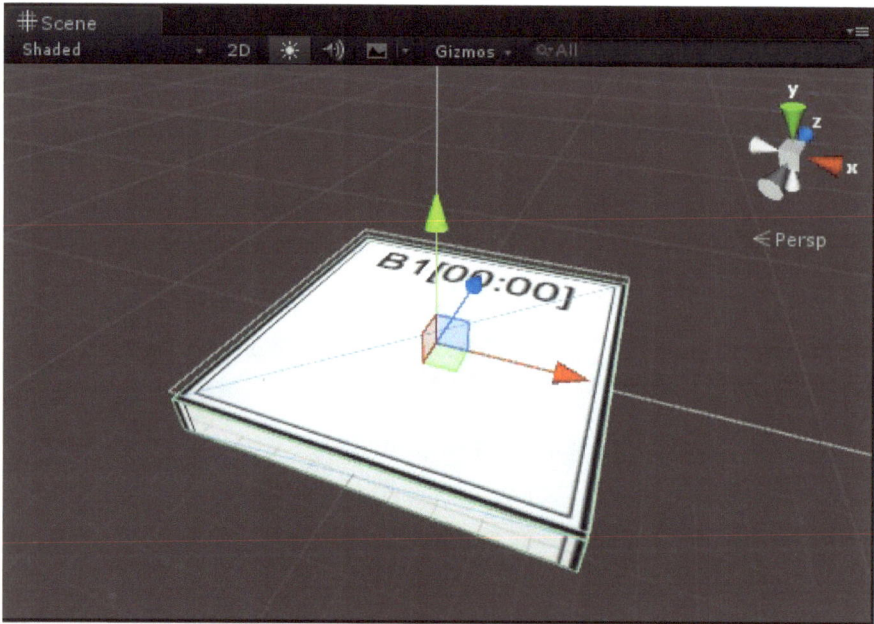

Figure 70-Board Unit with Texture and UI Elements Applied

Each board unit will look like Figure 70. B1 represents the name and id of the board, and [00:00] represent the row and column that will be used to identify the board unit. One more last piece that we need for completing our initial version of the board unit is a script that will represent the internal data for the unit itself. This will be called *BoardUIVer1.cs* and here is the listing for it:

```
using UnityEngine;
using UnityEngine.UI;

using System.Collections;

public class BoardUIVer1 : MonoBehaviour {
```

```
public Text lblBoardPosition;

public int ROW;
public int COL;

public bool OCCUPIED;

// Use this for initialization
void Start () {
    this.OCCUPIED = false;
}

// Update is called once per frame
void Update () {   }
}
```

Code Block 44-BoardUIVer1 Class Definition

A simple class that will store the row and column data for the unit. A reference to the UI Text Label for the unit so it can be updated when it has been instantiated, and finally a Boolean variable that indicates if the unit is occupied or not.

The Steps to Create Board Unit:

1. Create a Cube primitive GameObject, name it BoardUnit.
2. Change the scale to be <1,0.1,1> on the <x,y,z>
3. Create a new Material type called BoardUnit
4. Assign your preferred texture to the Albedo property under Main Maps.
5. Assign the new material to the BoardUnit GameObject
6. Create a new .cs script named BoardUIVer1.cs
7. Enter your script code and assign the script to BoardUnit GameObject

Once we are satisfied with our board unit, we would like to create the actual board consisting of the board units. For a board with dimensions of 10 x 10, we would need to use 100 board units!

There are two ways to achieve this. (1) Manually creating the board and placing one hundred units together, or (2) Creating a procedure that will take care of it for you! Obviously the choice would be to create a procedure to handle board creation for us.

We can represent our board with a two-dimensional array. There are two things that need to happen, we would need to create the board visually and also store the data per board unit. We can use our favorite loop method, *for … loop*, structure to iterate through our rows and columns.

```
// create a 10x10 board - Board 1
int row = 1;
int col = 1;
for(int i=0; i<10; i++)
{
    for(int j=0; j<10; j++)
    {
        // instantiate prefab and place it properly on the scene
        GameObject tmp = GameObject.Instantiate(this.BoardUnitPrefab,
                                    new Vector3(i, 0, j),
this.BoardUnitPrefab.transform.rotation) as GameObject;

        BoardUIVer1 tmpUI = tmp.GetComponent<BoardUIVer1>();
        string name = string.Format("B1:[{0:00},{1:00}]", row, col);
        tmpUI.lblBoardPosition.text = name;
        tmpUI.COL = j;
        tmpUI.ROW = i;

        board[i, j] = tmp;

        tmp.name = name;

        col++;
    }
    col = 1;
    row++;
}
```

Code Block 45-Creating the Board Dynamically

Let's take a look and see what is going on in Code Block 45. We have two for loops one for the rows in the board and the second for the columns in the board. Since our board is 10 x 10, each for loop will iterate 10 times. Within the body of the second loop, is where most of the magic happens.

We first instantiate our Board Unit Prefab GameObject at a specific position defined by the Vector3 object representing the position, and for rotation, we use the Prefab's default rotation orientation. Notice that the Vector3 object uses the (i, 0, j) for the positioning of the board unit. If you recall, Unity uses the metric system and by default the basic unity is 1 meter.

This makes it easy, as we start at position (0,0,0), and for each row and column we increment by 1unit. So we have (0,0,0), (0,0,1), (0,0,2) … (9,0,9). The final result look like the following:

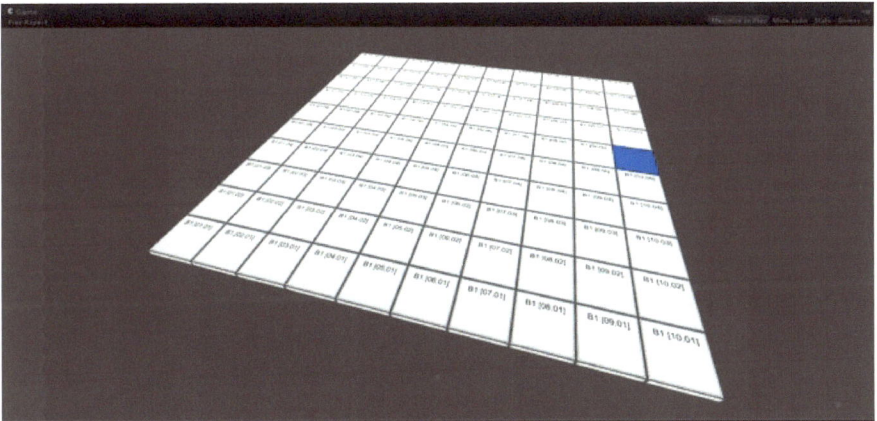

Figure 71-The Board

Since we are generating our board dynamically at runtime, we are going to rely on the UnitBoard Prefab we created and saved in the previous step. The actual board creation is going to be done by a script.

Steps to Create The Board:
1. Create a new cs file called BoardVer1.cs
2. In the Start() function implemented the code listed in Code Block 45-Creating the Board Dynamically
3. Attach the newly created script to the Camera GameObject.

4. Now you will need to assign the BoardUnit prefab to the public variable named BoardUnitPrefab.

When you run the game, you will notice the board that has been generated.

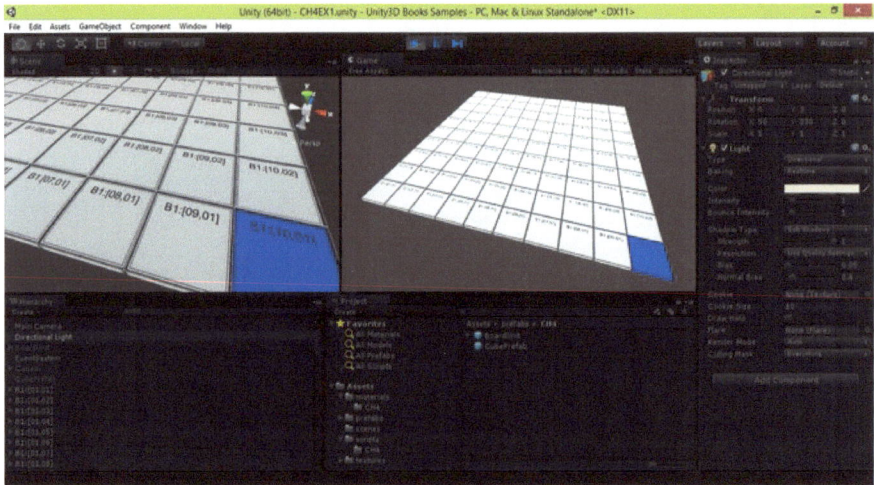

Figure 72-Showing Details per Board Unit

If you look closely, you will notice that information for each board unit is being displayed properly. There are many reason we would like to see these information. First, it is a visual way to pin-point each board unit, which leads to the more important reason, debugging! We can quickly debug our logic and identify the values we get behind the scene with the actual visual representation. You will see the benefit as we progress.

Since this is a board game, we need to somehow keep track of the state of the board throughout its life, and also be able to select a particular location on the main board for placing our GameObjects and interacting with them. So let's see how this portion would be done.

Assuming that we will use our mouse pointer to locate and position our pieces, and also submit the attack command, we will have to capture the mouse position and convert the mouse position into our 3D space. There are two features that will enable us to perform these operations, one is the actual Input object which will provide us with the mouse position, and the next is a combination of a Ray object and using the Physics engine to perform a Raycast to determine if we have hit an object in the scene or not. The following code-block will illustrate this operation.

NOTE: The code block is partial listing of the Update() function[18].

```
        if (Input.mousePosition != null)
        {
            // capture the mouse position and cast a ray to see what object we
hit
            Ray ray = Camera.main.ScreenPointToRay(Input.mousePosition);

            if (Physics.Raycast(ray, out tmpHitHighlight, 100))
            {
                BoardUIVer1 tmpUI = tmpHitHighlight.transform.GetCompo-
nent<BoardUIVer1>();
                if (tmpHitHighlight.transform.tag.Equals("board") &&
!tmpUI.OCCUPIED)
                {
                    BoardUIVer1 boardData = board[tmpUI.ROW,
tmpUI.COL].transform.GetComponent<BoardUIVer1>();

                    if (tmpHighlight != null)
                    {
                        if(boardData.OCCUPIED)
                            tmpHighlight.GetComponent<Renderer>().material.color =
Color.red;
                        else
                            tmpHighlight.GetComponent<Renderer>().material.color =
Color.white;

                    }

                    if(this.tmpBlockHolder != null)
                    {
                        Destroy(this.tmpBlockHolder);
                    }

                    if(this.PLACE_BLOCK)
                    {
                        this.tmpBlockHolder = new GameObject();
                        this.OK_TO_PLACE = true;
                        if (!this.vertical && (tmpUI.ROW<=10-this.blockSize))
                        {
                            for(int i=0; i<this.blockSize; i++)
                            {
```

---

[18] Full listing of the function will be provided in the upcoming sections.

```
                        GameObject visual = GameObject.Instantiate(this.Cub-
ePrefab,
                                                          new Vec-
tor3(tmpUI.ROW+i, this.CubePrefab.transform.position.y, tmpUI.COL),
                                                        this.Cub-
ePrefab.transform.rotation) as GameObject;

                        GameObject bp = board[tmpUI.ROW + i, tmpUI.COL];
                        BoardUIVer1 bpUI = bp.GetComponent<BoardUIVer1>();
                        if (!bpUI.OCCUPIED)
                        {
                            visual.GetComponent<Renderer>().material.color =
Color.gray; // ok to place
                            //this.OK_TO_PLACE = true;
                        }
                        else
                        {
                            visual.transform.localScale = new Vector3(0.6f,
0.6f, 0.6f);
                            visual.GetComponent<Renderer>().material.color =
Color.yellow; // not ok
                            this.OK_TO_PLACE = false;
                        }

                        visual.transform.parent = this.tmpBlockHolder.trans-
form;

                    }
                }
                if (this.vertical && (tmpUI.COL <= 10 - this.blockSize))
                {
                    for (int i = 0; i < this.blockSize; i++)
                    {
                        GameObject visual = GameObject.Instantiate(this.Cub-
ePrefab,
                                                          new Vec-
tor3(tmpUI.ROW, this.CubePrefab.transform.position.y, tmpUI.COL+i),
                                                        this.Cub-
ePrefab.transform.rotation) as GameObject;

                        GameObject bp = board[tmpUI.ROW, tmpUI.COL+i];
                        BoardUIVer1 bpUI = bp.GetComponent<BoardUIVer1>();
                        if (!bpUI.OCCUPIED)
                        {
                            visual.GetComponent<Renderer>().material.color =
Color.gray; // ok to place
                            //this.OK_TO_PLACE = true;
                        }
                        else
                        {
                            visual.transform.localScale = new Vector3(0.6f,
0.6f, 0.6f);
                            visual.GetComponent<Renderer>().material.color =
Color.yellow; // not ok
                            this.OK_TO_PLACE = false;
```

```
                    }

                    visual.transform.parent = this.tmpBlockHolder.trans-
form;

                }
            }
        }

        tmpHitHighlight.transform.GetComponent<Renderer>().mate-
rial.color = Color.blue;
                tmpHighlight = tmpHitHighlight.transform.gameObject;
            }
        }
    }
```

Code Block 46-Highlighted Lines for Mouse Position and Raycasting

Let's discuss only the section of the code that deal with the mouse position and Ray casting. The first if statement check to see if we have a mouse position. If we do, we convert that mouse position to a Ray object using the built in function provided by the Camera class. Once we have a ray object, we use the Physics engine's Raycast function to cast a ray and one of the parameters for the raycast function is an out variable named *tmpHitHighlight* that will return a GameObject if we do hit anything within the active camera view.

Remember, tmpHitHighlight is a GameObject that represents our board unit. The board unit Prefab has a script attached to it called *BoardUIVer1.cs* which is used to update the visuals of the board unit as well as store the state of that particular board unit. Therefore based on our design we know that we at this time, the only object we can technically hit through the raycast is the board unit. So what we are doing is getting the components attached to the board unit using the *GetComponent<>()* function and we store the returned object in a variable called *tmpUI*.

The next step is to detect if we are actually hitting a board GameObject. This is detected by checking the tag on the GameObject we just hit by the raycast. The idea here is that if we are a board type object and the board unit we are currently pointing to is not occupied, we execute the next logical block. First we get the board data from our two dimensional array by supplying the row and column of the hit board unit, retrieving and storing the data element in a variable of type **BoardUIVer1** named *boardData*.

The last two lines in Code Block 46 change the material color of the board unit we are pointing to from white to blue as an indicator.

Putting Everything Together - Game Objects

We would need to create several GameObjects that will be used to make our game. Some of the GameObjects are visual, and some are functional. Some are both! Here is a list:

Prefabs:	Scene Objects:	Scripts:
BoardUnit	_BackgroundMusic	BoardUIVer1
~~BoardUnitAttack~~	Main Camera	BoardVer1
BoardUnitEnemy	EventSystem	
BoardUnityPlayer	Directional Light	
~~CubePrefab~~	Canvas	
CubeWreck		

Let's go through each one of the GameObjects and see what they will be used for. Starting with BoardUnit, the GameObject was created as a base for demonstrating several concepts and ideas in the previous section, and it will be the base for the other components which will be used in the actual game.

BoardUnitPlayer, this GameObject is used to represent the Player's board. It has the following structure:

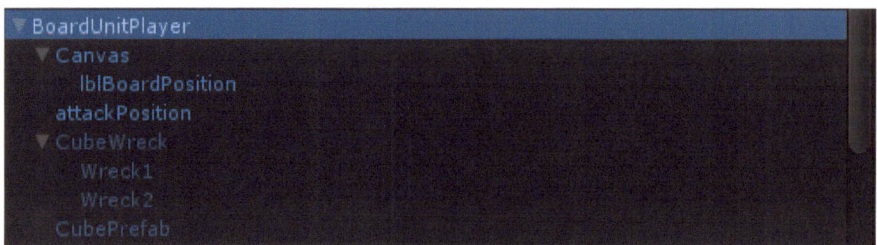

Figure 73 - BoardUnitPlayer Structure

Notice that the GameObject is composed of several other GameObjects. One is a Canvas which is used for displaying the label of the BoardUnit. AttackPosition is an empty GameObject used internally for rendering graphics. CubeWreck is another nested GameObject that represents the visual aspect of a hit on the BoardUnit. You will see how these items are being constructed and used when we start looking at the source code.

BoardUnitEnemy is a duplicate of BoardUnityPlayer, the structure is exactly the same. The only difference between the two is the Tag and a few other configuration elements. We will also take a look at them when discussing the source code.

CubeWreck is the prefab that represents the visual representation of a hit to a board unit that is occupied by a ship. It is the combination of two Cube primitives at specified angles to give us some nice visual effect.

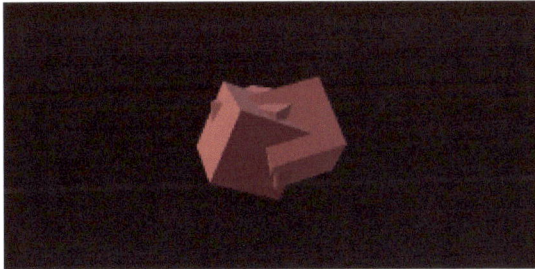

Figure 74 - CubeWreck Prefab

The Prefabs we just described are not present in the live scene during design time. They will be instantiated during the game play. Now let's take a look at the GameObjects that are going to be present at design time in the scene.

_BackgroundMusic is an empty GameObject that is solely used to store and manage an Audio Source. It basically plays the background music for the level.

Main Camera is the GameObject representing the camera in the scene. By default, whenever you create a scene, a Camera GameObject is created for you. There are a lot of configuration and properties for the camera, we will look at some of them in the given example.

Directional Light is the GameObject representing the lighting element in the scene. Like the camera, by default a Directional Light GameObject is created whenever you start a new scene. It also has a lot of properties that can be configured for lighting effects, we will take a look at some of them during our examples.

Canvas and Event System, the Canvas GameObject is used for the Graphical User Interface (GUI) design. It is the new way of designing and implementing your GUI for Unity. It has powerful features for building attractive interfaces. The Event System GameObject is responsible for the events raised within the GUI.

BoardUIVer1 is the c-sharp script that is used to handle the Board Unit user interface elements. It is also responsible on managing the state of the given board unit. That is, if it is occupied, hit and etc… It also manages the visual aspects of the board unit based on the state.

BoardVer1 is the main script for the game logic. It holds all of the necessary data elements, and logic for the game to function properly. It glues everything together. It is responsible to the initialization of the board units, it is responsible to keep track of the score, and also it is responsible for the thinking process of the computer opponent to make the next move.

Game Flow + Logic

The following diagram is a high level visual representation of the game flow. As a good rule of thumb, before you start any project, it is a good idea to sketch out and capture some high level representation of how your program will flow.

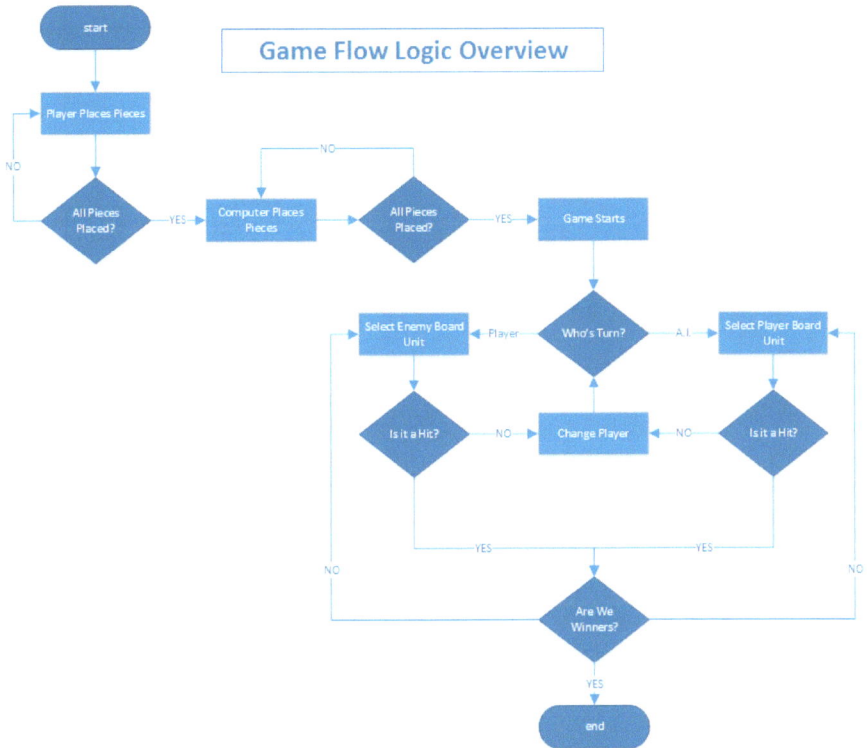

Figure 75 - Game Flow High Level

To quickly summarize the diagram, when the game initially starts, the player is asked to place his/her pieces on the designated board[19]. When the player has completed placing their pieces, then the computer will start to place its pieces. Once the player and the computer have placed all of the necessary pieces, the game starts!

---

[19] Note, that we have not captured the details of checking the board for proper placement of the pieces, nor did we capture the change of orientation while placing the pieces on the board.

When the game starts, the game manager decides which player's turn it is, once that is determined, if it is the player's turn, it will wait until the player selects a board unit, the game manager will handle the details of a hit and miss behind the scenes. If it is a hit, then some accounting is done and the player gets another turn, if it is a miss, then the computer A.I. selects a board unit on the player's board and the same process continuous until either the player or the computer wins the game.

Let's look at the internals of the logic more closely.

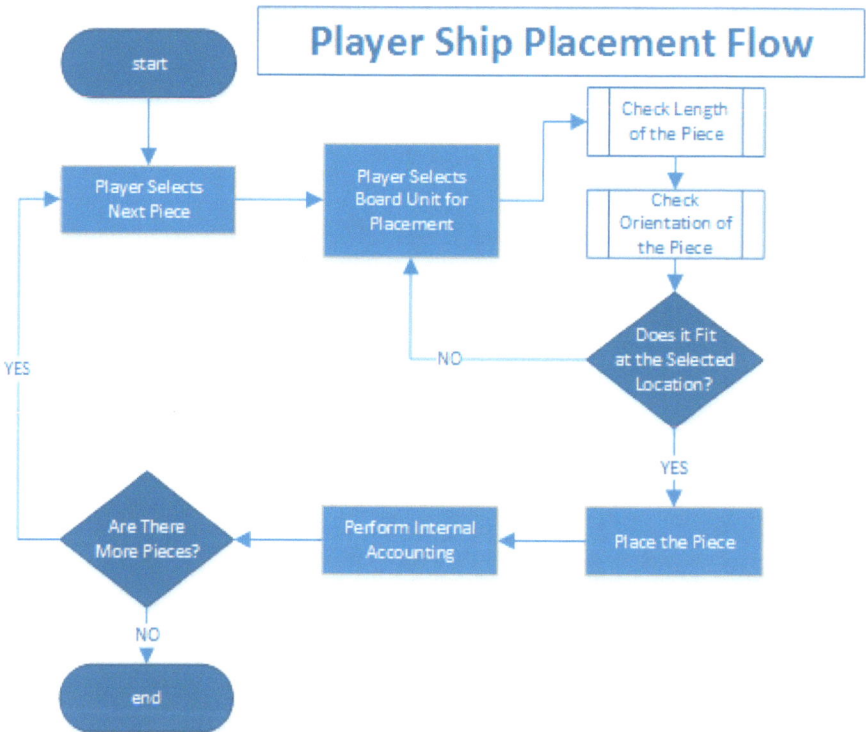

Figure 76 - Player Ship Placement Flow Diagram

Breaking down Figure 75, we will start by taking a closer look at what happens internally to the program logic when the player is asked to place his/her ships onto their board. Figure 76, illustrates the logical flow in more detail.

As illustrated, the player needs to first select a piece to be placed on the board. When a piece is selected, then he/she has to select where they would like to place the piece on the board, and in what orientation. There are only two orientations available, horizontal and vertical.

When a given board unit is selected, the computer checks to see if there is enough room for the placement of the piece, it also check to see if the whole length of the selected ship is clear for placement. That is, if there are no pieces placed already placed on the path of the newly selected piece. This process keeps repeating until all pieces have been successfully placed onto the board.

Next, the computer starts placing its pieces.

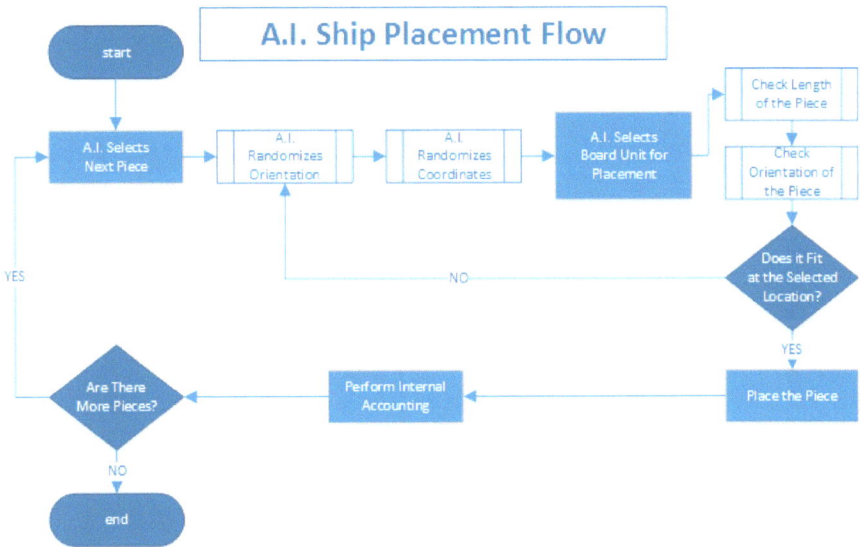

Figure 77 - A.I. Ship Placement Flow Diagram

The A.I. goes through a similar process when it is placing its own playing pieces onto the board. It starts by selecting the next available piece to be placed, then it randomly decides what orientation it wasn't to place the piece, next it decides the coordinates on the playing board, once that is determined, then it starts going through the process of checking and verifying if the selection is valid for placement or not. If it is, then all is good and the data is recorded, if not, it goes through steps to select another available position and orientation.

When all players have placed their pieces, the game start. The following diagram illustrates the detailed version of the game play logic.

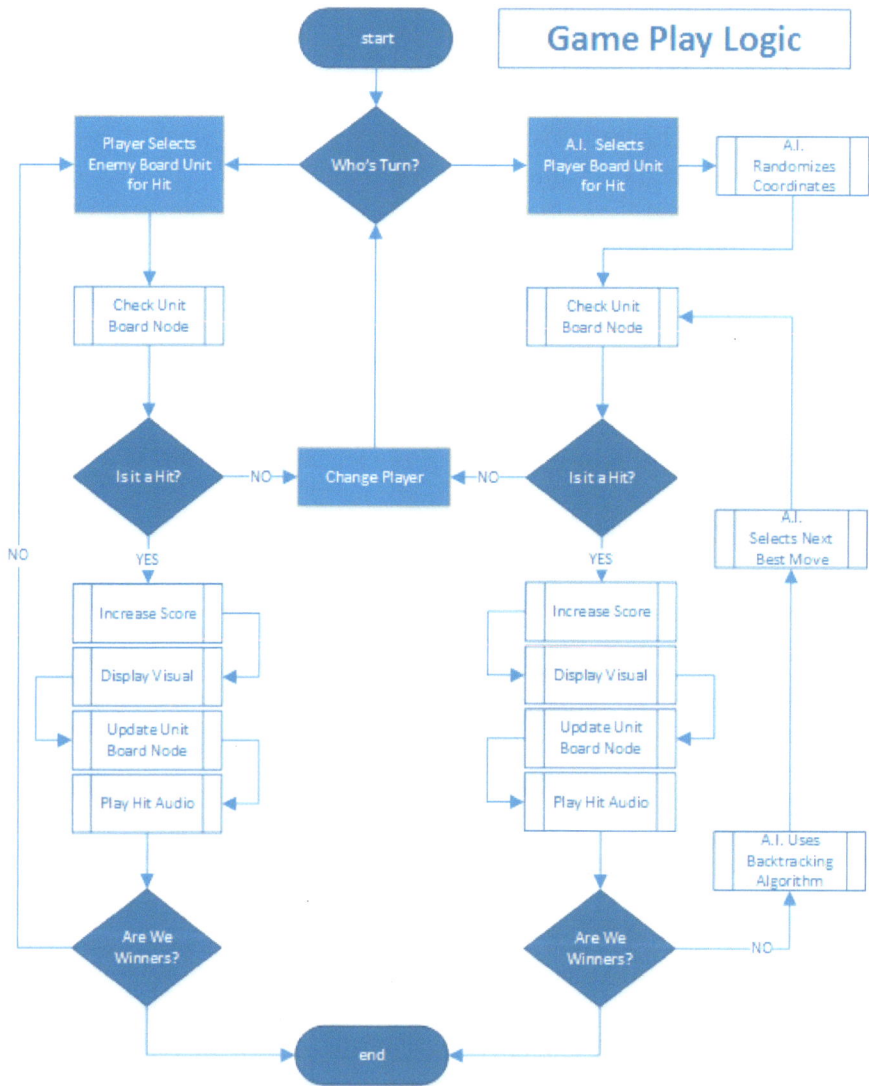

Figure 78 - Game Play Logic

Figure 78 provides a more detailed view of how the internal game logic is once both the player and the A.I. have placed their ships onto their respective boards. Each player gets a chance to select a board unit when it is their turn, if the selected board unit is occupied by the opponents piece, then we have a hit, several operations happen behind the scene by the game manager for accounting and also visual and audio representation, finally the game manager checks to see if the player has hit all of the opponent's pieces, and if so, the game is over.

The A.I. starts with similar logic and the program performs the same steps for the hit or miss criteria, however, there is a backtracking[20] algorithm developed for the A.I. if there is a hit! This is basically the code that actually give the A.I. its intelligence. It determines what the best next move is for the A.I. if the A.I. has a hit. In the meantime the game manager also checks to determine if the A.I. has hit all of the play's pieces, and if so, the game is terminated with the A.I. being the winner.

As you can see, even for a simple game, there is a lot of planning to do as a designer and programmer. The diagrams are provided to make it easier to visualize the flow of the program. We will look at the implementation in a different section.

Game User Interface

As any other application, a game also needs to provide a Graphical User Interface (GUI) to the user. The GUI of your game is a means of how the user will interact with your game. Generally speaking, the GUI of an application and or a game is driven by the features and goals of that particular application and or game.

Typically the GUI has to display meaningful information to the end user. The information are data related to the environment. For instance, in our game, we need a means for the player to select the pieces that are needed to be placed onto their board, we also need a means to

---

[20] Backtracking is a general algorithm for finding all (or some) solutions to some computational problems, notably constraint satisfaction problems, that incrementally builds candidates to the solutions, and abandons each partial candidate c ("backtracks") as soon as it determines that c cannot possibly be completed to a valid solution.

change the orientation of the piece before placing them onto the board, and finally we need to show the score for the player and also the A.I.

The GUI for the game is not very complex, but regardless, you still need to pay attention to the requirements of your project and design and implement a GUI that will be sufficient to the overall experience.

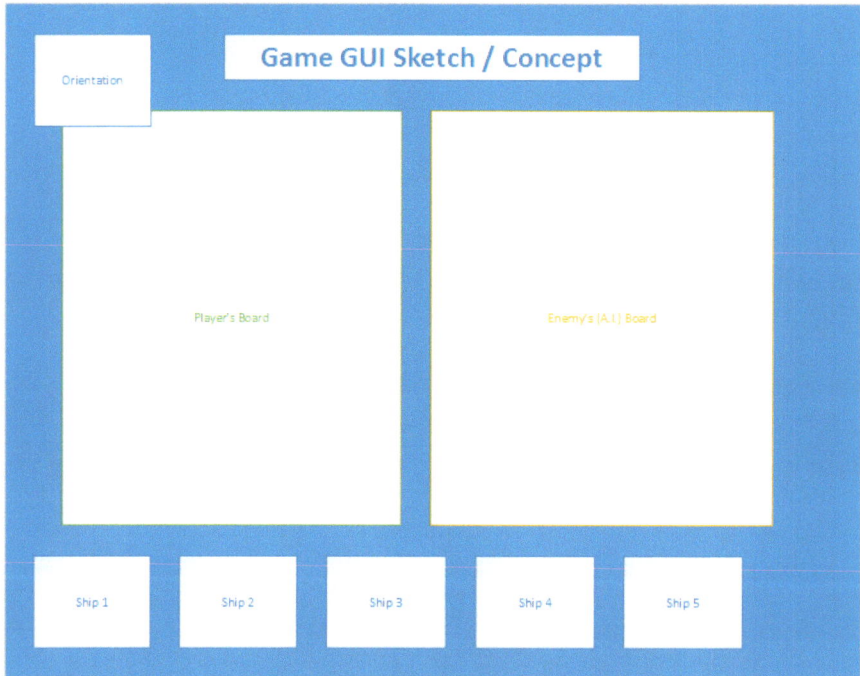

Figure 79 - Game GUI Concept

Here is a list of input and output that need to be handled:

Inputs:
- Select individual pieces.
- Change orientation of the piece (vertical/horizontal)
- Select location on player's board to place the piece.
- Select location on enemy's board to have a hit.

Output:
- Display player's / enemy's board(s)

- Display player's pieces to be placed onto the player's board before the game starts.
- Visually represent the board pieces after player has positioned them onto the board.
- Display scores for both the player and the enemy.
- Visually represent a hit on both the player's board and the enemy's board.
- Background music for the game.
- Sound FX when there is a hit on either the player's board or the enemy's board.

Given our list of inputs and outputs, we can come up with a sketch representing the layout of how we would like our GUI to be designed. These process usually will take some time and effort and it will most likely go through a few iterations before you settle down on a final design.

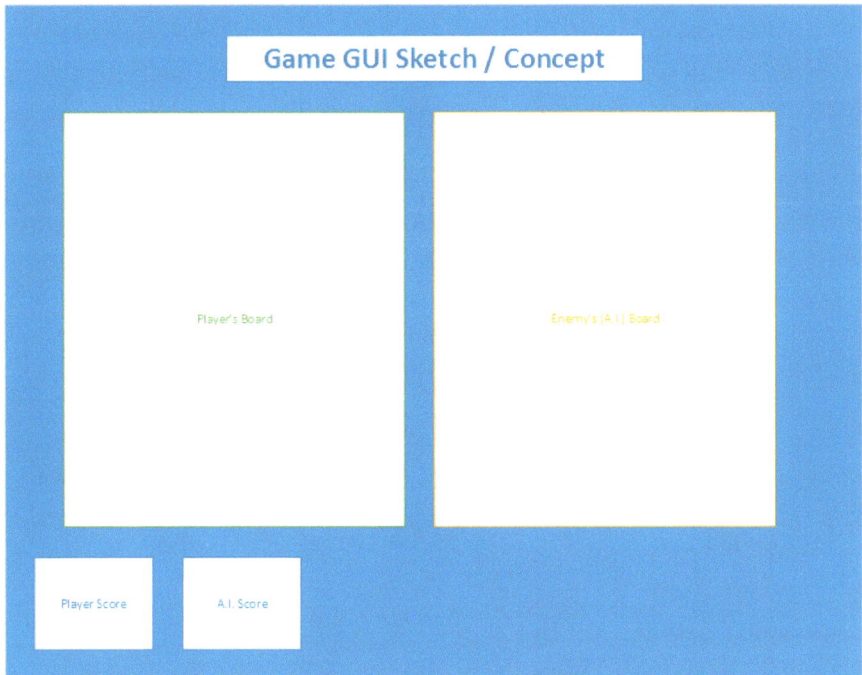

Game GUI Sketch / Concept

Player's Board

Enemy's (A.I.) Board

Player Score

A.I. Score

Figure 80 - Game GUI Score Display

Looking at Figure 79 we get a look at our desired GUI layout. As indicated in the diagram, we have five buttons representing the selection of our pieces for board placement at the bottom of the screen, we have a button for the change of orientation at the top left corner of the screen, and we have two big main blocks representing the game boards that we are going to use for our game.

If you notice Figure 79, does not display any information regarding the score in the game. This is captured in Figure 80. Here is how the UI logic works:

1. Player selects a given ship to be placed on his/her board.
2. After successful placement, the select piece will be removed from the UI.
3. This process repeats until all pieces have been placed onto the playing board.
4. At this point, when the game starts, all placement functional buttons are either removed or hidden from the UI.
5. Then the score UI is displayed to the user as indicated in the sketch.

This is another important concept when you are designing a GUI for a particular application. Due to the restrictions of screen real-estate, you will need to decide how to manage the information you want to display to the end user. Not only you will need to think about the size location and orientation of the UI elements, but also at what time you want to display specific information.

In some cases, you might have to continuously display a set of very important data to the player, hence, you will need to design the UI in a way that will be comfortable for the player to get the information he or she needs, but at the same time it does not interfere with the gameplay.

At other points, you might want to display information (more details) regarding a certain criteria upon a trigger by the player. This action will bring up a panel and or a window that will display data in more details.

Chapter 7 – Delving Into the Code

If you have following along in Chapter 3 – Game Objects and Components and Chapter 6 – Creating Battleship, you should have a good understanding of the concepts and a clear idea of our game objective. To do a quick recap, in Chapter 3, we covered the basics of Game Objects and Unity IDE, the key concept of the chapter was to get you started in the right direction, and allow you to jump start your own study and development of the IDE.

Chapter 6 was fully dedicated to the concept and the idea of the game called Battle Ship. We covered a lot of important ideas, approaches in general to software development, and we used Battle Board as an example for demonstration. In this chapter, we are going to delve into the code behind the game and see how it drives everything and glues everything together.

Script – BoardUIVer1.cs

Board UI Ver 1 script is used to control the individual board units of the given board within the game. If you recall from our earlier discussion regarding the approach we should take for the design and implementation of our game board, you will recall that we have a specific prefab dedicated for the visual representation of our board unit. The details of the prefab are discussed in the following section, Putting Everything Together - Game Objects, in Chapter 6 – Creating Battleship.

The prefab on its own is pretty useless. In order for us to be able to bring it to life and interact with the prefab we need some kind of scripting. The script is used to interact and modify the state of a given GameObject. In this particular case, this happens to be our Board Unit.

Let's take a look at the code listing, and go over each section and break down the logic and understand what it is trying to achieve.

```
using UnityEngine;
using UnityEngine.UI;

using System.Collections;

public class BoardUIVer1 : MonoBehaviour {

    public GameObject AttackPrefab;
    public GameObject WreckPrefab;
    public GameObject AttackPosition;
    public GameObject CubePrefab;

    float timeLimit = 4.0f; // 10 seconds.

    public Text lblBoardPosition;

    public int ROW;
    public int COL;

    public bool OCCUPIED;       // used to indicate if unit is occupied
    public bool ATTACKED;       // used to indicate if unit is attacked

    // Use this for initialization
    void Start () {
            this.OCCUPIED = false;
            this.ATTACKED = false;
    }

    private GameObject tmp = null;

    private GameObject tmp1 = null;
    private GameObject tmp2 = null;

    // Update is called once per frame
    void Update () {

        if(transform.tag.Equals("boardAttack") && this.ATTACKED &&
            this.OCCUPIED)
        {
            this.WreckPrefab.SetActive(true);

            if (timeLimit > 0)
            {
                // Decrease timeLimit.
                timeLimit -= Time.deltaTime;
                if(this.tmp==null)
                    tmp = GameObject.Instantiate(this.AttackPrefab,
                                                this.AttackPosition.trans-
form.position,
                                                this.AttackPosition.trans-
form.rotation) as GameObject;
                //Destroy(tmp, 3.0f);
            }
            else
```

```
            {
                Destroy(tmp);
                timeLimit = 4.0f;
            }
        }

        if (transform.tag.Equals("board") && this.ATTACKED && this.OCCUPIED)
        {

            this.CubePrefab.SetActive(false);

            if (timeLimit > 0)
            {
                // Decrease timeLimit.
                timeLimit -= Time.deltaTime;
                if (this.tmp2 == null)
                    tmp2 = GameObject.Instantiate(this.AttackPrefab,
                     new Vector3(transform.position.x, 1.0f, transform.position.z),
                     transform.rotation) as GameObject;
            }
            else
            {
                Destroy(tmp2);
                timeLimit = 4.0f;
            }
        }
    }

    public void PlaceEnableCubePrefab()
    {
        this.CubePrefab.SetActive(true);
    }

}
```

Code Block 47 - Listing for BoardUIVer1.cs

Let's start by stating that BoardUIVer1 is defined as a class that is inheriting from MonoBehaviour[21]. All C# scripts by default inherit from MonoBeviour. By default each script has a *Start()* and an *Update()* function defined.

The Start() function will be called by Unity before gameplay begins, i.e. before the Update() function is called for the first time, and it is the ideal place to do your initialization.

---

[21] MonoBehaviour is the base class every script derives from.

The Update() function is the place to put code that will handle the frame update for the GameObject. This might include movement, triggering actions and responding to user input. Basically anything that needs to be handled over time during gameplay.

Let's take a look at the class structure, and break it down for better understanding:

We have a class called BoardUIVer1, it contains the following properties / attributes:

- *AttackPrefab*, is of type GameObject and is a reference to the Prefab GameObject used for displaying the special FX for a hit on the player's board.
- *WreckPrefab*, is of type GameObject and is a reference to the Prefab GameObject used for displaying the visual wreck for a hit on the enemy board.
- *AttackPosition*, is of type GameObject and is a reference to the 3D position for instantiating the AttackPrefab visually onto the screen.
- *timeLimit*, is of type float and it is used as a timer for handling when to create a new instance of the special FX.
- *lblBoardPosition*, is of type Text and it is used to display the position of the Unit Board.
- *ROW*, is of type int and is used to hold the row number of the unit board.
- *COL*, is of type int and is used to hold the column number of the unit board.
- *OCCUPIED*, is of type bool and is used to indicate if the specific Unit Board is occupied or not.
- *ATTACKED*, is of type bool and is used to indicate if the specific Unit Board is attacked or not.

The class also has the following three functions defined:

- *Start()*, in the Start() function the two variable OCCUPIED and ATTACKED are initialized to false. This is because by default none of the board units are occupied or attacked.
- *Update()*, the Update() function is a little more involved. It is used to manage the visual aspect of the board unit based on the state.
- *PlaceEnableCubePrefab()*, this function is used to enable the prefab defined in the board unit.

Let's look at the *Update()* function in more depth. This is where most of the action is happening for this particular class. There are two main conditions that we are checking:

```
if(transform.tag.Equals("boardAttack") && this.ATTACKED && this.OCCUPIED)
{
    this.WreckPrefab.SetActive(true);

    if (timeLimit > 0)
    {
        // Decrease timeLimit.
        timeLimit -= Time.deltaTime;
        if(this.tmp==null)
            tmp = GameObject.Instantiate(this.AttackPrefab,
                    this.AttackPosition.transform.position,
                    this.AttackPosition.transform.rotation) as GameObject;
    }
    else
    {
        Destroy(tmp);
        timeLimit = 4.0f;
    }
}
// This code block here is used for the enemny player placeholder ...
if (transform.tag.Equals("board") && this.ATTACKED && this.OCCUPIED)
{
    this.CubePrefab.SetActive(false);

    if (timeLimit > 0)
    {
        // Decrease timeLimit.
        timeLimit -= Time.deltaTime;
        if (this.tmp2 == null)
            tmp2 = GameObject.Instantiate(this.AttackPrefab,
                new Vector3(transform.position.x, 1.0f, transform.position.z),
                transform.rotation) as GameObject;
    }
    else
    {
        Destroy(tmp2);
```

```
        timeLimit = 4.0f;
    }
}
```

If you notice, both of the if conditions check for the same criteria: the board unit must be attacked and it must be occupied. These criteria are checked through the *this.ATTACKED* and *this.OCCUPIED* properties. The main difference between the two blocks is done through the tag property associated to the unit board prefab.

We need to be able to somehow identify whose board we are interacting with, and this is done through the tag property that is associated to the unit board prefab. For the player's board, the tag property is defined as *"boardAttack"* and for the enemy's board, the tag property is defined as *"board"*. The tag property is defined and assigned at design time. In other words, since we are using one single script to handle both the player's board units and the enemy's board units, we need to somehow distinguish between the two, and hence we are doing that through the tag property.

Since that is now out of the way, the actual structure and logic for both *if blocks* are similar, if the conditions are met, we activate/enable the prefab used for visually representing a hit. The next step is to check a timer variable, the timer is set to reset every four (4) seconds, we instantiate the defined visual FX prefab on the attack position transform associated with the unit board prefab. Notice that every four seconds we destroy the visual FX GameObject from the scene.

Script – BoardVer1.cs

This script is the main driving force behind the Battle Board game. It is used to control the game logic and game flow from start to finish. It is the script that brings everything together and acts as the glue between all of the different pieces. It is a complex script, so I will try to break it down as much as possible. Let's take a look and list all of the internal variables that have been defined in the BoardVer1[22] class.

---

[22] The code-block is showing only the declared variables, full listing of the code is provided later on.

```
• …
• …
  public Camera cameraEndGame;

  public AudioClip explosionPlayerBlast;
  public AudioClip explosionEnemyBlast;
  private AudioSource audioSource;

  public GameObject BoardUnitPrefab;
  public GameObject BoardUnitAttackPrefab;

  public GameObject CubePrefab;

  // this variable will be used for chapter 5 ... enhancements of the code
  public GameObject IverHuitfeldt;
  public GameObject IverHuitfeldtAnchorPosition;

  public GameObject AdmiralSergeyGorshkov;
  public GameObject AdmiralSergeyGorshkovAnchorPosition;

  public GameObject MRVikhrIFQ;
  public GameObject MRVikhrIFQAnchorPosition;

  public GameObject Steregushchiy;
  public GameObject SteregushchiyAnchorPosition;

  public GameObject AdmiralKuznetsov;
  public GameObject AdmiralKuznetsovAnchorPosition;
  // ------------------------------------------------------------------

  public GameObject[,] boardPlayer = new GameObject[10,10];
  public GameObject[,] boardEnemy = new GameObject[10, 10];

  // used for placing enemy ships (by size)
  private int[] ships = new int[5] {2,3,3,4,5};

  private int maxNumberOfHits = 17;

  private int playerHitCount = 0;
  private int enemyHitCount = 0;

  public int  blockSize = 3;
  public bool vertical = false;

  public GameObject myWater;

  #region BUTTON REF
  public Button butAircraftCarrier;
  public Button butBattleship;
  public Button butSubmarine;
  public Button butDestroyer;
  public Button butPatrolBoat;

  public Button butUIReset;
  public Button butExit;
```

```
public Button butHorizontal;
public Button butVertical;

public Canvas canvasScoreBoard;
public Text lblPlayerScore;
public Text lblAIScore;

public Image imgYouWin;
public Image imgYouLose;
#endregion
    …
.   …
```

Code Block 48 - BoardVer1 Variables

Here are the variables responsible for the main game play.

- *cameraEndGame*, is of type Camera, and is used to display the ending scene of the game.
- *explosionPlayerBlast*, is of type AudioClip, and is used to play the sound FX when the player gets hit.
- *explosionEnemyBlast*, is of type AudioClip, and is used to play the sound FX when the enemy gets hit.
- *audioSource*, is of type AudioSource, is it used for the playback of the audio in the level.
- *BoardUnitPrefab*, is of type GameObject, it is the reference to the prefab used to hold the player's unit board.
- *BoardUnitAttackPrefab*, is of type GameObject, it is the reference to the prefab used to hold the enemy's unit board.
- *CubePrefab*, is of type GameObject, this variable is used to dynamically generate a cube prefab for visual clues.
- *boardPlayer*, is a two dimensional array data type, representing the player's board. The dimension of the array are 10x10.
- *boardEnemy*, is a two dimensional array data type, representing the enemy's board. The dimension of the array are 10x10.
- *ships*, is a one dimensional array data type, holds the length of each piece that will need to be placed on the board. This variable is specifically used by the A.I. when it is placing it's pieces onto the board.

- *maxNumberOfHits*, is of type int, and is used to represent the maximum value attainable for a win.
- *playerHitCount*, is of type int, it is the counter for the player's score.
- *enemyHitCount*, is of type int, it is the counter for the A.I.'s score.
- *blockSize*, is of type int, it is used for measuring and computing the boundary of ship placement on the game boards. Think of it as a margin or a padding measurement.
- *vertical*, is of type bool, it is used to identify if the current piece to be placed is going to be vertical or horizontal.

As you can see, the list of variables to manage the game is pretty extensive. We will see how each one is being used when we cover the functions in the class.

Advanced Graphic Variables

The following variables are all of type GameObject. They are a reference to the prefabs that represent the 3D model for each ship that will be placed on the player's board.

- IverHuitfeldt
- IverHuitfeldtAnchorPosition
- AdmiralSergeyGorshkov
- AdmiralSergeyGorshkovAnchorPosition
- MRVikhrIFQ
- MRVikhrIFQAnchorPosition
- Steregushchiy
- SteregushchiyAnchorPosition
- AdmiralKuznetsov
- AdmiralKuznetsovAnchorPosition

Graphical User Interface Variables

The following variables are used to reference the UI elements in the game. The variables starting with *butXXX* are representing the buttons defined in the UI that the user can interact with. The variables starting with *lblXXX* are referencing labels in the UI, the variables starting with *imgXXX* are referencing images in the UI. The variable *canvasScoreBoard* is of type Canvas and is used to reference the score board in the game. We will also look at these in more detail in the next section.

- butAircraftCarrier
- butBattleship
- butSubmarine
- butDestroyer
- butPatrolBoat
- butUIReset
- butExit
- butHorizontal
- butVertical
- canvasScoreBoard
- lblPlayerScore
- lblAIScore
- imgYouWin
- imgYouLose

Functions Defined in BoardVer1 Class

The game has a few functions that are necessary for it to function. In this section, we will list each function and go over the code and describe what the functions are performing.

- *Awake()*, the Awake() function is called once and it is the first function that will be executed in the lifecycle of the game. It is used to grab a reference to the AudioSource in the level.
- *Start()*, the *Start()* function is called once as well, it is called after the *Awake()* function. The *Start()* function is responsible for initializing all of the game variables. It is also responsible for generating both of the game boards, one for the player and one for the enemy.

- *CheckPlayerBoard()*, is responsible for handing the placement of the game pieces onto the player's game board.
- *CheckAttackBoard()*, is responsible for handling the attack and detection of a hit for both the player and the enemy.
- *Wait4Me()*, is a function used for time delay.
- *Update()*, is a function that is called every frame. The *Update()* function is the main body of the game program. It determines the state of the game and calls the appropriate functions as needed during the lifetime of the game.
- *ChangeHitDirection()*, this function is used by the A.I. to make a decision about the direction its next move will be.
- *PlaceEnemyShips()*, this function is used by the A.I. to decide where it wants to place its ships on the game board before the game starts.
- *CheckBoardForEnemyPlacement(row,col,size,hor)*, this function is used by the A.I. to determine if the placement of the ship is valid or not. It is a recursive function. It is based on the original row and column data the size of the ship and the orientation.
- *CheckWhichShipWasPlaced(row,col)*, this function is used by the A.I. to determine which ship is has placed onto the game board.
- *butCreateBattleship(size)*, this function is triggered when the player selects the UI button defined for a specific ship for placement.
- *butCreateBattleShipSetID(shipID)*, this function is triggered when the player selects the UI button defined for a specific ship for placement. The two function together provide the size and the ID of the selected ship.
- *butRestart()*, this functions does some cleanup work and restarts the game.
- *butExitClick()*, this functions terminates the game.
- *butChangeOrientation()*, this function changes the orientation of the player's piece placement onto the game board.
- *ResetGUIButtons()*, this function resets all of the GUI buttons when the user restarts the game.

Awake() Function Implementation

Now that we have a brief overview of what each function is designed for, we can look at the actual implementation and start absorbing the details further. The first and simplest of all functions is the *Awake()* function.

```
void Awake()
{
    this.audioSource = GetComponent<AudioSource>();
}
```

Code Block 49 - Awake() function in BoardVer1 class

There is only one line of code in this method, and it is used to get the AudioSource components attached to the GameObject where this script itself is attached to. The GameObject happens to be the *Main Camera* defined in the scene. We need a reference to the AudioSource so that we can directly access what audio we want to play at a given time. You will see how this variable is utilized in the other functions listed below.

Start() Function Implementation

The next function we want to look at is the *Start()* function.

```
void Start ()
{
    #region GAME ACCOUNTING
    Water tmpWater = this.myWater.gameObject.GetComponent<Water>();
    tmpWater.waterMode = Water.WaterMode.Refractive;

    this.cameraEndGame.gameObject.SetActive(false);
    this.canvasScoreBoard.enabled = false;

    this.count = 0;

    this.currentShipID = 0;
    this.blockSize = 0;

    this.placeEnemyShips = true;

    this.START_GAME = false;
    this.PLAYER_TURN = true;

    this.maxNumberOfHits = 17;

    this.playerHitCount = 0;
```

```
    this.enemyHitCount = 0;

    this.hit_row = -1;
    this.hit_col = -1;
    this.hit_dir = HitDirection.none;
    this.IsBusy = false;
    this.gotoLastHit = false;

    this.imgYouLose.enabled = false;
    this.imgYouWin.enabled = false;

    this.butUIReset.gameObject.SetActive(false);

#if UNITY_WEBPLAYER
    // for web player we do not need to display the exit button!!!
    this.butExit.gameObject.SetActive(false);
    this.butUIReset.GetComponent<RectTransform>().Translate(new Vector3(75,
0, 0));
#endif

    if(this.vertical)
    {
        this.butVertical.gameObject.SetActive(true);
        this.butHorizontal.gameObject.SetActive(false);
    }
    else
    {
        this.butVertical.gameObject.SetActive(false);
        this.butHorizontal.gameObject.SetActive(true);
    }

    #endregion

    // clear the board(s)
    for (int i = 0; i < 10; i++)
    {
        for (int j = 0; j < 10; j++)
        {
            boardPlayer[i, j] = null;
            boardEnemy[i, j] = null;
        }
    }

    // create a 10x10 board - Board 1
    int row = 1;
    int col = 1;
    for(int i=0; i<10; i++)
    {
        for(int j=0; j<10; j++)
        {
            // instantiate prefab and place it properly on the scene
            GameObject tmp = GameObject.Instantiate(this.BoardUnitPrefab,
                    new Vector3(i, 0, j), this.BoardUnitPrefab.transform.rota-
tion) as GameObject;

            BoardUIVer1 tmpUI = tmp.GetComponent<BoardUIVer1>();
```

```
            string name = string.Format("B1:[{0:00},{1:00}]", row, col);
            tmpUI.lblBoardPosition.text = name;
            tmpUI.COL = j;
            tmpUI.ROW = i;

            boardPlayer[i, j] = tmp;

            tmp.name = name;

            col++;
        }
        col = 1;
        row++;
    }

    // create a 10x10 board - Board 2
    row = 1; col = 1;
    for (int i = 11; i < 21; i++)
    {
        for (int j = 0; j < 10; j++)
        {
            // instantiate prefab and place it properly on the scene
            GameObject tmp = GameObject.Instantiate(this.BoardUnitAttackPrefab,
                    new Vector3(i, 0, j), this.BoardUnitAttackPrefab.trans-
form.rotation) as GameObject;

            BoardUIVer1 tmpUI = tmp.GetComponent<BoardUIVer1>();
            string name = string.Format("B2:[{0:00},{1:00}]", row, col);
            tmpUI.lblBoardPosition.text = name;
            tmpUI.COL = col-1;
            tmpUI.ROW = row-1;

            boardEnemy[tmpUI.ROW, tmpUI.COL] = tmp;

            tmp.name = name;

            col++;
        }
        col = 1;
        row++;
    }
}
```

Code Block 50 - Start() function in BoardVer1 class

The first two lines in the function get a reference to the Water component in the *myWater* variable, and we change the *WaterMode* to *Refractive*. This changes the rendering mode of the water and hence the appearance changes in the level.

The next two lines of code disables the end game camera we have setup through the variable *cameraEndGame*. We also disable the canvas object that is referencing the score board through the *canvasScoreBoard* variable. The next few lines initialize all of the variables that are used for handing the game data.

Going to the first for loop, we are initializing the game boards for both the player and the enemy. Here we have two for loops, one embedded in the other representing the rows and the columns of our boards. They are set to iterate 10 times each, as that is the size of our board. Notice that we are nullifying each position in the matrix/board, hence preparing it for the actual creation of the board in the next step.

```
// create a 10x10 board - Board 1
int row = 1;
int col = 1;
for(int i=0; i<10; i++)
{
    for(int j=0; j<10; j++)
    {
        // instantiate prefab and place it properly on the scene
        GameObject tmp = GameObject.Instantiate(this.BoardUnitPrefab,
            new Vector3(i, 0, j), this.BoardUnitPrefab.transform.rotation) as
GameObject;

        BoardUIVer1 tmpUI = tmp.GetComponent<BoardUIVer1>();
        string name = string.Format("B1:[{0:00},{1:00}]", row, col);
        tmpUI.lblBoardPosition.text = name;
        tmpUI.COL = j;
        tmpUI.ROW = i;

        boardPlayer[i, j] = tmp;

        tmp.name = name;

        col++;
    }
    col = 1;
    row++;
}
```

Code Block 51 - Code for Construction of Player's Board

All this code is doing is instantiating our prefab referenced by the variable *BoardUnitPrefab*, it is located a position $<i,0,j>$ where i is the row, and j is the column, and the Vector3 object is the 3D position of the Board Unit in 3D space. The rotation is set to the default of the transform of the object.

That one line is where the Board Unit prefab gets instantiated and placed in the 3D world. The next few lines of code, format the name for the board unit, that is, they apply a label for identification such as, *B1[00,00]* and etc… the *i* and *j* values are assigned to the internal data variables of the *BoardUIVer1* class, *ROW* and *COL* respectively. And finally, the newly instantiated Board Unit is stored into the 2-dimensional array that represents the player's board at the specific location again identified by the values of *i* and *j*.

NOTE: *When the Board Unit gets instantiated, it has a script attached to it called BoardUIVer1.cs. Each time a GameObject is introduced into the scene, the process is to have all scripts, that are enabled, attached to it be executed, and in this case, the Awake() and the Start() function will be called first and only once, if they are defined. This is mentioned, as a reminder that those scripts would probably have their own initializations and etc…*

The second block of the for loop creates the board for the enemy. The logic of the code works similarly, the accounting is done a bit different. Here is the listing for the enemy board creation:

```
// create a 10x10 board - Board 2
row = 1; col = 1;
for (int i = 11; i < 21; i++)
{
    for (int j = 0; j < 10; j++)
    {
        // instantiate prefab and place it properly on the scene
        GameObject tmp = GameObject.Instantiate(this.BoardUnitAttackPrefab,
            new Vector3(i, 0, j), this.BoardUnitAttackPrefab.transform.rota-
tion) as GameObject;

        BoardUIVer1 tmpUI = tmp.GetComponent<BoardUIVer1>();
        string name = string.Format("B2:[{0:00},{1:00}]", row, col);
        tmpUI.lblBoardPosition.text = name;
        tmpUI.COL = col-1;
        tmpUI.ROW = row-1;

        boardEnemy[tmpUI.ROW, tmpUI.COL] = tmp;
        tmp.name = name;
        col++;
    }
    col = 1;
    row++;
}
```

Code Block 52 - Code for Enemy Board Construction

The biggest difference you will notice here is the starting point for the variable *i*. This is because we need to displace the actual creation of the GameObject at a specific coordinate. This is specifically used only for the placement of the object in the 3D world.

If you notice, we use the row and col variables for the actual data assignment for the Board Unit, and not the, *i* and *j* variables as before. This is because, the *row* and *col* represent the numbers we want internally for the unit board and also the storing of the GameObject in the 2-dimensionsl array representing the Enemy's game board. Other than that, everything else is the same logic.

Update() Function Implementation

The next function we should look at is the *Update()* function. This function is the heart of the script. It gets called every single frame by the Unity Game Engine. It also controls the flow of the game.

```
// Update is called once per frame
void Update ()
{

    if (this.IsBusy)
        return;

    if (this.count < 5)
    {
        // If the up arrow or the right mouse button has been clicked, then
switch between
        // vertical and horizontal
        if (Input.GetKeyDown(KeyCode.UpArrow) || Input.GetMouseButtonUp(1))
            this.vertical = !this.vertical;

        if (this.vertical)
        {
            this.butVertical.gameObject.SetActive(true);
            this.butHorizontal.gameObject.SetActive(false);
        }
        else
        {
            this.butVertical.gameObject.SetActive(false);
            this.butHorizontal.gameObject.SetActive(true);
        }

        this.CheckPlayerBoard();
    }
    else
    {
        if (placeEnemyShips)
```

```
    {
        // disable orientation buttons
        this.butHorizontal.gameObject.SetActive(false);
        this.butVertical.gameObject.SetActive(false);

        //Debug.Log("I AM GOING TO PLACE ENEMY SHIPS NOW");
        // place the enemy ships
        this.PlaceEnemyShips();

        this.START_GAME = true;
    }

    if(this.START_GAME)
    {
        this.butUIReset.gameObject.SetActive(true);

        this.canvasScoreBoard.enabled = true;

        this.CheckAttackBoard();

        if(this.playerHitCount>=this.maxNumberOfHits || this.ene-
myHitCount>=this.maxNumberOfHits)
        {
            this.START_GAME = false;
        }

        this.lblPlayerScore.text = string.Format("{0:00}", this.play-
erHitCount);
        this.lblAIScore.text = string.Format("{0:00}", this.enemyHitCount);
    }
    else
    {
        // some one has won the game!
        if (this.playerHitCount >= this.maxNumberOfHits)
        {
            // make another graphic to represent the winner icon
            this.lblPlayerScore.text = string.Format("{0:00}", this.play-
erHitCount);
            this.imgYouWin.enabled = true;
        }
        if (this.enemyHitCount >= this.maxNumberOfHits)
        {
            // make another graphic to represent the winner icon
            this.lblAIScore.text = string.Format("{0:00}", this.ene-
myHitCount);
            this.imgYouLose.enabled = true;

            // display the remaining enemy ship parts
            for (int i = 0; i < 10; i++)
            {
                for (int j = 0; j < 10; j++)
                {
                    GameObject tmp = boardEnemy[i, j];
```

```
                    if (tmp.GetComponent<BoardUIVer1>().OCCUPIED && !tmp.Get-
Component<BoardUIVer1>().ATTACKED)
                    {
                        tmp.transform.GetComponent<Renderer>().material.color =
Color.cyan;
                    }
                }
            }
        }

        // change the water rendering mode
        Water tmpWater = this.myWater.gameObject.GetComponent<Water>();
        tmpWater.waterMode = Water.WaterMode.Reflective;

        this.cameraEndGame.gameObject.SetActive(true);
    }
  }
}
```

Code Block 53 - Update() function defined in BoardVer1 class

The *Update()* function is somewhat complex, but it is manageable. The first if condition checks to see if the thread is busy based on a Boolean variable named *IsBusy*, and if so, it exits the function until the next cycle. This variable is updated by the A.I.'s ship placement process.

The next condition block `if (this.count < 5)` handles the Player's ship placement. The *count* variable is used to keep track of the placement of the player's pieces. So starting at 0, it increments each time there is a successful placement of a game piece onto the board. Within the if block, the code check for mouse input from the user to see if the right-button on the mouse or the up arrow key has been pressed, if either one of this conditions is true, then the orientation of the piece placement will be inversed. This is done using the `this.vertical` variable.

The next set of if blocks are used for updating the GUI interface based on the user input for the orientation button. Finally, the code calls the `this.CheckPlayerBoard();` function which then takes care of the actual placement of the game piece. This function will be covered separately.

In the else section of the if condition, we determine if the A.I. needs to start placing its game pieces or the game is ready to start.

Within the body of the else condition, we see the first if condision `if`
`(placeEnemyShips)`. This condition checks the variable *placeEnemy-*
Ships to determine if the computer A.I. still has game pieces for
placement, and if so then it calls the `this.PlaceEnemyShips();` function
to complete the placement of the pieces accordingly. This function will
be covered separately in detail. Once the function return, it sets the variable to identify the start of the game.

This takes us to the next if condition within the else block
`if(this.START_GAME)`. This code block is where the actual game starts,
and the main function for handling the input from the user and also the
A.I. is `this.CheckAttackBoard();`. This function is very involved, and
will be covered separately. Each time through the *Update()* function,
the code checks to see if there is a winner in the game.

The else section of the code block properly displays the scores to
the user. If the computer A.I. is the winner of the game, it also display
all of the game pieces on the board, this includes the hit and the no-hit
game pieces.

CheckPlayerBoard() Function Implementation

Going down in the order of how the functions are being called from
within the *Update()* function, we will cover our next function called
CheckPlayerBoard().

```
private void CheckPlayerBoard()
{
    if (Input.mousePosition != null)
    {
        // capture the mouse position and cast a ray to see what object we hit
        Ray ray = Camera.main.ScreenPointToRay(Input.mousePosition);

        if (Physics.Raycast(ray, out tmpHitHighlight, 100))
        {
            BoardUIVer1 tmpUI = tmpHitHighlight.transform.GetCompo-
nent<BoardUIVer1>();
            if (tmpHitHighlight.transform.tag.Equals("board") &&
!tmpUI.OCCUPIED)
            {
                BoardUIVer1 boardData = boardPlayer[tmpUI.ROW,
tmpUI.COL].transform.GetComponent<BoardUIVer1>();

                if (tmpHighlight != null)
```

```
            {
                if (boardData.OCCUPIED)
                tmpHighlight.GetComponent<Renderer>().material.color =
Color.red;
                else
                    tmpHighlight.GetComponent<Renderer>().material.color =
Color.white;
            }

            if (this.tmpBlockHolder != null)
            {
                Destroy(this.tmpBlockHolder);
            }

            if (this.PLACE_BLOCK)
            {
                this.tmpBlockHolder = new GameObject();
                this.OK_TO_PLACE = true;
                if (!this.vertical && (tmpUI.ROW <= 10 - this.blockSize))
                {
                    for (int i = 0; i < this.blockSize; i++)
                    {
                        GameObject visual = GameObject.Instantiate(this.CubeP-
refab, new Vector3(tmpUI.ROW + i, this.CubePrefab.transform.position.y,
tmpUI.COL), this.CubePrefab.transform.rotation) as GameObject;

                        GameObject bp = boardPlayer[tmpUI.ROW + i, tmpUI.COL];
                        BoardUIVer1 bpUI = bp.GetComponent<BoardUIVer1>();
                        if (!bpUI.OCCUPIED)
                        {
                            visual.GetComponent<Renderer>().material.color =
Color.gray; // ok to place
                        }
                        else
                        {
                            visual.transform.localScale = new Vector3(0.6f,
0.6f, 0.6f);
                            visual.GetComponent<Renderer>().material.color =
Color.yellow; // not ok
                            this.OK_TO_PLACE = false;
                        }

                        visual.transform.parent = this.tmpBlockHolder.trans-
form;

                    }
                }
                if (this.vertical && (tmpUI.COL <= 10 - this.blockSize))
                {
                    for (int i = 0; i < this.blockSize; i++)
                    {
                        GameObject visual = GameObject.Instantiate(this.CubeP-
refab, new Vector3(tmpUI.ROW, this.CubePrefab.transform.position.y,
tmpUI.COL + i), this.CubePrefab.transform.rotation) as GameObject;

                        GameObject bp = boardPlayer[tmpUI.ROW, tmpUI.COL + i];
```

```
                        BoardUIVer1 bpUI = bp.GetComponent<BoardUIVer1>();
                        if (!bpUI.OCCUPIED)
                        {
                            visual.GetComponent<Renderer>().material.color =
Color.gray; // ok to place
                        }
                        else
                        {
                            visual.transform.localScale = new Vector3(0.6f,
0.6f, 0.6f);
                            visual.GetComponent<Renderer>().material.color =
Color.yellow; // not ok
                            this.OK_TO_PLACE = false;
                        }

                        visual.transform.parent = this.tmpBlockHolder.trans-
form;

                    }
                }
            }

            tmpHitHighlight.transform.GetComponent<Renderer>().mate-
rial.color = Color.blue;
            tmpHighlight = tmpHitHighlight.transform.gameObject;
        }
    }
}

if (Input.GetMouseButton(0))
{
    // capture the mouse position and cast a ray to see what object we hit
    Ray ray = Camera.main.ScreenPointToRay(Input.mousePosition);
    RaycastHit hit;

    if (Physics.Raycast(ray, out hit, 100))
    {
        Debug.Log(hit.transform.gameObject.name);

        if (hit.transform.tag.Equals("board"))
        {

            BoardUIVer1 tmpUI = hit.transform.GetComponent<BoardUIVer1>();

            if (this.PLACE_BLOCK && this.OK_TO_PLACE)
            {
                if (!this.vertical)
                {
                    for (int i = 0; i < this.blockSize; i++)
                    {
                        GameObject sB = boardPlayer[tmpUI.ROW + i, tmpUI.COL];
                        sB.transform.GetComponent<Renderer>().material.color =
Color.green;

                        sB.GetComponent<BoardUIVer1>().OCCUPIED = true;
```

```
                    sB.GetComponent<BoardUIVer1>().CubePrefab.gameOb-
ject.GetComponent<Renderer>().material.color = Color.green;
                    boardPlayer[tmpUI.ROW + i, tmpUI.COL] = sB;
                }

            }
            if (this.vertical)
            {
                for (int i = 0; i < this.blockSize; i++)
                {
                    GameObject sB = boardPlayer[tmpUI.ROW, tmpUI.COL + i];
                    sB.transform.GetComponent<Renderer>().material.color =
Color.green;

                    sB.GetComponent<BoardUIVer1>().OCCUPIED = true;

                    sB.GetComponent<BoardUIVer1>().CubePrefab.gameOb-
ject.GetComponent<Renderer>().material.color = Color.green;
                    boardPlayer[tmpUI.ROW, tmpUI.COL + i] = sB;

                }
            }

            this.CheckWhichShipWasPlaced(tmpUI.ROW, tmpUI.COL);

            this.OK_TO_PLACE = true;
            tmpHighlight = null;
        }

        // block group on the board
        if(this.count>=5)
        {
            if (this.tmpBlockHolder != null)
            {
                Destroy(this.tmpBlockHolder);
            }
        }

    }

  }

 }
}
```

Code Block 54 - CheckPlayerBoard() Function Definition

So the first thing this function does is check to see if the *In-put.mousePosition* is not null. This is important, because the user needs to use the mouse to place his or her game piece onto the board.

The next line of code is very important. We are creating a *Ray* object using the mouse position.

Mathematical Definition of a Ray: A portion of a line which starts at a point and goes off in a particular direction to infinity.

A ray is used in Unity, in conjunction with the *Raycast()* function defined in the *Physics* object, to generate a logical line in the 3D space and when you shoot the ray, it actually will provide information regarding any object in its path. It is basically used for Ray Casting[23].

This particular satetement if (Physics.Raycast(ray, out tmpHitHighlight, 100)), is what makes our Raycast work and also returns the necessary data needed. The hit data is stored in *tmpHighligh* variable. Before continuing, we should also list some temporary variables that are used specifically within the *CheckPlayerBoard()* function.

```
GameObject tmpHighlight = null;
RaycastHit tmpHitHighlight;

GameObject tmpBlockHolder = null;

private bool OK_TO_PLACE = true;
```

Code Block 55 - Temporary variables used by CheckPlayerBoard()

NOTE: *The variables listed in Code Block 55 are all also part of the class data, however, they have been listed right above the CheckPlayerBoard() function for clarification.*

Due to the nature of the scene setup we know that the only objects that can be hit by the Raycast are going to be the Unit Boards and also the other game pieces. What we would like to do is extract the *BoardUIVer1* component from the *tmpHitHighlight* variable, and start processing the object.

There is two conditions we are looking for, first, we want to make sure that the raycast hit registered a board unit. This is done with the identification of the tag. The second condition is to make sure that the given board unit is not occupied. If these two conditions are met, we

---

[23] Ray casting is the use of ray-surface intersection tests to solve a variety of problems in computer graphics and computational geometry. The term was first used in computer graphics in a 1982 paper by Scott Roth to describe a method for rendering constructive solid geometry models.

proceed with processing the actual data in the *boardPlayer[,]* 2-dimentional array storing the actual data node.

The code gets pretty complex here, so let's take it section by section.

```
        if (Physics.Raycast(ray, out tmpHitHighlight, 100))
        {
            BoardUIVer1 tmpUI = tmpHitHighlight.transform.GetCompo-
nent<BoardUIVer1>();
            if (tmpHitHighlight.transform.tag.Equals("board") &&
!tmpUI.OCCUPIED)
            {
                BoardUIVer1 boardData = boardPlayer[tmpUI.ROW,
tmpUI.COL].transform.GetComponent<BoardUIVer1>();

                if (tmpHighlight != null)
                {
                    if (boardData.OCCUPIED)
                    tmpHighlight.GetComponent<Renderer>().material.color =
Color.red;

                    else
                        tmpHighlight.GetComponent<Renderer>().material.color =
Color.white;
                }

                if (this.tmpBlockHolder != null)
                {
                    Destroy(this.tmpBlockHolder);
                }

                if (this.PLACE_BLOCK)
                {
                    this.tmpBlockHolder = new GameObject();
                    this.OK_TO_PLACE = true;
                    if (!this.vertical && (tmpUI.ROW <= 10 - this.blockSize))
                    {
                        for (int i = 0; i < this.blockSize; i++)
                        {
                            GameObject visual = GameObject.Instantiate(this.CubeP-
refab, new Vector3(tmpUI.ROW + i, this.CubePrefab.transform.position.y,
tmpUI.COL), this.CubePrefab.transform.rotation) as GameObject;

                            GameObject bp = boardPlayer[tmpUI.ROW + i, tmpUI.COL];
                            BoardUIVer1 bpUI = bp.GetComponent<BoardUIVer1>();
                            if (!bpUI.OCCUPIED)
                            {
                                visual.GetComponent<Renderer>().material.color =
Color.gray; // ok to place
                            }
                            else
                            {
```

```
                        visual.transform.localScale = new Vector3(0.6f,
0.6f, 0.6f);
                        visual.GetComponent<Renderer>().material.color =
Color.yellow; // not ok
                        this.OK_TO_PLACE = false;
                    }

                    visual.transform.parent = this.tmpBlockHolder.trans-
form;

                }
            }
            if (this.vertical && (tmpUI.COL <= 10 - this.blockSize))
            {
                for (int i = 0; i < this.blockSize; i++)
                {
                    GameObject visual = GameObject.Instantiate(this.CubeP-
refab, new Vector3(tmpUI.ROW, this.CubePrefab.transform.position.y,
tmpUI.COL + i), this.CubePrefab.transform.rotation) as GameObject;

                    GameObject bp = boardPlayer[tmpUI.ROW, tmpUI.COL + i];
                    BoardUIVer1 bpUI = bp.GetComponent<BoardUIVer1>();
                    if (!bpUI.OCCUPIED)
                    {
                        visual.GetComponent<Renderer>().material.color =
Color.gray; // ok to place
                    }
                    else
                    {
                        visual.transform.localScale = new Vector3(0.6f,
0.6f, 0.6f);
                        visual.GetComponent<Renderer>().material.color =
Color.yellow; // not ok
                        this.OK_TO_PLACE = false;
                    }

                    visual.transform.parent = this.tmpBlockHolder.trans-
form;

                }
            }
        }

        tmpHitHighlight.transform.GetComponent<Renderer>().mate-
rial.color = Color.blue;
        tmpHighlight = tmpHitHighlight.transform.gameObject;
    }
  }
}
```

Code Block 56 - Determining what object we have hit by ray casting.

Trying to explain what is going on line-by-line will be a little overwhelming. It would make more sense to give you an overall informative view on the code block and have you dig through it for the details.

Code Block 56 does a few things for us. The first thing that it performs is our ray cast. We get the data returned by the raycasting functino to determine what type of GameObjects we have hit. If the GameObject returned is a Board Unit belonging to the player, and the Board Unit is not occupied, we start the main process of retrieving the main data from the 2-dimensional array holding actual game board data. Based on the state of the board unit hit, we change the color of the board unit to either red if it is occupied, visually notifying the user that they cannot place a unit at that particular location, or white which is the default color for an empty unit board.

Next, if the player is able to place their block, the code iterates through and dynamically generates visual clues for the placement of the game piece, in this case the select ship piece. Throughout the iteration and checking of the availability of board units along the pathway, it determines if the game piece can be placed at the selected location or not. If all checks and verifications are O.K. the program then actually takes the data and records it on the player's game board. This process repeats until all game pieces have been placed onto the board.

CheckWhichShipWasPlaced() Function Implementation

This function is used for initializing the prefabs of the selected ship to be placed on the board. It used the row and column positions as the origin for placement, and the actual identification of the ship is done through the ID that has been assigned at design time.

```
private void CheckWhichShipWasPlaced(int row, int col)
{
    switch(this.currentShipID)
    {
      case 1:
      {
         if (!this.vertical)
         {
            // place it as vertical
            GameObject testingVisual = GameObject.Instantiate(this.Admi-
ralKuznetsov, new Vector3(row + 2,
```

```
this.AdmiralKuznetsov.transform.position.y, col), this.AdmiralKuz-
netsov.transform.rotation) as GameObject;

                testingVisual.transform.RotateAround(testingVisual.transform.po-
sition, Vector3.up, 90.0f);
        }
        else
        {
            GameObject testingVisual = GameObject.Instantiate(this.Admi-
ralKuznetsov, new Vector3(row, this.AdmiralKuznetsov.transform.position.y,
col + 2), this.AdmiralKuznetsov.transform.rotation) as GameObject;
        }

        // Aircraft Carrier was placed, disable button
        this.butAircraftCarrier.gameObject.SetActive(false);
        this.count++;
        break;
    }
    case 2:
    {
        if (!this.vertical)
        {
            // place it as vertical
            GameObject testingVisual = GameObject.Instantiate(this.Stere-
gushchiy, new Vector3(row + 1.5f, this.Steregushchiy.transform.position.y,
col), this.Steregushchiy.transform.rotation) as GameObject;

                testingVisual.transform.RotateAround(testingVisual.transform.po-
sition, Vector3.up, 90.0f);
        }
        else
        {
            GameObject testingVisual = GameObject.Instantiate(this.Stere-
gushchiy, new Vector3(row, this.Steregushchiy.transform.position.y,
col + 1.5f), this.Steregushchiy.transform.rotation) as GameObject;
        }

        // Battle ship was placed, disable button
        this.butBattleship.gameObject.SetActive(false);
        this.count++;
        break;
    }
    case 3:
    {
        if (!this.vertical)
        {
            // place it as vertical
            GameObject testingVisual = GameObject.Instantiate(this.Admiral-
SergeyGorshkov, new Vector3(row + 1,
this.AdmiralSergeyGorshkov.transform.position.y, col),
this.AdmiralSergeyGorshkov.transform.rotation) as GameObject;

                testingVisual.transform.RotateAround(testingVisual.transform.po-
sition, Vector3.up, 90.0f);
        }
```

```
            else
            {
                GameObject testingVisual = GameObject.Instantiate(this.Admiral-
SergeyGorshkov, new Vector3(row,
this.AdmiralSergeyGorshkov.transform.position.y, col + 1),
this.AdmiralSergeyGorshkov.transform.rotation) as GameObject;
            }

            // Submarine was placed, disable the button
            this.butSubmarine.gameObject.SetActive(false);
            this.count++;
            break;
        }
        case 4:
        {
            if (!this.vertical)
            {
                // place it as vertical
                GameObject testingVisual = GameObject.Instantiate(this.IverHuit-
feldt, new Vector3(row + 1,
this.IverHuitfeldt.transform.position.y, col),
this.IverHuitfeldt.transform.rotation) as GameObject;

                testingVisual.transform.RotateAround(testingVisual.transform.po-
sition, Vector3.up, 90.0f);
            }
            else
            {
                GameObject testingVisual = GameObject.Instantiate(this.IverHuit-
feldt, new Vector3(row,
this.IverHuitfeldt.transform.position.y, col + 1),
this.IverHuitfeldt.transform.rotation) as GameObject;
            }

            // Destroyer was placed, disable the button
            this.butDestroyer.gameObject.SetActive(false);
            this.count++;
            break;
        }
        case 5:
        {
            if (!this.vertical)
            {
                // place it as vertical
                GameObject testingVisual = GameObject.Instanti-
ate(this.MRVikhrIFQ, new Vector3(row + 0.5f,
this.MRVikhrIFQ.transform.position.y, col), this.MRVikhrIFQ.transform.rota-
tion) as GameObject;

                testingVisual.transform.RotateAround(testingVisual.transform.po-
sition, Vector3.up, 90.0f);
            }
            else
            {
                GameObject testingVisual = GameObject.Instanti-
ate(this.MRVikhrIFQ, new Vector3(row,
```

```
this.MRVikhrIFQ.transform.position.y, col + 0.5f), this.MRVikhrIFQ.trans-
form.rotation) as GameObject;
        }

        // Patrol Boat was placed, disable the button
        this.butPatrolBoat.gameObject.SetActive(false);
        this.count++;
        break;
    }
}

// clear internal data
this.currentShipID = 0;
this.blockSize = 0;
}
```

Code Block 57 - Visually placing the selected piece onto the game board

The main logic in the code here is to identify the ID of the ship and properly instantiate the associated prefab onto the game board.

PlaceEnemyShips() Function Implementation

Once all of the player's game pieces have been placed onto the board, the A.I. needs to do the same. The *PlaceEnemyShips()* function is used to place the pieces for the computer opponent.

```
private void PlaceEnemyShips()
{
    this.placeEnemyShips = false;
    for(int i=0; i<this.ships.Length; i++)
    {
        int row = Random.Range(0,9);
        int col = Random.Range(0,9);

        bool ori = (Random.Range(0, 9) > 5) ? true : false;

        this.CheckBoardForEnemyPlacement(row, col, this.ships[i], ori);
    }
}
```

Code Block 58 - Function for A.I. to place game pieces

The function uses a for loop to iterate through all of the game pieces that need to be placed onto the A.I. game board. Within the for loop, the logic generates a random row and a random column position and a random orientation for the current piece that is being prepared for placement.

CheckBoardForEnemyPlacement() Function Implementation

The actual work is done by a supporting function called *Check-BoardForEnemyPlacement()*. This is a recursive function and here is the listing for it.

```
private void CheckBoardForEnemyPlacement(int row, int col, int size, bool hor)
{
    GameObject checkUnit = boardEnemy[row, col];

    if (checkUnit.GetComponent<BoardUIVer1>().OCCUPIED || (row + size > 9) || (col + size > 9))
    {
        int r1 = Random.Range(0, 9);
        int c1 = Random.Range(0, 9);
        this.CheckBoardForEnemyPlacement(r1, c1, size, hor);
        return;
    }

    bool okToPlace = true;

    if (!hor && (row+size < 10))
    {
        for (int i = 0; i < size; i++)
        {
            GameObject bp = boardEnemy[row + i, col];
            BoardUIVer1 bpUI = bp.GetComponent<BoardUIVer1>();
            if (!bpUI.OCCUPIED)
            {
                //okToPlace = true;
            }
            else
            {
                okToPlace = false;
            }
        }
    }

    if (hor && (col + size < 10))
    {
        for (int i = 0; i < size; i++)
        {
            GameObject bp = boardEnemy[row, col + i];
            BoardUIVer1 bpUI = bp.GetComponent<BoardUIVer1>();
            if (!bpUI.OCCUPIED)
            {
                //okToPlace = true;
            }
            else
            {
                okToPlace = false;
            }
        }
```

```
        }

    if (okToPlace)
    {
        if (!hor)
        {
            for (int i = 0; i < size; i++)
            {
                GameObject visual = GameObject.Instantiate(this.CubePrefab,
                    new Vector3(row + i, 11.9f, col),
                    this.CubePrefab.transform.rotation) as GameObject;

                visual.GetComponent<Renderer>().material.color = Color.yellow;
                visual.tag = "enemyPrefabPH";

                GameObject sB = boardEnemy[row + i, col];
                sB.GetComponent<BoardUIVer1>().OCCUPIED = true;
                boardEnemy[row + i, col] = sB;

                visual.gameObject.name = string.Format("EN-R-[{0},{1}]", row +
i, col);
            }
        }
        if (hor)
        {
            for (int i = 0; i < size; i++)
            {
                GameObject visual = GameObject.Instantiate(this.CubePrefab,
                    new Vector3(row, 11.9f, col + i),
                    this.CubePrefab.transform.rotation) as GameObject;

                visual.GetComponent<Renderer>().material.color = Color.magenta;

                GameObject sB = boardEnemy[row, col + i];
                sB.GetComponent<BoardUIVer1>().OCCUPIED = true;
                boardEnemy[row, col + i] = sB;

                visual.gameObject.name = string.Format("EN-C-[{0},{1}]", row,
col+i);
            }
        }
    }
    else
    {

        int r1 = Random.Range(0, 9);
        int c1 = Random.Range(0, 9);

        this.CheckBoardForEnemyPlacement(r1, c1, size, hor);
    }
}
```

Code Block 59 - Function responsible for A.I. game piece placement

Going through the function you notice that we use the row and col that were passed to the function to get the data from the 2-dimensional array representing the computer's game board. The next check is to determine if the selected position is already occupied or not, and if the row and column plus the size of the piece are within bounds of the game board given the position. If this is not the case, the program re-generates these values and calls itself again.

If the first check is passed, we move on to the second check. Just like when we were placing the player's game pieces, we need a way to determine if the selected position by the computer is valid for placement.

If we are O.K. to place the piece, then the program updates the identified unit boards with the latest status. Otherwise, it generates a new set of row and column and calls the function once more, and goes through the whole process again. This continues of until all of the pieces have been properly placed onto the computer's board. If there is a miss, then the turn to attack is changed to the player.

CheckAttackBoard() Function Implementation

Moving on, the next function we have listing of is the *CheckAttackBoard()* function.

```
private void CheckAttackBoard()
{
    // check to see who's turn it is
    if(this.PLAYER_TURN)
    {
        if (Input.mousePosition != null)
        {
            // capture the mouse position and cast a ray to see what object we
hit
            Ray ray = Camera.main.ScreenPointToRay(Input.mousePosition);

            if (Physics.Raycast(ray, out tmpAttackHitHighlight, 200))
            {
                BoardUIVer1 tmpUI = tmpAttackHitHighlight.transform.GetCompo-
nent<BoardUIVer1>();
                if (tmpAttackHitHighlight.transform.tag.Equals("boardAttack") &&
!tmpUI.ATTACKED)
                {
                    GameObject bp = boardEnemy[tmpUI.ROW, tmpUI.COL];
                    BoardUIVer1 bpUI = bp.GetComponent<BoardUIVer1>();
```

```
                if (tmpAttackHighlight != null)
                {
                    if (bpUI.ATTACKED)
                    {
                        if (bpUI.ATTACKED)
                        {
                            tmpAttackHighlight.GetComponent<Renderer>().mate-
rial.color = Color.gray;
                        }
                    }
                    else
                    {
                        tmpAttackHighlight.GetComponent<Renderer>().mate-
rial.color = Color.white;
                    }
                }

                tmpAttackHitHighlight.transform.GetComponent<Renderer>().ma-
terial.color = Color.blue;
                tmpAttackHighlight = tmpAttackHitHighlight.transform.gameOb-
ject;
            }
        }
    }

    if (Input.GetMouseButton(0))
    {
        Ray ray1 = Camera.main.ScreenPointToRay(Input.mousePosition);
        RaycastHit hit;

        if (Physics.Raycast(ray1, out hit, 200))
        {
            Debug.Log(hit.transform.gameObject.name);

            if (hit.transform.tag.Equals("boardAttack"))
            {
                BoardUIVer1 tmpUI = hit.transform.GetCompo-
nent<BoardUIVer1>();
                GameObject enemyBoard = boardEnemy[tmpUI.ROW, tmpUI.COL];

                Debug.Log(string.Format("Enemy Board: {0}", enemyBoard.trans-
form.name));

                // check to see if we have a hit on the player board
                // we need to make sure that we don't increase just because
we are hitting the board
                if (enemyBoard.GetComponent<BoardUIVer1>().OCCUPIED && !ene-
myBoard.GetComponent<BoardUIVer1>().ATTACKED)
                {
                    // we have a hit
                    enemyBoard.transform.GetComponent<BoardUIVer1>().OCCUPIED
= true;
                    enemyBoard.transform.GetComponent<BoardUIVer1>().ATTACKED
= true;
```

```
                        enemyBoard.transform.GetComponent<Renderer>().mate-
rial.color = Color.red;

                        hit.transform.GetComponent<Renderer>().material.color =
Color.red;

                        // we have a hit, play explosion audio
                        this.audioSource.PlayOneShot(this.explosionEnemyBlast,
0.75f);

                        this.playerHitCount += 1;
                        this.playerHadHit = true;
                    }
                    else
                    {
                        enemyBoard.transform.GetComponent<BoardUIVer1>().ATTACKED
= true;
                        enemyBoard.transform.GetComponent<Renderer>().mate-
rial.color = Color.gray;

                        hit.transform.GetComponent<Renderer>().material.color =
Color.gray;

                        this.playerHadHit = false;
                    }

                    boardEnemy[tmpUI.ROW, tmpUI.COL] = enemyBoard;

                    tmpAttackHighlight = null;
                }
            }
        }
        if(Input.GetMouseButtonUp(0))
        {
            if (!this.playerHadHit)
            {
                // now we will capture the true aspect for turn of player vs.
A.I.
                this.PLAYER_TURN = !this.PLAYER_TURN;
                this.playerHadHit = false;
            }
        }
    }
    else
    {
        int r1 = 0;
        int c1 = 0;

        if(this.gotoLastHit)
        {
            this.hit_dir = this.hit_dir_last;
            this.hit_row = this.hit_row_last;
            this.hit_col = this.hit_col_last;

            this.gotoLastHit = false;
        }

        switch (this.hit_dir)
```

```
    {
        // make sure to check the bounds ...

        case HitDirection.up:
        {
            r1 = this.hit_row + 1;
            c1 = this.hit_col;
            break;
        }
        case HitDirection.right:
        {
            c1 = this.hit_col + 1;
            r1 = this.hit_row;
            break;
        }
        case HitDirection.down:
        {
            r1 = this.hit_row - 1;
            c1 = this.hit_col;
            break;
        }
        case HitDirection.left:
        {
            c1 = this.hit_col - 1;
            r1 = this.hit_row;
            break;
        }
        default:
        {
            r1 = Random.Range(0, 9);
            c1 = Random.Range(0, 9);
            break;
        }
    }

    if((r1<0 || r1>9) || (c1<0 || c1 > 9))
    {
        // we aldo need to check and change hit_direction in here ...
        this.ChangeHitDirection();

        this.CheckAttackBoard();        // try a new unit
        return;                         // exit after the call back
    }

    Debug.Log(string.Format("R1={0}, C1={1}", r1, c1));

    GameObject playerBoard = boardPlayer[r1, c1];

    // check to see if the unit has been attacked before, if it has been
then try a new location
    if(playerBoard.GetComponent<BoardUIVer1>().ATTACKED)
    {

        // we aldo need to check and change hit_direction in here ...
        this.ChangeHitDirection();
```

```
      this.CheckAttackBoard();         // try a new unit
      return;                          // exit after the call back
   }

   // check to see if we have a hit on the player board
   if (playerBoard.GetComponent<BoardUIVer1>().OCCUPIED)
   {
      // we have a hit
      playerBoard.transform.GetComponent<BoardUIVer1>().OCCUPIED = true;
      playerBoard.transform.GetComponent<BoardUIVer1>().ATTACKED = true;
      playerBoard.transform.GetComponent<Renderer>().material.color =
Color.red;

      // we have a hit, play explosion audio
      this.audioSource.PlayOneShot(this.explosionPlayerBlast, 0.75f);
      this.enemyHitCount += 1;

      // we have a hit
      this.hit_col = c1;
      this.hit_row = r1;

      this.hit_col_last = c1;
      this.hit_row_last = r1;
      this.hit_dir_last = this.hit_dir;

      if (this.hit_dir == HitDirection.none)
         this.hit_dir = HitDirection.up;

      StartCoroutine(this.Wait4Me());

   }
   else
   {
      playerBoard.transform.GetComponent<BoardUIVer1>().ATTACKED = true;
      playerBoard.transform.GetComponent<Renderer>().material.color =
Color.gray;

      this.ChangeHitDirection();

      this.PLAYER_TURN = !this.PLAYER_TURN;

      this.gotoLastHit = true;
   }

   boardPlayer[r1, c1] = playerBoard;
   }
}
```

Code Block 60 - CheckAttackBoard function listing

The function *CheckAttachBoard()* is used by both the player and also the A.I. during game time. Which means that when the player picks a unit board on the enemy game board, or the A.I. select a unit board on the player's game board, then this function is used as the starting point. As before, the function is dependent on some more variables for accounting and etc… The following is a list of the variables used within the function:

```
GameObject tmpAttackHighlight = null;
RaycastHit tmpAttackHitHighlight;

GameObject tmpAttackBlockHolder = null;

#region A.I. Memory for Hit success
public enum HitDirection { none, up, right, down, left };

public int hit_row;                   // used for current hit row
public int hit_col;                   // used for current hit col
public HitDirection hit_dir;          // used for current hit dir

public int hit_row_last;              // used for last known hit row
public int hit_col_last;              // used for last known hit col
public HitDirection hit_dir_last;     // used for last known hit dir

public bool playerHadHit = false;
public bool gotoLastHit = false;
#endregion
```

Code Block 61 - Variables used by CheckAttackBoard() function

The variables listed in Code Block 61 are specifically used by the *CheckAttackBoard()* function. As stated previously, they have been defined before the function for clarity.

One big difference that should catch your eye, while you review the code, is the variables defined for the A.I. operations. The A.I. needs to represent the current hit selection, and it also needs to keep track of its previous move so that it can determine what location and direction to move next. The variables defined in Code Block 61 help with these operations.

The first if block checks to see who's turn it is for the attack. Assuming that it is the player's turn, the program once again uses the ray cast operation to grab the board unit that has been returned through the *tmpAttackHighlight* variable. The logic here is almost the same as that defined in the *CheckPlayerBoard()* function. But notice that our conditions are different. We are checking to make sure we are selecting the enemy's board for the attack movement, and that the selected board unit has not been attacked before.

244

If the condition is met, we use the 2-dimensional data array that stores the enemy's board data to retrieve the current state of the board unit and make modifications to it based on a hit or a miss. During the process we also use visual notification based on the state of the board. This logic happens during the selection / movement of the mouse on the enemy's board. Once the left mouse button has been clicked, then the actual operations start for registering a hit or a miss.

```
if (hit.transform.tag.Equals("boardAttack"))
{
    BoardUIVer1 tmpUI = hit.transform.GetComponent<BoardUIVer1>();
    GameObject enemyBoard = boardEnemy[tmpUI.ROW, tmpUI.COL];

    Debug.Log(string.Format("Enemy Board: {0}", enemyBoard.transform.name));

    // check to see if we have a hit on the player board
    // we need to make sure that we don't increase just because we are hit-
ting the board
    if (enemyBoard.GetComponent<BoardUIVer1>().OCCUPIED && !enemyBoard.Get-
Component<BoardUIVer1>().ATTACKED)
    {
        // we have a hit
        enemyBoard.transform.GetComponent<BoardUIVer1>().OCCUPIED = true;
        enemyBoard.transform.GetComponent<BoardUIVer1>().ATTACKED = true;
        enemyBoard.transform.GetComponent<Renderer>().material.color =
Color.red;

        hit.transform.GetComponent<Renderer>().material.color = Color.red;

        // we have a hit, play explosion audio
        this.audioSource.PlayOneShot(this.explosionEnemyBlast, 0.75f);
        this.playerHitCount += 1;
        this.playerHadHit = true;
    }
    else
    {
        enemyBoard.transform.GetComponent<BoardUIVer1>().ATTACKED = true;
        enemyBoard.transform.GetComponent<Renderer>().material.color =
Color.gray;

        hit.transform.GetComponent<Renderer>().material.color = Color.gray;
        this.playerHadHit = false;
    }

    boardEnemy[tmpUI.ROW, tmpUI.COL] = enemyBoard;

    tmpAttackHighlight = null;
}
```

Code Block 62 - Registering a hit or a miss by the Player

In Code Block 62, we have isolated the code responsible for the registration of a hit or a miss by the player. If we have a hit, we update the state of the unit board accordingly on the display as well as the data that represents the board in the 2-dimensional array. Likewise we do the same if the attack is a miss.

There is one last condition we need to check, if the player has a hit, then it will be again the player's turn to select the next attack position. Otherwise, we give the turn to the A.I.

```
if(Input.GetMouseButtonUp(0))
{
    if (!this.playerHadHit)
    {
        // now we will capture the true aspect for turn of player vs. A.I.
        this.PLAYER_TURN = !this.PLAYER_TURN;
        this.playerHadHit = false;
    }
}
```

Code Block 63 - Changing Turns after Player's selection

Looking at the scenario where it is the A.I.'s turn to attack, the A.I. checks to see if it had a hit from the previous move, and if so, it gets the hit direction, the hit row and the hit column. Based on the information provided, it decides where to make its next move. After the move we check to make sure we are in the boundaries of the board. If not, we recursively call the function to get a new attack position.

If all is well, we grab the player's unit board data, and check to see if it was previously attacked, if so we get a new position.

Finally, we check to see if the position selected is occupied, this determines if we have a hit for the move. The program performs the necessary accounting, saves the updated data into the 2-dimensional array representing the player's board and the process goes to the next step.

ChangeHitDirection() Function Implementation

The A.I. uses another function for determining the direction to hit on the board. This is done through the *ChangeHitDirection()* function. Here is a listing of the function:

```csharp
private void ChangeHitDirection()
{
    switch (this.hit_dir)
    {
        // change direction based on logic
        case HitDirection.none:
        {
            this.hit_dir = HitDirection.up;
            break;
        }
        case HitDirection.up:
        {
            this.hit_dir = HitDirection.right;
            break;
        }
        case HitDirection.right:
        {
            this.hit_dir = HitDirection.down;
            break;
        }
        case HitDirection.down:
        {
            this.hit_dir = HitDirection.left;
            break;
        }
        case HitDirection.left:
        {
            this.hit_dir = HitDirection.none;
            break;
        }
    }
}
```

Code Block 64 - Function used to change the hit direction for the A.I.

The function is pretty straight forward. It changes the direction of the hit based on the pattern that has been pre-defined[24].

The next section will cover the user interface functions and events.

---

[24] This is very basic, and it was implemented for simplicity. For better A.I. performance you might want to consider implementing a backtracking algorithm to make the best move based on historical data.

Game User Interface

The following variables are used to reference the UI elements in the game. The variables starting with *butXXX* are representing the buttons defined in the UI that the user can interact with. The variables starting with *lblXXX* are referencing labels in the UI, the variables starting with *imgXXX* are referencing images in the UI. The variable *canvasScoreBoard* is of type Canvas and is used to reference the score board in the game. We will also look at these in more detail in the next section.

- butAircraftCarrier
- butBattleship
- butSubmarine
- butDestroyer
- butPatrolBoat
- butUIReset
- butExit

- butHorizontal
- butVertical
- canvasScoreBoard
- lblPlayerScore
- lblAIScore
- imgYouWin
- imgYouLose

The following figures will illustrate the UI concepts:

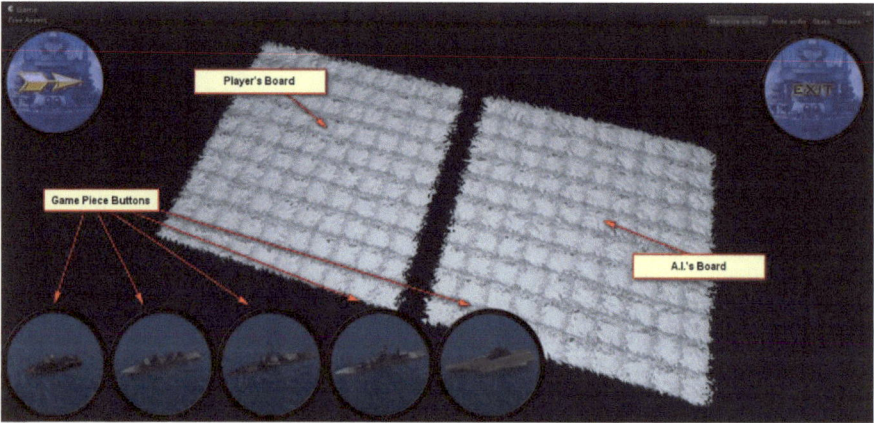

Figure 81 - User Interface - Player game piece placement

In Figure 81 you will notice the position of the primary buttons presented to the player at the start of the game. The players is shows five buttons for each game piece that needs to be placed onto the game

248

board. Once the player selects a particular ship, the UI will trigger the necessary functions that provide the size of the game piece as well as the ID associated with it. The details of this is covered in the following sections.

The button on the top left corner of the screen is used for the orientation of the ship that is going to be places on the board, and the button on the top right corner is the exit button. This is only visible on non-web deployments. In other words, you need a way to exit the application on a computer or a mobile device, this button will take care of that for you!

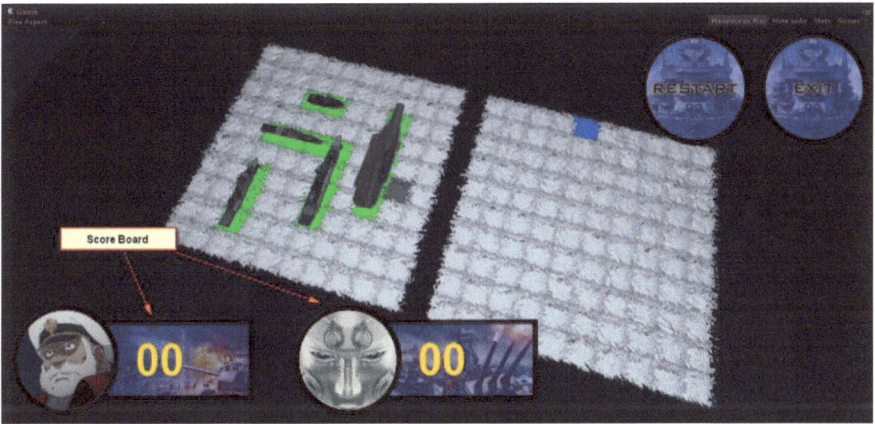

Figure 82 - User Interface Game Play

Figure 82 the player places all the game pieces, the User Interface of the game changes to reflect appropriately. All UI elements associated with placements of game pieces are replaced with the UI elements associated with the score board and the ability to restart the game and or exit the game. This is illustrated in Figure 82. In the next section we will discuss the details of the functions and the design time elements of the GUI.

Button Events for Placing Game Pieces

There are two supporting function that are used at the beginning of the game to allow the player for placing his/her game pieces. These two function are:

- butCreateBattleShip(size)
- butCreateBattleShipSetID(shipID)

The first function sets the size of the selected game piece, and the second function sets the ID. The size variable is used by the *Check-PlayerBoard()* function to determine the placement boundaries of the game piece, and the ID variable is used by the *CheckWhichShip-WasPlaced()* function to instantiate the appropriate prefab.

```
#region BUTTON EVENTS FOR PLACING BATTLE SHIPS
    public void butCreateBattleShip(int size)
    {
        //this.PLACE_BLOCK = !this.PLACE_BLOCK;
        this.blockSize = size;
    }

    public void butCreateBattleShipSetID(int shipID)
    {
        this.currentShipID = shipID;
    }
#endregion
```

Code Block 65 - Function to handle UI portion of ship placement by player

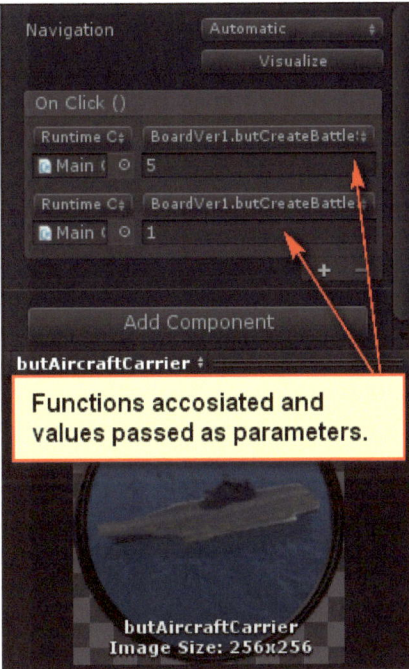

Figure 83 - Functions Ref. by Buttons

In order for the concept to work, you need to setup the environment in a specific way in the designer. When you are setting up the button components for each game piece, you will need to also include the two parameters values that are then used in the code to correctly work in the logic.

Figure 83, demonstrates the design time setup of the button object defined under the canvas. Notice, that on the click event, we have attached the two functions[25] that need to be triggered. Each function takes a single value, one for the size and the other for the ID.

Following this concept, you will have each button trigger both of these functions on the click event, and for each button the values for the parameters are going to be different.

Type of Ship	Size	Id
Aircraft Carrier	5	1
Battleship	4	2
Submarine	3	3
Destroyer	3	4
Patrol Boat	2	5

Next we should look at the restart function.

---

[25] As of the writing of this book, Unity only supports single value function calls for events. Therefore we need to setup it in this fashion to pass multiple parameters.

Button Event for Restart

The restart button is used to clean out the game and reset all of the variables to their default values. This gives the player the ability to reset the game at any time during the game play. Here is the code listing for the reset function.

```csharp
public void butRestart()
{
    GameObject[] playerBoardGO = GameObject.FindGameObjectsWithTag("board");
    foreach(var go in playerBoardGO)
    {
        Destroy(go);
    }

    GameObject[] enemyBoardGO = GameObject.FindGameOb-
jectsWithTag("boardAttack");
    foreach(var go in enemyBoardGO)
    {
        Destroy(go);
    }

    GameObject[] enemyPrefabPH = GameObject.FindGameObjectsWithTag("ene-
myPrefabPH");
    foreach(var go in enemyPrefabPH)
    {
        Destroy(go);
    }

    GameObject[] shipModels = GameObject.FindGameObjectsWithTag("shipModel");
    foreach (var go in shipModels)
    {
        Destroy(go);
    }

    this.ResetGUIButtons();
    Start();
}
```

Code Block 66 - Reset function listing

In this function, you will notice that the first for loop is iterating through the player's board units and destroying them one by one. This process happens for all of the other Game Objects present in the 3D world. Once the Game Objects have been destroyed, the *ResetGUIButtons()* function is called to reset the GUI elements.

```csharp
private void ResetGUIButtons()
{
    this.butAircraftCarrier.gameObject.SetActive(true);
```

```
    this.butBattleship.gameObject.SetActive(true);
    this.butSubmarine.gameObject.SetActive(true);
    this.butDestroyer.gameObject.SetActive(true);
    this.butPatrolBoat.gameObject.SetActive(true);

    this.lblPlayerScore.text = string.Format("00");
    this.lblAIScore.text = string.Format("00");
}
```

Code Block 67 - GUI Reset Function

The GUI Reset function makes sure that the default UI elements are visible and it also resets the score labels.

In Chapter 6 – Creating Battleship, we discussed the requirements and specifications of the game called Battle Ship. Gave some historical background on the game, introduced the game play, and presented plan for implementation. This was followed by identifying the game objects we would need for our game, and more importantly the game flow and the game logic needed to achieve our objectives.

In Chapter 7 – Delving Into the Code, we looked at the scripts that were created to make all of the pieces in our game work with one another. We started by looking at the *BoardUIVer1.cs* script that is responsible for the state management of the individual unit board on the board game. We then looked at the implementation of *BoardVer1.cs* script which handles everything in the game.

You are now ready to create some cool games!

Appendix 1 – Table of Figures

Table of Figures

Figure 1 - for loop diagram.. 9
Figure 2 - foreach loop diagram 10
Figure 3 - while loop diagram.. 11
Figure 4 - do-while loop diagram 11
Figure 5-Car Object... 18
Figure 6-Airplane Composite Object.. 23
Figure 7-Inheritance Example 25
Figure 8-Unity 5 Editor 35
Figure 9-Cube Primitive 38
Figure 10-Inspector Window 40
Figure 11-Transform Tools... 41
Figure 12-Position 41
Figure 13-Rotation 41
Figure 14-Scale... 41
Figure 15-New Material names CH1EX1MAT 42
Figure 16-Applying the CH1EX1MAT material to the Cube GameObject 44
Figure 17-Cube2 Position, Rotation, Scale 46
Figure 18-Script Attached to Game Object.. 49
Figure 19 - Property Types, Reference and Value 53
Figure 20 - Car Class Properties 54
Figure 21 - NavMesh Components 57
Figure 22 - Prefab Concept 59
Figure 23 - Simple 50x50 Terrain.. 67
Figure 24 - Snap shot of Terrain Tool 68
Figure 25 - Terrain Design 68
Figure 26 - Terrain with texture applied 69
Figure 27 - Search and collect game objects.. 70
Figure 28 - Cube Prefab with Cube Collider 75
Figure 29 - Inspector Window showing Box Collider 76
Figure 30 - Rigidbody Freeze Rotation 79
Figure 31 - Third Person Camera Setup... 80
Figure 32 - Collider Interaction after IsTrigger is Enabled............................... 81
Figure 33 - Console output for collision detection... 82
Figure 34 - Drop-Off Platform... 85
Figure 35 - Drop Off Zone in action.. 88
Figure 36 - Visual Representation of a Stack 89
Figure 37 - Console Window Showing Stack Ouput after Successful Order 95
Figure 38 - Just a Concept for Level 2... 96
Figure 39 - Level 2 Design 97
Figure 40 - 3D Room Model... 98
Figure 41 - 3D Model in Unity Scene.. 98
Figure 42 - Hierarchy of the Room 99
Figure 43 - Design Sample of Storage and Collector Units............................. 112

Figure 44 - User Interface Sample 1 131
Figure 45 - User Interface Sample 2 132
Figure 46 - Rect Tool Toolbar Buttons 134
Figure 47 - Rect Transform Component 135
Figure 48 - Pivot Interface 135
Figure 49 - Anchor UI Elements 136
Figure 50 - Preset Anchor Component...137
Figure 51 - Canvas with Panel Attached 143
Figure 52 - UI Panel and Text Element..145
Figure 53 - Collectables UI Implemented 146
Figure 54 - Additional UI for Matching...147
Figure 55 - Additional UI Elements for Level 1 148
Figure 56 - Button OnClick Event 149
Figure 57 - Level 2 Level Concept..154
Figure 58 - Level 3 UI Concept 160
Figure 59 - Another UI Sample 175
Figure 60 - Status Panel Background...177
Figure 61 - Message Panel Background..177
Figure 62 - Enemy Panel Background 177
Figure 63 - Panel Textures Applied to Level 3 178
Figure 64 - Level 3 UI Enhancement 179
Figure 65 - World Space Canvas Properties...180
Figure 66 - UI Concept for Health Bar..182
Figure 67 - World Space Canvas Hierarchy...182
Figure 68-Grid Sample Layout 185
Figure 69-Base Board Unit 187
Figure 70-Board Unit with Texture and UI Elements Applied..................................188
Figure 71-The Board...191
Figure 72-Showing Details per Board Unit..192
Figure 73 - BoardUnitPlayer Structure..196
Figure 74 - CubeWreck Prefab..197
Figure 75 - Game Flow High Level 199
Figure 76 - Player Ship Placement Flow Diagram 200
Figure 77 - A.I. Ship Placement Flow Diagram 201
Figure 78 - Game Play Logic 202
Figure 79 - Game GUI Concept 204
Figure 80 - Game GUI Score Display 205
Figure 81 - User Interface - Player game piece placement...248
Figure 82 - User Interface Game Play..249
Figure 83 - Functions Ref. by Buttons 251

Appendix 2 – Code Block Table

Code Block Table

Code Block 1-variables assignment and data types 5
Code Block 2-if ... else structure example 5
Code Block 3 - Nested if..else statement 6
Code Block 4-switch statement structure example 7
Code Block 5-loop structure samples 12
Code Block 6-example of a method.. 13
Code Block 7 - Method parameter pass by reference 14
Code Block 8-simple calculator program demo... 16
Code Block 9 - Sample Car Class... 19
Code Block 10 - Car class using properties 21
Code Block 11 - MyStack Data Structure.. 27
Code Block 12 - Generics Code Sample... 28
Code Block 13 - Simple Event Handler Example.. 32
Code Block 14 - Car Class with Event handler... 34
Code Block 15 - SerializeField for Inspector Window 54
Code Block 16 - MyCollectable.cs listing 77
Code Block 17 - PlayerInput() initial version 79
Code Block 18 - MyCollectable.cs ver 2 82
Code Block 19 - MyCollectableData.cs.. 83
Code Block 20 - PlayerInput.cs ver. 2 84
Code Block 21 - PlayerInput.cs ver. 3 88
Code Block 22 - Stack Data Structure 90
Code Block 23 - PlayerInput.cs ver. 4 94
Code Block 24 - Room Selection Code Listing 100
Code Block 25 - Sliding Door Code Listing 102
Code Block 26 - RoomSelection Script Update to Include Timer 105
Code Block 27 - PlayerInput.cs Update to include Timer Condition.......... 107
Code Block 28 - SlidingDoor.cs Script update for Timer function............. 108
Code Block 29 - Room Visited addition to SlidingDorr.cs script............... 109
Code Block 30 - Addition to PlayerInput.cs script to handle rooms visited 110
Code Block 31 - MyStorage.cs initial version 114
Code Block 32 - MyCollector.cs version 1.. 116
Code Block 33 - MyResource.cs version 1.. 117
Code Block 34 - MyEnemy.cs version 1 121
Code Block 35 - PlayerInput.cs with Attack Enemy function 126
Code Block 36 - MyEnemy.cs with Attack Function 129
Code Block 37 - Level 1 Match Canvas Variables 148
Code Block 38 - Button triggers for Level 1... 149
Code Block 39 - Level 2 Timer and Objective UI Code............................... 157
Code Block 40 - Revised RoomVisited() function for Level 2..................... 159
Code Block 41 - MyStorage.cs Listing for UI Design 163
Code Block 42 - MyCollector.cs Listing for UI Design 165
Code Block 43 - MyResource.cs Listing for UI Design 166

Code Block 44-BoardUIVer1 Class Definition..189
Code Block 45-Creating the Board Dynamically..190
Code Block 46-Highlighted Lines for Mouse Position and Raycasting 195
Code Block 47 - Listing for BoardUIVer1.cs...209
Code Block 48 - BoardVer1 Variables..214
Code Block 49 - Awake() function in BoardVer1 class 218
Code Block 50 - Start() function in BoardVer1 class...220
Code Block 51 - Code for Construction of Player's Board...221
Code Block 52 - Code for Enemy Board Construction 222
Code Block 53 - Update() function defined in BoardVer1 class 225
Code Block 54 - CheckPlayerBoard() Function Definition..229
Code Block 55 - Temporary variables used by CheckPlayerBoard() 230
Code Block 56 - Determining what object we have hit by ray casting.......................232
Code Block 57 - Visually placing the selected piece onto the game board 236
Code Block 58 - Function for A.I. to place game pieces..236
Code Block 59 - Function responsible for A.I. game piece placement.......................238
Code Block 60 - CheckAttackBoard function listing...243
Code Block 61 - Variables used by CheckAttackBoard() function 244
Code Block 62 - Registering a hit or a miss by the Player 245
Code Block 63 - Changing Turns after Player's selection 246
Code Block 64 - Function used to change the hit direction for the A.I. 247
Code Block 65 - Function to handle UI portion of ship placement by player 250
Code Block 66 - Reset function listing..252
Code Block 67 - GUI Reset Function 253

www.ingramcontent.com/pod-product-compliance
Lightning Source LLC
Chambersburg PA
CBHW041303210326
41598CB00005B/14